ON WINGS OF PRAYER

ON WINGS
OF PRAYER

by

GLENN CLARK

Macalester Park Publishing Company

Saint Paul   Minnesota

ON WINGS OF PRAYER

Copyright 1955
by
Macalester Park Publishing Company

First Edition

*Published in the United States of Amer-
ica by Macalester Park Publishing Company, 1571 Grand Avenue, Saint Paul 5,
Minnesota*

ACKNOWLEDGMENTS

The author gratefully acknowledges the following sources from which he has quoted in this book after receiving permission to do so.

Louis Fischer: quotation from his book *Gandhi: His Life and Message for the World*. Signet Books, The New American Library of World Literature, Inc., New York 22, New York.

Dwight D. Eisenhower: quotation from his speech before The World Council of Churches in Evanston.

William O. Douglas: quotation from his article "Morocco" in *Look Magazine* of October 19, 1954.

The Rotarian: quotation from "Dynamics of Free Enterprise" in the February 1954 issue.

Roland J. Brown: for the photographs contained in this book which make up such a vital part of the book.

The host of personal friends who have read and offered suggestions regarding the book while in manuscript and galley forms.

ON WINGS OF PRAYER

Book I

A BELT OF PRAYER AROUND THE WORLD

Book II

THREE WAYS OF SOLVING WORLD PROBLEMS

8 CONTENTS

BOOK I

A Belt of Prayer
Around the World

PROLOGUE: THE WORLD AT PRAYER

A STORY IS TOLD THAT ONE DAY A MAN WAS STROLLING WITH THE famous historian, Charles A. Beard, when suddenly he turned to Beard and asked, "If you were writing a condensed history of the world, how many volumes would it take?"

Mr. Beard hesitated and then answered, "Four."

Later in the walk Beard turned to his friend and said, "If all the unessentials were left out, the history of the world could be condensed into four chapters."

Still later when they were returning home, Beard stopped again and said, "I have been turning your question over in my mind and I have come to the conclusion that the entire history of the world could be told in four sentences."

Naturally the friend asked for the four sentences, and the historian replied:

"First, 'The mills of the gods grind slowly but they grind exceedingly small!'

"Second, 'The bees carry pollen where they gather honey.'

"Third, 'The meek shall inherit the earth.'

"Fourth, 'When the night grows dark the stars come out.'"

One day I told this incident to my Bible class in Minneapolis, a class which I had been teaching for thirty years, and then added, "I am about to start on a journey that will take me around the world. As one who travels by air must travel light, I shall carry instead of heavy volumes only those four sentences. Through them as through the amplifying lens of a telescope I shall expect to read the history of every nation I enter, not only the record of its past but also the prognosis of its future. For the more I consider these four sentences the more I am convinced that in them can be found not only the key that explains what has been but the key to what shall be. When focused on the past we read history; when focused on the future we become prophets.

"Looking through this glass of prophecy I can definitely foretell, even before I leave these shores, that France will lose Indo-China. It is foretold in the words, 'The mills of the gods grind slowly, but they grind exceedingly small.' The knell of colonialism has sounded. While Britain, Holland, and other governments have been liberating their colonies, France has been hanging on to hers with a death grip.

"In contrast to this dark picture for France, the second prophecy, 'Where the bees gather honey, they carry pollen,' is bringing good news about the Philippines. Even before I go there I can foresee freedom from Communism and loyalty to the United States. For while we extracted honey from the islands, we also carried pollen. Unlike other nations that exploited their colonies we sent thousands of teachers, many of whom died of tropical diseases, lifting the Philippines to 90 per cent literacy. We developed the industry of the nation, and crowned it all by granting the independence we had promised.

"When it comes to, 'The meek shall inherit the earth,' it does not require a soothsayer nor a prophet to foretell that one hundred years from now India and China—but not Red China—will inherit the earth. They won't have to conquer it; all they will need to do is to remain meek enough. It will fall like a ripe plum into their laps. And our own great nation—if we, too, grow meek enough, righteous enough, and generous enough—will also share in this heritage.

"Today we face the darkest night in history. Our hope is that when things get bad enough they will have to get better. When hydrogen bombs threaten to destroy the destroyer, wars may cease. Friends, I am leaving you when the night is growing dark. When I return I hope to tell you about the stars."

It was Sunday, the 27th of December, 1953, when I made those remarks. The next two days, Monday and Tuesday, found me in Chicago addressing a group of people gathered together from eighteen states; men and women who joined in dedicating me in glorious abandon to the purpose for which my world journey was intended.

Two evenings later, New Year's Eve, I found myself standing before a full sanctuary in the National Presbyterian Church in Washington where a dozen presidents had had their pews. The

President's pastor, Dr. Edward Elson, in introducing me said, "Every year for six years, on the first Sunday of the year, Dr. Clark has given the evening address in this church. This year he will be in England on that date so we have invited him to address us now."

I told them that in an hour of world confusion like this a dream may seem a very small thing, but just as the greatest forests grow out of tiny seeds, so the greatest art and beauty of the world take their rise from dreams in the hearts of simple men. Nations, empires, and civilizations that have endured have grown out of dreams in the hearts of men, coinciding with the Dreams in the heart of God. Because poets can say these things better than ordinary men, I quoted Alfred Noyes' poem which I always carry tucked away in the vest pocket of my memory:

WIZARDS

There's many a mighty wizardry in Araby and Egypt
Can read the silver writing of the stars as they run;
And many a dark gypsy, with a pheasant in his knapsack,
Has gathered more by moonlight than wiser men have won;
But I know a Wizardry
Can take a buried acorn
And whisper forests out of it, to tower against the sun.

There's many a magician in Bagdad and Benares
Can read you—for a penny—what your future is to be;
And a flock of crazy prophets that by staring in a crystal
Can fill it with more fancies than there's herrings in the sea;
But I know a Wizardry
Can break a speckled egg-shell,
And shake thrushes out of it, in every hawthorne tree.

There's many a crafty alchemist in Mecca and Jerusalem;
And Michael Scott and Merlin were reckoned very wise;
But I know a Wizardry can take a wisp of sun-fire
And round it roll a planet, and spin it through the skies,
With cities and seaports, and little shining windows,
And hedgerows and gardens, and loving human eyes. . . .

The theme of my address was that on this journey, in which Roland and Marcia Brown were to be my team-mates, we would expect to find lands which the Lord had prepared: fields planted by faith, deserts watered by hope, and cities saved by love.

New Year's Day I spent at Koinonia Estate just outside of Baltimore meeting in discussion and prayer with twelve men of God. The day following, January 2, I boarded a plane at the International Airport and my journey around the world began.

CHAPTER *I*

I FIND THE SOUL OF BRITAIN

"FASTEN SEAT BELTS. NO SMOKING." THE HUM OF THE MOTORS
muffled; the plane was coming down in Ireland. This was the first
time I had ever set foot in Ireland. Hills and meadows clothed
in green grass. Never had I seen lusher greens.

A snug little island is Ireland filled with warm, affectionate
folk, an island that should be filled with harmony. That was what
I was encircling the globe to find—harmony. What the world
needed right now was love and harmony—love that produces
harmony and harmony that produces love.

In this snug green island, harmony has proved to be the one
thing lacking. An Irishman himself put his finger on the cause.
"They will never have peace in Ireland because one half is Catholic
and one half Protestant. Now if they were all heathen they could
live together like Christians."

As we were rising off the ground on our magic carpet and heading
toward our goal, England; I felt as I have always felt when approaching England, as if I were going home. From here my ancestors came; indeed, half the ancestors of all America came from
England. Some of them came in crude sailing vessels with Captain
John Smith and Sebastian Cabot. How different these trans-Atlantic
journeys now! In 1907 I crossed steerage to England in the *Empress
of Ireland,* returning second class in the *Deutschland.* We had no
gyroscope, no radio contact with home, no movies on the vessel to
entertain us. Forty years later I crossed first-class in the *Mauretania*
with all the known modern devices for safety, speed, comfort, and
entertainment. Now I was arriving in England flying in air. We
shudder at the perils of the crossing of those early explorers and
settlers and congratulate ourselves upon the security of our modern
majesties of the seas and miracles of the skies. But perhaps Sebastian
Cabot's old tubs were no more perilous than the modern con-

veyances I have travelled on, for the *Empress of Ireland* and the *Deutschland* both were destined to go down, on subsequent voyages, carrying hundreds of passengers with them.

Four centuries of continuous war lay before the passengers of those first Cabot ships. First with the redskins, next with the red-coats, and now with the reds. Will the time ever come when Americans will cease to "see red"!

As our plane circled over England a great admiration for that little island welled up in my heart. Here was a land where conflict flourished and political parties competed vigorously, but here too was a stable people of amazing maturity and self-control, a people who had mastered the art of composing their conflicts and living together in peace.

I reset my watch to match Big Ben as the great plane, weighing many tons, touched the earth with hardly a jar. I pondered in awe at those twin wonders of human ingenuity—this immense plane which had roared so steadily across the miles, and my tiny automatic watch that had kept ticking without once rewinding during the six years since I bought it in Lucerne. There was a basic secret underlying the production of these two wonders; the same secret that underlies all the wonders of God—the mystery of rhythm. As I disembarked, my heart quickened in anticipation of what lay before me and yet it beat in perfect rhythm; my breath was coming faster, but still in rhythm. All around the little island of Britain the ocean was moving in wonderful rhythm, so obvious during the hours of the ebb and flow of the tides. I recalled the waxing and waning of the moon, the alternation of day and night. Enough to say that all life is based on rhythm, and the art of living consists of accepting this great fundamental law and working with it; never against it. I first became acquainted with that tremendous law when as a boy I "worked myself up" in the backyard swing. The quickest way "to make the old cat die" was to work against the alternating forward and backward pendulum motion of the swing, while the way to mount into the heights was to work in harmony with it.

Just as great achievements of individuals come from the right application of the law of rhythm, so do the achievements of nations depend upon right application of the same law. The Israelites stepped into God's rhythm materially and spiritually because they "remembered the Sabbath day to keep it holy." They fitted their entire living into a time rhythm of work and rest, a rhythm as dependable and sure as the rhythm of moon and tide. Out of this work-rest rhythm was born a great religion, a great Book, a great line of seers and prophets, a great Savior with a great program of bringing God's Kingdom—which is the doing of His will—here on earth.

The Greeks also knew the significance of rhythm. They produced their significant works of art, from the epics of Homer and the dramas of Sophocles to the Acropolis of Athens and the sculpture of Phidias, because one third of their education was devoted to a study of the principles of rhythm. Aristotle said that if any subject was ever omitted from the Greek curriculum it should not be rhythm which he considered the most essential of all. Finally it burst upon me as one of those heavenly revelations that the secret of England's stability and maturity in political science and jurisprudence lay in the fact that she, above all nations, had in those fields mastered the art of rhythm.

Just as there is a normal rhythm in every individual's life, as well as in the life of the earth, so is there also a normal rhythm in the life of every nation. The problem is not to let that natural rhythm get out of hand as it sometimes does in the life of the individual when his high periods stay too high too long, and his low periods stay too low too long. An individual, when the pendulum swings too high and then too low, is said to be neurotic or, when it goes to a greater extreme, even psychopathic. The same with nations. Under the Tsars of Russia when the pendulum toward tyranny and oppression was allowed to swing too wide an arc, it was to be expected that the return swing of the pendulum would also go too far. If at times our shift from one political administration to the other with the subsequent alternation between conservatism and liberalism makes our policies appear a shade neurotic, we should not be surprised that Russia and China, after their tumultuous pasts, seem at present to be verging on a very deep form of neurosis. When the drive of colonialism with its exploitation of dark races by the white races had continued too long, we should have been prepared to see the back swing of resentment and revenge bordering on the psychopathic. No wonder the world today is a pretty sick world.

Great Britain mastered the science of healthy government through her two party system—a constant swing of the pendulum between the Labour Party and the Tories. Few people realize that since 1945 a full scale revolution has taken place in Britain. But instead of its being accompanied by terrorism and bloodshed, as have the revolutions in China and Russia, Britain's revolution has been bloodless and peaceful. Nevertheless its consequences have been far reaching. During the war the Tories, the Conservatives, were in control. They are the administrators, the conservers of Britain. Then at the end of the war the Labour government was returned to power, not so much because the people had turned "socialist," as because by tradition, the "Whigs," or Liberals are the ones who come out with new ideas; and after the grim grind of the long war the people in Britain wanted new ideas. As a result of this return swing of the pendulum, India was granted its independence; the forty hour week was introduced; the age-level for compulsory education was raised to sixteen years; hospitals became state-owned; a National Health Service was introduced granting free treatment to all, including foreign visitors; steel, coal, and railways were nationalized and all within the space of five short years.

To carry this load, taxes went up, consumer goods rose in price to meet the added taxation, and the spiral of inflation began. By 1951 the British people felt it was time for the traditional administrators to consolidate these far-reaching changes and so they returned the Conservatives to power. The new government's first move was to denationalize steel, and next by rigid austerity to bring the inflation under control.

By means of this normal pendulum swing, by utilizing in turn the peculiar gifts of each party, Britain has digested the best part of a major revolution without the usual aftermath of an all-out inflation and its consequent ills. After smoothing out her domestic problems, the next step was for Britain to consolidate her interests abroad. The Labour Party had proved that voluntary evacuation of India did not necessarily mean the loss of its friendship, so why should voluntary military evacuation of Egypt necessarily mean loss of security? Indeed, the loyalty of India to the British Commonwealth is greater now than before, and the same may be true of Egypt. If that happens it will convincingly demonstrate that in this age of nuclear fission nations can cooperate far more effectively when bound together by justice, understanding, and good will than by political dictatorships and military might.

Yes, Britain has something. She is a living example of Hegel's law, that one party takes its *position,* the other party produces the *opposition,* the two points of view resolve their differences and the result is *composition.* If balance is necessary to composition, Great Britain has that balance.

And the secret of that balance is that she has a fulcrum—a fulcrum firmly embedded in tradition, law, and justice. Just as a children's see-saw needs a fulcrum across which the board is placed, so does a nation need a stationary pillar of support for its teetering political parties. In the British Commonwealth the office of the Royal Family is that fulcrum. The peculiar special duty of the monarch is to represent the spirit of the nation, to favor no party or individual, but to accept the fealty and loyalty of every subject and bestow the royal blessing upon all alike.

In the United States the fulcrum is the Constitution, a less dramatic symbol. The United States is also blessed with a two-party system, although, unfortunately, the lines are not as clearly drawn as in Britain. For instance, under Franklin D. Roosevelt the new-dealers, the avowed liberals among the Democrats, made strange yoke-mates with the old-line conservatives of the solid South. But the party on the whole is regarded as our liberal party and after sixteen years of power it was recently succeeded by the traditionally more conservative Republicans—again a healthy rhythm between periods of new ideas of reform and periods of conservation and consolidation.

France, on the other hand, with its multiplicity of parties, does not know what a healthy rhythm is. In fact, more adequate words to describe the situation in the French government is vibration, or even palpitation. Most French premiers are vibrated, or shall we say jarred, out of office, almost before they get safely seated.

This rhythm which functions in such a wholesome, normal way in Great Britain and the United States, and in what appears at present to be a more or less "neurotic" way in France, has startled the world in the present generation by manifesting itself in an actual "psychopathic" form in Russia, resulting in the vast pendulum swing from the most tyrannical of monarchial dictatorships under the

Tsars to the most tyrannical of proletarian dictatorships under the Kremlin. Some political scientists would diagnose France as a fit subject for a hospital, and Russia and Red China as fit subjects for an asylum. But when we take a fair appraisal of all the nations, including ourselves, after the past half century of costly wars I think we will agree that we have all been a little bit mad.

After this appraisal we might take some lessons from our own psychiatrists who have dealt with human madness and, using the methods they have found successful with sick individuals, apply them to sick nations. At the Menninger Institute in Topeka, for instance, they have discovered the best of all cures for psychopathic cases is love. While there is yet time could we not do a little experimenting and take this same cure found efficacious in dealing with mad-men, and apply it to mad-nations? That was the purpose of our journey around the globe—to explore and demonstrate the practicability and efficacy of this power of love, when combined with the power of prayer, to solve the problems of the world. If all the so-called Christian nations would "turn-off" fear and hate for a while and "turn-on" a vast, overflowing flood of love expressed in forms of amazing kindness to all our Communist brothers, what a miracle might come to pass! I was thinking these thoughts while we three travelers, Roland and Marcia Brown and I, with the shelves of our railroad train compartment loaded with our baggage, were traveling rapidly from London toward Swanwick where two hundred and thirty sturdy Britons were gathering for our first Camp Farthest Out on foreign soil. We were about to put this hypothesis to a test. The Great Experiment was about to begin.

And what was this experiment? What was this camp we were going to? What was the purpose of our coming? And who did we think we were—three ordinary run-of-the-mill Americans—starting on a journey to build a Belt of Prayer around the world? And whom did we expect to reach? And what would come of it if we did reach them?

Yes, we were just ordinary Americans in one sense. We were just ordinary citizens with ordinary passports and visas—from the ordinary middle class ranks—therefore run-of-the-mill. But we were filled with a vision—a vision of spreading the Kingdom of Heaven on earth among our friends and also on earth everywhere. We knew

we were being led of the Spirit within. And as long as we were im-
pelled and empowered by that Spirit, we could be used in ways
which were more than "just ordinary."

Twenty-five years ago I had started a camp, the purpose of which
was to go all the way out in teaching people how to pray and live
Christianity victoriously so they could go all the way out in love,
faith, and obedience, with their spirit-filled lives a demonstration
of the effectiveness of prayer and the trustworthiness of God. My
intention was to hold one camp, but the people who came seemed
to achieve such release in finding the joy of God, and the love of
God and the inspiration of communicating with God that, on its
twenty-fifth anniversary, the one camp had multiplied into forty in
the United States and they were overflowing into Canada, Mexico,
and Hawaii. So, when people began to beg us to start some in Europe and Asia, we decided to accept the call.

In 1948 I had led a "Spiritual Odyssey" of forty-two people on
a prospective journey through Europe. In 1950 Rev. Roland Brown
and his wife Marcia led a similar group. While in Great Britain,
Holland, and Germany, Roland Brown won the hearts of ministers
and church members so completely that, on their insistence, for
five consecutive years he has made preaching excursions to Britain
and other European nations, and the effect of his missions have
been so quickening and have produced such cumulating spiritual
growth that wherever he went they begged him to return.

After one seven-months' mission among the cities of England,
the clergy published a special souvenir edition of the Christian
Herald devoted entirely to recounting the wonderful transformation of the churches by "Pastor Brown," as they affectionately called
him. While his chief ministry was in England he was equally
effective in every nation he visited, for three reasons: his Christ-
centered message, his contagious personality, and his natural elo-
quence which win audiences in every land, no matter how poor
the interpreters might be.

One of the most unique characteristics of the Camps Farthest Out
is that they make use of many avenues for reaching God beside the
spoken word, and in every one of these avenues Marcia Brown
excells. Leading Meditations or Prayer Groups, or Creative Arts,
or Counselling, or Creative Devotion—she is an entire Camp Far-

thest Out in herself. As a matter of fact, if I had not written a book or two that had penetrated some of these far off places we were going to there would be little need of my going at all.

And now that we had come, what kind of reception would we receive?

Gathered together for our first English Camp Farthest Out at Swanwick we found some of the finest people of England—two hundred and thirty Christians, all of whom were seeking to put God first. Thirty-three of them were ministers and clergymen, titles which are synonymous in America, but very distinctive in England, where the title *ministers* is applied to those of the free churches while the title *clergymen* is reserved for Anglicans only. Behind these two hundred and thirty persons lay centuries of self-discipline, self-control, reverence for law, training in democracy, and in freedom of thought, freedom of religion, freedom of speech. Of course I expected to find some pride, some snobbishness, and a lot of repression and reserve, and perhaps a little stubborn reluctance to participate in the various activities offered. But I was in for a happy surprise.

Our question, can the English unbend and slip out of their reserve, was answered almost before we asked it. They were like a river long held in check by a mighty dam, which, when the water has finally risen high enough, pours with such irresistible power that it turns turbines to furnish light and power in cities hundreds of miles away.

Not only did they listen eagerly to the messages brought by Roland and me, but they tossed dignity aside and participated with alacrity and abandon when Marcia led them in "devotion through motion." Many of the most staid clergymen exclaimed, "We haven't had so much fun since we were children!"

When it came to the creative writing class, which all two hundred and thirty attended faithfully, their outpouring in prose and poetry was superb. Not in all my thirty years of teaching creative writing in colleges have I found anything to surpass it. Dr. John Maillard accounted for it thus: "Never before have we English people attended a gathering like this where everyone has been given opportunity for self-expression—especially in the field of creative writing." And there was some real "literature" turned out. Who shall say what muted Miltons found new tongues, how many silent Wordsworths found new voices, how many Emily Brontës found new release? If Camps Farthest Out should spread all over Great Britain in the next twenty-five years as they have spread over the United States we might see a new Renaissance of literature or, more appropriately, a new Elizabethan Age to rival the great Age of Elizabeth I.

Among my great spiritual friends in England, in addition to those pictured in this book, I would list these as worthy of the prophet's mantle: John Henry Hamlin, Norman Grubb, William Sangster, Leslie Weatherhead and Muriel Lester.

For that matter I discovered that every one of the thirty-three ministers and clergymen at this Camp was of high caliber. The seven pictured in this book met late at night with Roland Brown and me in special consecration meetings and will be potential instruments for spreading these training Camps in prayer all over Great Britain. Two of them, John Maillard and Norman Renshaw, made a pilgrimage to America the following summer, attending many Camps Farthest Out in preparation for carrying on these Camps in England in the years to come.

But it was not the intellectual fiber of the British that impressed me as much as their moral fiber. As I have mentioned, I doubt if any nation surpasses Britain in true integrity, sound discipline, and genuine self-control. England has mastered the delicate art of union in diversity. At the center is a marvelous unity; at the periphery is amazing freedom and flexibility. In politics and religion, at the outer fringes one is at liberty to speak his mind from any soap-box or pulpit, but debate and controversy fades before the loyalty to the Queen and the Magna Charta. Somehow everyone feels safe the moment he steps into England. He is on solid ground. Here one finds a maturity, a stability, a dependability unmatched by any other nation in the world.

But from an international point of view England has had one conspicuous shortcoming. With an almost fanatical faith she has believed that she is God-ordained to spread the fruits of her maturity—her law and order—to less matured nations of the world and has a God-given right to take in return whatever she thinks she deserves. When I cycled through England in 1907 every third person I met was supported by India. Today, blighted by two world wars and deprived of billions of revenue from her colonies, the English people, turning to God as we saw them at Swanwick, stand forth as far more magnificent in their hour of impoverishment than ever in their hours of opulence and success. Have no fear. England will carry on!

CHAPTER II

HOLLAND FINDS HER SOUL

AND NOW OUR "MAGIC CARPET" BROUGHT US DOWN IN AMSTERDAM in the midst of a people just one step removed from the English. The rhythm of the English is just a little slower and more placid than the rhythm of the Scotch and Irish, and the rhythm of the Dutch is still more placid and leisurely than that of the English. But all these great peoples I find are brothers under the skin.

In both England and Holland I found true integrity, sound discipline, and genuine self-control. For centuries these two nations have been schooled and disciplined in political and economic techniques under democratic regimes. For centuries they have grown in religious and moral maturity through a Protestant faith that gives each individual an open Bible with the social incentives to put its teachings into practice.

Their common error was their over-enthusiastic attempt to apply that discipline and control to under-developed peoples in a manner which produced modern imperialism. Their missionaries preached a call to surrender, and as long as the center of that surrender was Christ, the call was good. But when the center was a foreign imperialistic government enforced by traders, moneylenders, and politicians, the call was not so good.

England and Holland both clung to their dream of Empire for a long time, but both saw the handwriting on the wall and let go just in time to avoid the terrible repercussions that came upon France in Indo-China. The Lord is telling us as nations, just as the fairy godmother told Cinderella, "You may dance with your dream as long as the minute hands move steadily *upward* toward honesty, integrity, justice, and good will; but the moment the minute hands start traveling *downward* toward unfairness, injustice, and exploitation, the hour has struck and you must leave your dream behind and dash back to your home or all your borrowed garments of pre-

25

tended benevolence and self-righteousness will turn to rags and tatters."

England's last years in India had their periods of storm and of calm, but her departure from Ceylon was so peaceful that she left a "glass slipper" of good will that holds Ceylon by happy bonds of affection and loyalty within the British Commonwealth. Because violence and force were necessary to get Holland out of Indonesia the riches and personal holdings of the Dutch inhabitants were lost to them forever.

The loss to Holland of Indonesia was very great. For instance the pre-war trade included a large share of the world's quinine, and barely less of the kapok, and almost an equal proportion of the world's rubber, teak, and tea. Holland had risked fortunes in building a great shipping industry and with determination, imagination, and intrepid zeal had built a world trade that lifted her standard of living above many nations. While England's reputation as a colonizer was the best, and Holland's about the worst, Holland was the best of all colonizers from the point of respecting native customs, common law, and religion. Unfortunately, this *laissez faire* policy had one hole in it. Indonesia was 93 per cent illiterate and Holland made no effort to change that condition. As a matter of fact, she discouraged any attempt to educate the people, on the theory that the less they knew the easier they could be controlled. Part of the bitterness of these islanders against Holland today stems from the fact that they are 7 per cent literate while the neighboring islands of the Philippines are 95 per cent literate.

Another unique thing about Holland's control was that the Christian Churches in Indonesia were government supported, not church supported, so when the government was ousted, the financial undergirding of the Christian Churches went with it. From the religious viewpoint, this was the greatest calamity of the revolution.

The loss of Indonesia was a tremendous shock to Holland economically and psychologically. She took it badly. There is no telling how long her bull-dog grip might have held if the United States (through the United Nations) had not intervened.

Riding from Amsterdam to The Hague, passing miles and miles of palatial residences, I turned to my driver, who, by the way, was a high national official, director of all the government printing of the Netherlands, and asked him where these Holland people made their wealth. Instantly he replied, "From the colonies. Young men went by the scores to the East Indies and there made their fortunes in rubber, sugar, tobacco, and the shipping trades. Now that this source of wealth is gone we must develop home industries."

And so Holland, since the loss of Indonesia and since the more recent flooding of the dikes, has been girding herself for more frugal times and through hard work has been bravely carrying on. This stringency was brought forcibly to my attention through the occasion of my being the house guest, during my stay in The Hague, of a splendid lawyer, Gaele Van der Veen, who had been for twenty-five years president of an association of tobacco companies in Indonesia with a combined capitalization of $50,000,000. He had made his fortune there but the Japanese invasion confiscated everything he had. For three and a half years during the war he and his family of wife and four children were in Japanese concentration camps, separated from one another. Now back in Holland he has to start all over again. He has written a book on relations between employer and employees and since his return has now written another book dealing with aiding underdeveloped countries through international cooperation in what I would call a thoroughly Christian way, showing how to avoid the mistakes of the past. He is now European President of the International Council for Christian Leadership, which has established men's breakfast groups all over the world. I have had the privilege of addressing many of these, including the two which are made up of Senators and members of the House of Representatives.

We were surprised and pleased when Mr. Van der Veen told us that Princess Wilhelmina had heard of our mission of "Spreading a belt of prayer around the world," and had cordially invited us to spend an hour with her.

"Have you a dark suit?" asked Van der Veen.

"Only a light-weight navy blue summer suit," I replied, "that I am carrying for the hot weather of India and the Philippines."

His wife kindly pressed it, and I braved the January blasts to meet the only ex-Queen I have ever met face to face in all my life.

With mounting anticipation adding wings to our taxi, Roland, Marcia, and I arrived at the palace of Her Royal Highness promptly at 11:00 o'clock. We didn't have to knock. The Great Door opened and two men in uniform, evidently expecting us, showed us to the broad staircase. At the top of the stairs Mrs. Lowe, a kindly woman well over six feet tall, with a loving spiritual face, the Lady in Waiting, greeted us and took us into the parlor to meet the Queen. Had I walked into the home of my nearest neighbor I could not have felt more at ease. The Queen Mother, the Princess Wilhelmina, had the same direct, genuine, sincere cordiality and eagerness that we have witnessed in meeting some of our truly spiritual American friends. Of course we had a few little hurdles to overcome, wondering whether we should bow, or how often we should say "Your Royal Highness." We knew "Your Majesty" was not appropriate since she ceased to be the reigning Queen. We compromised by returning smile for smile. Of course Roland was best at the amenities, but quickly the conversation got going. We told her of the belt of prayer groups around the world and I spoke of President Eisenhower's interest in prayer. She has great respect for Abraham Vereide who founded the International Christian Leadership Movement, and she knows Senator Carlson, the close friend of the President. As I know both these men, we had much in common.

I commended her for her humility in all her relations with her people. She instantly responded by saying that the most important thing for a queen to learn was to be absolutely humble, to keep self completely out and to let God have all the credit. Such a spirit won our hearts. Then Roland asked about her little granddaughter, whose serious eye trouble had caused Queen Juliana such grief and for whom we had prayed. "She is much, much better," said the Princess. She regretted not coming to our meeting the evening before because of her cold, but she added, "This visit is better." We told her that *Time* magazine, just out, had quotations from Rev. Edward Elson telling what influence President Eisenhower's spiritual practices in private and public life were having on the nation. She nodded approvingly.

But above all she wanted us to tell her about the Camps Farthest Out.* "Are they democratic? Open to all classes, rich and poor alike? To all races? To all denominations?" We explained that they were interdenominational, open to all who wanted to go as far out as possible in obeying and following the teachings of Jesus, not only in their religious practices but in all phases of their lives—

---

* See Appendix A.

their homes, their business, their citizenship, and their recreation.

She was deeply interested in the fact that the camps had only two or three lectures a day and the rest of the time was devoted to creative prayer through creative silence, creative worship, creative arts, creative song. "Our entire purpose," we explained, "is to serve the churches through developing a more dedicated and loyal constituency, eager to assist the ministers in the work they are doing for the Lord. We feel that the 'saviours' of the world in the future will not be the military leaders nor the political leaders but the spiritual leaders, and the hope of the world lies in the Christian churches."

We left this stalwart Christian woman, who had been for half a century Queen of the Netherlands, feeling anew that if all the Christians of the world, regardless of denomination, worked humbly together in love and harmony, then the forces of evil would have no power. Indeed, one purpose of our journey around the world was to stimulate that kind of spiritual harmony, and Holland proved a splendid proving ground for just that thing.

The high water marks of our stay in Holland were the two Camps Farthest Out we held at de Hezenberg, a Retreat Center presided over by two saintly people, Rev. William Plug and his wife, Barbara. The first camp was for young people and when it closed on a Sunday night I realized I had never met a finer, cleaner, more substantial group of young men and women than those one hundred young folks of Holland. I knew there were some who would carry the impact of those meetings all through their lives.

The experience of "devotion in motion" and the picturing of their spiritual experiences on paper in the creative art led by Marcia Brown captivated them in a way they had never experienced before, while Roland Brown and I tried to make Christ a living force and Jesus a living reality. But all these things were appreciated in a more vital way because of the loving influence of the host and hostess, William and Barbara Plug.

I had caught a slight cold from living in unheated houses, so welcomed two days of rest before the second conference of Netherlanders assembled in the friendly (but chilly) Conference Halls of de Hezenberg. Fifty spiritual leaders, men and women, were in this second group so this time the CFO emphasis was introduced to a company of adults.

One night in Amsterdam we addressed the International Council of Christian Laymen and had a deeply responsive audience. Roland, as usual, spoke first. During the coffee period that followed I had a long visit with a member of Parliament. Then I gave my talk, telling of the western frontiers of America, and of the Dutch frontiers in the East Indies, pointing out that those frontiers were closing, but that the unclosable frontiers of spiritual life were opening. The challenge before the Christian leaders today is to enter these new frontiers and chart the paths for the whole world to follow. The audience followed closely as I took them "above the clouds of doubt —above the sun," for only as we rise above the sun of this mundane universe do we really reach the Son of God.

Miss Richards, an English woman, under John Maillard's influence, had started thirty-five prayer groups in The Hague, and these prayer groups were gathered together in a second very vital meeting for us to address.

These meetings are worth recording because something much deeper than the meetings themselves is involved. They illustrated, as you will see as our journey proceeds, what our whole trip around the world points up: that tremendous power for the Kingdom can be released when all Christian groups work together in harmony. Give Jesus eleven dedicated Christian men of different denominations and creeds who will work together like eleven men on a football team, and He can change the world. Or give Him eleven Christian lay-organizations, or eleven Christian denominations following His coaching and working together even to the point of "in honor preferring one another," and God and they will change the world. The International Christian Leaders in America opened the door and prepared the way for us to reach these Christian leaders in The Hague. John Maillard, of Milton Abbey fame, through Miss Richards, prepared the prayer groups. Roland Brown's meetings in Holland in previous years drew ministers to meet us in The Hague. The seven months' crusade Roland Brown had conducted in English churches in 1952 and 1953 helped plough the ground for Billy Graham's sensational achievements in 1954 and 1955. Everywhere we went we found individuals and groups that Jesus had been training for that Team which can change the world.

CHAPTER III

WE INVADE NAZI LANDS

UNLIKE ENGLAND AND HOLLAND WHOSE ECONOMIES WERE BUILT upon the fruits of colonialism, Germany had to build her economy upon the genius and industry of her own people. Whether that fact put the fiber and muscle into their way of doing things I do not know, but this I do know, that at the start of this century no nation in the world surpassed Germany in her output in science and industry. Had Germany not grown jealous of the "land grabbing nations," and had she foreseen how within one generation colonization would be a thing of the past, and had she appreciated her own good fortune in escaping the painful amputations the colonizing nations would have to undergo, Germany would today be riding high as the most prosperous and powerful nation of modern times.

During the eighteenth century while the other nations were building their colonial empires, Germany was absorbed in civil wars between petty princes. When she finally attained unification under Bismarck and took a good look around her, she found herself hemmed in by prosperous nations whose merchant fleets were loaded with precious raw materials from lands far away.

Nations, as well as individuals, can become victims of jealousy, of resentment and of greed, and Germany was no exception. With her it took the form of a sort of claustrophobia—shut in as she was in all directions from the sea. Frantically she looked toward the south where she dreamed of a railroad from Berlin to Bagdad, and toward the north where she dreamed of a Polish Corridor giving access to the sea. Great Britain, jealous of her own "life line" to India, checkmated the railroad dream by moving in as "financial advisor" to Persia. France and Russia threw up a "road-block" toward Poland. Within this situation can be found the real causes of World War I—the chance pistol shot in Serbia being merely the precipitating incident.

Never did a nation fight with more skill and courage than did Germany, but in time the weight of numbers was too great, and she lay crushed and bleeding at the feet of the Allied Powers. France, who had never forgotten her own humiliation under Bismarck in the seventies, insisted on having the German blockade continued until the treaty of peace was signed, resulting in the death of nine out of every ten babies born in Germany for lack of milk during that period of waiting.

This heart-rending humiliation, piled upon the humiliation of losing the war, finally culminated in a third great humiliation—the total collapse of the German economy following the United States depression of 1929. When our government was unwilling to secure the German mark, the disaster in Germany was beyond words, the consequent suffering (not the sorrow) being even greater than during the war.

During the nineteenth century the best safeguard against the evils of depression was the possession of a frontier. From 1790 to 1890 whenever an economic collapse occurred in America, the unemployed got into covered wagons and sought new homesteads in our great Western frontier. When the younger sons in England or Holland couldn't find employment in their native land, they took passage to the East Indies, India, or South Africa, and returned as men of opulence.

When frontiers are closed, explosions begin. When the frontier in America was officially closed in 1890, the need for mental hospitals doubled and tripled, and psychiatrists for the first time came into style. A whole new vocabulary was born, such as "inferiority complex" and "repressed desires." In Europe, with no frontiers for the unemployed to emigrate to, the rulers found the easiest way to prevent internal revolts was to put men in uniform with guns in their hands and start them marching. The chief argument that the Communists raise against capitalistic nations is that they are natural "war mongers"—they say war is their favorite solution to the recurring hard times whenever production has outstripped distribution.

Since the only safeguard of nations is to have a frontier, it naturally follows that when frontiers are closed in one direction they must open in another or the nation will go psychopathic. That is what happened to Germany. After the series of humiliations referred to above, the soil of Germany was prepared for the rise of Hitler, the greatest psychopath of modern times. With almost uncanny genius, he opened the doors, not only to one frontier, but to two—one geographical, the other psychological.

The most penetrating and revealing analysis of Hitler was made by Dr. Karl Gustav Jung, the world's greatest psychiatrist, while Hitler was at the height of his power.

> Hitler belongs in the category of the truly mystic medicine men. He is the mirror of every German's unconscious. He is the loudspeaker which magnifies the inaudible whispers of the German soul until they can be heard by the German's conscious ear. He is the first man to tell every German what he has been thinking and feeling all along in his unconscious about German fate, especially since the defeat in the first World War; and the one characteristic which colors every German soul is the typically German inferiority complex, the complex of the younger brother, of the one who is always a bit late to the feast. Hitler's power is not political; it is *magic*.
>
> Now the secret of Hitler's power is not that Hitler has an unconscious more plentifully stored than yours or mine. Hitler's secret is twofold: first, that his unconscious has exceptional access to his consciousness; and second, that he allows himself to be moved by it. He is like a man who listens intently to a stream of suggestions in a whispered voice from a mysterious source and then acts upon them.
>
> In our case, even if occasionally our unconscious does reach us through dreams, we have too much rationality, too much cerebrum to obey it—but Hitler listens and obeys. The true leader is always *led*.
>
> We can see it work in him. He himself has referred to his Voice. His Voice is nothing other than his own unconscious, into which the German people have projected their own selves; that is, the unconscious of seventy-eight million Germans. That is what makes him powerful. Without the German people he would be nothing. It is literally true when he says that whatever he is able to do is only because he has the German people behind him, or, as he sometimes says, because he *is* Germany. So with his unconscious being the receptacle of the souls of seventy-eight million Germans, he is powerful, and with his unconscious perception of the true balance of political forces at home and in the world, he has so far been infallible.

That is why he makes political judgments which turn out
to be right against the opinions of all his advisers and against
the opinions of all foreign observers. When this happens it
means only that the information gathered by his unconscious
and reaching his unconsciousness by means of his exceptional
talent, has been more nearly correct than that of all others,
German or foreign, who attempted to judge the situation and
who reached conclusions different from his.*

We entered World War II in the last days of 1941. In the early
days of 1942 while our War Staff were devising ways and means of
ending the war on the military frontier a number of us came together to devise ways and means of hastening the coming of peace
on the psychological and spiritual frontier.

Studying Jung's analysis of Hitler, the secret of Hitler's unbroken
series of successes became very clear to us. It lay in the fact that
Hitler's intuitive plans, plots, and strokes took their inception at
deeper levels than the calculated steps of Daladier and Chamberlain. While these two limited their strategy to the levels of logic
and conscious thinking, Hitler let his strategy be born in his own
subconscious and in the subconscious of all Germany. He definitely
made himself the focus of that power. To lose his contact for one
hour would cripple all his capacities, and effects and influences.
Himself a man of very mediocre abilities and of very unstable emotions, so long as he held his door open to the subconscious of his
people and reflected it with fidelity, he was almost irresistible. His
intuitive judgements, his timing of attacks, his programs and
speeches might not be honest or even logical, they might not seemingly make sense, but they "accomplished that whereunto they
were sent."

We came to the conclusion that the way to bring the war to a
conclusion quicker than anything else would be a recognition of
what the true nature of the war was, and the recognition of the
planes upon which it was being fought. The only way to counter
the powerful attacks of the enemy that were initiated on these subconscious levels, would be to launch a defensive movement on a
higher level of the SUPERCONSCIOUS plane, bringing into play

* From *A Man's Reach,* by Glenn Clark. Harper & Brothers, N. Y. $3.00.
Copyright, 1949. By permission.

the full use of the power of prayer and the full use of the power of love.

Glenn Harding and Starr Daily offered to drop all their other plans and go with me on a seven month journey to all the large cities of America with the purpose of marshalling an "army" of dedicated Christians who would join us in our campaign not to bring the kind of victory God would approve on the level of the conscious or the subconscious, but on the level of the SUPERCON-SCIOUS where love and prayer would be substituted for guns and tanks.

We would go above the level of Daladier, Chamberlain, Stalin, and Roosevelt; we would soar way above the level of Hitler who was out there in the "no man's land" of the psychic, surrounded by astrologers and delving in the occult, trusting to the magic of his subconscious mind. We frankly told our audiences that as long as we trusted merely to the mental powers of men, Hitler would continue to keep the advantage he already held; but the moment enough people, an entire army of them, would mount to a higher level, the level of the spiritual which is as high above the psychic as the psychic is above the mental, the power of Hitler would be short-circuited and every move that he would henceforth make would bring the war more rapidly to an end.

Whether our logic was right many might question, but whether the logic is sound or not, this much is a matter of history: before we started this campaign, November 1, 1942, nearly all our battles were defeats; after that nearly all our battles were victories; before that date every move Hitler made had the power of magic; he seemed incapable of making mistakes; after that date nearly everything he did boomeranged against him.

As I was recalling these incidents to Roland and Marcia Brown, it came to us with tremendous force that the most effective way to bring a great spiritual awakening in Germany would be to find some youth who had been led into the psychic frontier and lead him on a step farther into the spiritual frontiers of Jesus. Having been initiated into the powers generated by the subconscious it should not be an impossible task to initiate him into the immensely greater powers generated by the superconscious. If we could set one young German on fire with the flame of the spiritual realm as Hitler was set on fire with the flame of the psychic realm, the spiritual awakening in Germany might begin.

Then it was that God sent us the man. Letters had just arrived cancelling our prospective three-day meetings in Geneva, Switzerland and four days of meetings in Heidelberg, Germany, when out of a clear sky came a letter from a young minister near Hanover, Germany. Arnim Reimenschnieder had been a leader of Hitler Youth in the second World War. During the war he was a combat pilot against American forces; he was shot down behind American lines and held in American prison camps for eighteen months. It was there, in prison, that he learned English. Five years ago, when Roland was in Germany, Arnim's father, a prominent clergyman and leader among the churches of the Ruhr, had insisted that Arnim serve as Roland's interpreter for his speaking engagements. It was while he was interpreting that his new spiritual enlightenment began and, from a Hitler henchman, he became a bondservant of Jesus. I feel convinced that he is destined to become a leader in German spiritual life.

The letter of Arnim was an urgent request to come over into the very heart of Germany. Although written in modern terms, its effect upon us was exactly like the effect upon Paul of the call to come over to Macedonia. As we rode on the plane, Roland Brown told me more of the background of this young man.

Arnim was one of the organizers of the young people, zealously trying to bring the world under a totalitarianism in which he positively believed. That totalitarianism failed and in exchange Arnim found another totalitarianism to cleave to. The new unfailing center for his devotion was Jesus. Now with passionate zeal he is devoting his life to bringing the world under a spiritual government of which Jesus is the head. Young people, like Arnim, need goals to make life worthwhile. Otherwise there is a vacuum. They need goals they can strive toward passionately. Jesus set the goal for us in the Kingdom of Heaven, not only for attainment in the life to come, but to strive to bring into manifestation here on earth. That is the only goal that can enlist a man's entire being. And paradoxical as it may sound, that is the goal of the good life—albeit in a very inverted or perverted sense—which the Fascists, Nazis and Communists sought. They attempted to found a "Utopia" on earth—but alas, cut to their measure, not to God's measure.

Disillusioned with the Utopia of his master, Hitler, Arnim's new passion to bring in the Kingdom of Heaven of his very real Lord and Savior Jesus Christ was moving. The hope of Germany lies not in strong armed governments and what they shall do, but in young men like Arnim, who are striving to put the government on God's shoulders.

We flew in a hurricane wind to Hanover and were literally blown into the airport waiting room. Arnim and his uncle met us and drove us through the city spotted with vacant lots where buildings had crumbled beneath American bombs, and then south seventy-five miles to the village of Bodenfelder.

We were taken to the home of the Muellers. Before breakfast each day the Christian patriarch of the family read from a German translation of Stanley Jones' *How To Be A Transformed Person*, then from another book of daily readings, and then gave a prayer. At supper he read a chapter from the Bible. On our second day he took us through his cheese factory where one hundred employees produce fifteen tons of cheese a day. Nearby was the village's other large factory where vinegar was produced from lumber.

Surveying this tiny mountain village, I could foresee sparse hope of gathering an audience for the messages we were so eager to give. But little did I realize how this young man "on fire" was going to use us to awaken this whole section of Germany. That Sunday night we went to the large Lutheran Church in the adjoining village and found it packed to the doors with people who had come from miles around. While Roland was speaking from the High Pulpit I wondered how I, not a clergyman, could bring, through an interpreter, a message which these staid, theologically-minded Germans would appreciate. I would have given anything to escape the ordeal. During the singing of the choir following Roland's address, I realized my turn had come and though I knew I was inadequate I would have to go through with my assignment. As I climbed into the High Pulpit with Arnim beside me, I prayed, "Lord, this is it. Help me." After the opening sentences, I found the Lord speaking through me. The most thrilling part of this trip around the world was the expectancy with which people listened to talks on how to pray in order to carry out the purpose of God. Jesus knew what He was talking about when He said to His apostles as they started their speaking trips, "If they receive you as a righteous man, they will receive a righteous man's reward. If they receive you as a prophet, they will receive a prophet's reward." The audience creates the speaker more than the speaker creates his audience.

The next afternoon Arnim gathered a dozen clergymen from a wide area and after tea in the Mueller home, we had a remarkably inspiring afternoon, Roland with his unique sensitivity to the needs of clergymen, leading the way. That evening we were driven to another neighboring village where in a Baptist Church, on a week day, an amazing congregation of over five hundred were waiting. So ended two days of very worthwhile meetings in the very heart of Germany. In addition we prayed with many heavily burdened people, the most heartbreaking being two women whose husbands have been missing since the war. They were certain their husbands were still alive in one of Russia's prison camps. Of the two million Germans thus held, it is anticipated that less than a hundred thousand will ever return. The children, deprived of their fathers and deprived of the years of love and provision their fathers would give them, suffer along with the wives. War is hell, and seven years after the fighting is over the hell still exists.

My thought journeyed away to those three million unfortunates behind the stockades, or in the mines of Siberia, most of whom would never return to their wives and children. Suddenly between that picture and me, there loomed another picture—of three million, seventy-five thousand hopeless alcohol addicts in our land, many of whom would gladly exchange the hell they live in for the lesser hell of the Russian camps. Of the sixty-five million liquor drinkers in the United States, over three million have become enslaved beyond human recall. The Alcoholics Anonymous rescues one hundred thousand, but alas, that is a mere drop in the bucket. The addiction trusts through their control of every avenue of publicity, deifying profit as their god, have created a hell for millions in a land that abhors slavery of any kind. Two beloved alcoholic friends of mine, who later committed suicide, told me they would gladly have traded masters—John Barleycorn for a Russian prison camp—any time.

To catch our plane for Rome necessitated arising the next morning at 4:00 a.m. for it would take three hours to drive to the Hanover airport. Imagine our surprise to have the entire Mueller family up before we were, preparing breakfast for us. Their loving hospitality had been inexhaustible and the devotion revealed in their "Godspeed" lingered like a benediction. It was given "as unto pilgrims of the King."

As I left this home of God-fearing, hard-working, devoted folk, representative of the majority of the people of Germany, I knew that nothing could stop this great nation from re-establishing itself among the great nations of the world.

Since then, from many sources, I have learned that this "come back" has been faster than anyone dreamed. Ask those who have been in Germany recently and they will tell you that gleaming new cities have sprouted from rubble, acres of factories are humming, highways are crowded, threadbare Germans are now well dressed.

When you ask how has this come to pass so soon, the reply will be quick and to the point: Because of—first, three billion U. S. aid; second, no outlay needed for military purposes.

In other words, Germany's good fortune is that she lost the war. Two months later I made the same discovery in Japan. All Japan's great cities, except two, were completely destroyed by bombs, and now they are rebuilt far better than before. And the reasons for their quick come back are the same as Germany's: American aid and no outlay needed for military purposes.

Two other reasons can be added to those cited above: third, a passion for hard work, and fourth, a discipline in Germany unmatched in Europe, and a discipline in Japan unmatched in Asia.

A German named Siebel who has been a leader in his nation's recovery made this statement in regard to Germany's capacity for discipline and hard work: "It's part of our upbringing as children for we are taught that work is a virtue—almost an end in itself. And in our homes we have discipline; wise, sturdy discipline, and the things we are taught, we do not forget. There is a saying, 'the French work in order to live; the Germans live in order to work.' It is a question of pride, also. Other nations doubted that we could rebuild Germany. We did."

When you add to this capacity for discipline and hard work, faith in God, you have the bricks and the mortar for rebuilding a world; not for conquering, thank the Lord, but for rebuilding the world!

At 8:05 a.m. our plane was airborne and at 3:15 p.m. we reached Rome, having changed planes in Amsterdam and lunching on the ground in Frankfort en route. From winter-bound Northern Germany to blossoming Southern Italy on our magic carpet in only a few hours! It was a perfect sunny day with no clouds, so Roland was able to take colored pictures of the snow-clad Alps as they stretched in all their magnificent grandeur from one end of Switzerland to the other. Flying over the Swiss-Italian border, we watched the snow on the southern slopes of the mountains give way to green grass. We looked down on Florence and Assisi and finally, as our plane circled before landing, Roland took magnificent pictures of St. Peter's and the Coliseum.

CHAPTER IV

WE SEE ROME THROUGH
PROTESTANT EYES

WE WENT TO THE ANGLO-AMERICAN HOTEL, AND THE NEXT MORNING Rev. Dewey Moore, in charge of Baptist work in that part of Italy, picked us up by car to take us to the Catacombs. I have often spoken of my dream-wish to start forth one day on a hitchhiking journey which will take me from one end of the world to the other, going wherever the Spirit takes me. Well, this was such a day. As we had no plans for Rome, we let Dewey Moore take us wherever he wished. He chose first to pick up Miss Juliett Mather, who is editorial secretary of the Southern Baptist Missionary Union, and two other American women who were on a trip around the world, traveling in the opposite direction from which we were going. We were packed in the car like chummy sardines. I knew God was directing Dewey Moore's choice of companions for immediately after the introductions Miss Juliett exclaimed, "Fifteen years ago I heard Mr. Clark at Ridgecrest, at a Retreat where I was director." So we were old friends!

Dr. Moore next took us to the Cathedral of Loyola and the Counter Reformation which contains remarkable sculpture depicting Loyola with one foot treading on Luther and the other on the old woman who represented all non-Catholic Christian faiths. Loyola is revered because he helped to save Catholicism, after Luther's upheaval, by introducing a system of discipline through meditation on the *dying* Christ. The Camp Farthest Out has been striving to bring blessings on the world by getting Protestants to meditate on the *living* Christ. Unfortunately Loyola's Jesuits carried his militant discipline (he had been a Roman soldier) so far that it stimulated the persecutions known in history as the Inquisition, and its influence seems dominant even today in many Latin nations. We paused to survey the Roman Forum and then Dewey Moore took us down into the dungeon where St. Paul wrote the last of his letters to the churches. In this place, where St. Paul had sent up many prayers for the seven little churches he had started, we seven took hands and sent up a prayer for the seven hundred thousand churches which those seven little ones had now grown into.

Then we went to the Catacombs which I had visited before, but now for the first time with a Protestant guide. Dewey Moore proved an expert; he has studied the Catacombs for years. Among other things we learned how the Catacombs grew out of the underground home of Hermes, who is greeted in the last chapter of Paul's letter to the Romans.

Then Moore drove us to the Baptist Orphanage which he and his wife direct, and, after taking pictures of some of the children playing during the noon recess and others all combed and neatly uniformed in black smocks and white collars ready to march to school, we sat down to an excellent dinner prepared by Mrs. Moore. Our dinner conversation was God-directed, for it was there that Dewey Moore outlined a plan for Roland to spend a week, on his next trip if possible, with the young Protestant ministers in Italy who are hungry for a deeper spiritual life. Also Juliett Mather briefed us further on Southern Baptist contacts she was eager for us to make in Asia. Among the names she gave us were Eugene Hill in Singapore, Gladys Hopewell in Bangkok, and Maurice Anderson in Hong Kong. We were deeply interested in her account of the remarkable work carried on by Southern Baptist missionaries. We were inspired to hear that last year the American Southern Baptists received three million dollars for missions in a single day following their annual week of prayer for missions which is held every December.

In the evening, Moore took us to a Baptist prayer meeting where the men outnumbered the women four to one. Roland spoke first, and I followed, both interpreted by Rev. Ronge, the most influential Baptist minister in Italy. "If you win him to your cause, all Italy will be open to your future missions," Dewey Moore had said. I am sure Roland's address won him. And Roland will be returning for many future missions—not only to Rome but to dozens of other places hungry for deeper spiritual living.

My address was inspired somewhat as Paul's was on Mars Hill when he referred to the altar to the unknown god. I began by saying, "The greatest praise Jesus gave to any human being was directed to a man who was born in Rome, a Roman Captain, whose faith led Jesus to exclaim, 'I have not seen such faith, no not in all Israel.' " Little did I realize that a Roman Captain was sitting in *the seat right before me.* How those men did listen! When the meeting was over they crowded around us and we did not get away for almost an hour. And so this unpremeditated journey through Rome proved to be among the richest in our entire world-wide trip in its potential, far-reaching influences.

Up to that point on our journey, Italy was the first nation where we found the danger of a whole country's going Communistic. And the danger there is very real. Lacking the open Bible and freedom of thought that Protestantism inspires, bottle-fed by Emperors and dictators and spoon-fed by priests and popes, the people lack the political and spiritual maturity of such nations as England, Holland, and the United States.

Our friends told us that the great open sore in Italy today is its complete corruption in the field of taxes. Their government has no sure way of computing the income of the very rich so the wealthy blatantly falsify their income reports and pay only a percentage of what their real income tax should be. The wages of the poor, on the other hand, are easily checked, so upon the poor rests almost all the burden of taxation. Wherever corruption exists Communism walks in. As one passes through Italy he can already hear Communism knocking on the door.

Thursday morning, with nothing on the agenda and an obviously growing need for a haircut, I stepped into a barber shop where no one spoke English. As my hair was being removed (and I mean removed) I was asked many questions to all of which I said, "No." "Shampoo?" "No." So I was shampooed. "Manicure?" "No." So a girl pulled up a stool and proceeded to make my hands look like the Prince of Wales' hands.

I then went into the National Gallery beside our hotel, an immense palace that could have held all the finest pictures of the world, but is currently almost empty. I climbed three stories in this ghostly building, opened a door, and after paying fifty cents found only six rooms filled with treasures of art. There were Holbeins and Tintorettos and other famous paintings but it was not a canvas that impressed me most. In one room was a statue of a madonna and child, and I noticed the large number of people that paused and stood staring at it for long periods of time, especially the visiting priests. This was the year that Mary had been lifted to a new status by the Pope's pronouncement of the Assumption of the Virgin. One young moon-faced priest sat motionless, not once removing his eyes from the figure. When I returned some time later he had moved to another part of the room and again his eyes were glued upon the same statue.

This elevation of Mary to what amounts to equal status with Jesus has widened still further the breach that exists between Catholics and Protestants today.

CHAPTER V

A NEW GREECE IS BORN

AS DARKNESS WAS CLOSING IN WE FOUND OURSELVES FLYING OVER a portion of the same sea that Paul had sailed when on his missionary journeys that made Christian history; the same sea Odysseus had sailed during his ten years of wanderings which, at Homer's hands, made literary history. Soon we were circling over brilliantly illumined Athens. After landing and clearing customs, we checked our next day's noon-time flight for Cairo and discovered that the Arabian airplane company had been banned for smuggling and no longer flew to Cairo. However, T.W.A. had available space the next evening at 8:50. That gave us a whole day for seeing Athens.

Now our purposes in coming to Athens could be realized. From the inception of the idea to encircle the world on a mission of prayer we had envisioned climbing Mars Hill to stand where Paul stood and reconstructing in imagination the splendor of the Acropolis, temples, stadium, and market places of those days. So Athens was included in our round-the-world schedule. But when the round-the-world tickets were placed in my hand I discovered our time of arrival and departure permitted us but a few daylight hours in that history-laden city. There would not be time enough even to climb the Hill or mount to the Acropolis! We thanked God for arranging this day in ways which our organized planners could not have foreseen. But now, due to this readjustment of plane schedules, our dream of seeing Athens would be realized. As in every other forced change in this journey, our disappointments became God's appointments.

Never have I enjoyed sightseeing more. In college I had majored in Greek, and although I had made two previous trips to Europe I had never before seen Athens. The thrill of standing on Mars Hill and exploring the Acropolis is simply beyond words to describe. From these two heights we were able to see all of the city. On Mars

Hill our guide took our pictures while Roland "preached" the full address of St. Paul from the very spot where Paul stood. Then I recited the central portion of the same address and there-and-then we asked God to mold and guide us and the Belt of Prayer we were undertaking to construct, so that our messages, even as Paul's, might bless the whole world. In imagination we could see the transforming of all the altars, to known and unknown gods, into one grand altar totally dedicated to the one God—the God of Love, giver of every good and perfect gift, in whom there is no variation, neither shadow that is cast by turning.

Nineteen hundred years ago, it was upon that little mountain of Mars Hill that the nine judges held supreme court under the open sky, winter and summer, and there they brought the "babbler," Paul, that he might tell them further about this "new doctrine." So radiantly did he expound his faith that while some said it was foolishness, others said, "We will hear this further."

Then we climbed a still higher "mountain" only a few hundred yards away—the Acropolis. There on that famous five-acre plateau overlooking all Athens we stood in awe before the lovely remains of the world's greatest triumph of architecture, the Parthenon, created by the greatest architect of all time, Ictinus. Next to the Parthenon, with its Doric pillars, stands the greatest example of Ionian architecture, the Erechtheum. From these heights we could see far below us the immense stadium with a seating capacity of 50,000, carved out of a natural amphitheater formed by the Grecian hills; the mounting tiers of seats were of white marble, the only grandstand in the world entirely of marble. Marble is cheaper in Athens than wood. We could see the Agora, or market place, where Paul talked to poor and rich alike and in the opposite direction the prison where Socrates spent his last days.

We also saw one of the earliest theaters of history where the Attic tragedies were first created and staged. It is very interesting the way the drama began, first as a religious festival with a chorus and its leader, who often interrupted the music to make a speech to the audience. As these talks grew in importance, it became a full time job for one man, and the leading of the chorus was turned over to another. This led to frequent dialogues between actor and chorus-leader until two full time actors evolved, but their dialogues were always introduced and followed by choral hymns that embodied the spirit and followed the theme of the play. The actors always wore masks which could be easily changed to match any part they were to play. Aeschylus and Sophocles, who were the greatest dramatists of all time, second only to Shakespeare, continued to use only two actors, obeying the law of dynamic symmetry which I describe in detail in my book, *God's Reach*. Not until Euripides, was the third actor added to the cast. Until Shakespeare no dramatist excelled the masterpieces of Aeschylus and Sophocles, all of whose plays I had read in college days. Now for the first time I was looking down upon the theater where the story of the drama began.

I cut a branch from the root shoots of the olive tree transplanted from Olympia from which wreaths were made for victors in the Olympic games. Every four years, when the new Olympics start, a flame is carried from Olympus by relay runners who pause here by this olive tree and then, still bearing the flame, race on to wherever the games are to be held so that fire from Olympus may light the torch that burns throughout the period of the games.

Having majored in Greek I know something of Greek history, Greek literature and Greek life, so as I stood on this "mountain" I lived a thousand years and my heart beat in unison with the thousand heroes of the classic past. Upon the thousand boys I have coached in track during twenty years of college coaching, I here, in imagination, bestowed the olive wreath of victory.

We saw Athens first from that high vantage point, and later, as we walked the streets, we contemplated the excavations and recalled the familiar legends of the past. The Greeks, unlike the Romans who planted a Catholic Church over every historic landmark, have reverently preserved, in its natural state, every shrine or relic of ancient days.

In this city of Athens the development of the intellect reached the highest point in the history of the world. The greatest orators of all time were Demosthenes and Pericles; the greatest philosophers were Socrates, Plato, and Aristotle; the greatest architect, Ictinus; the greatest sculptor, Phidias; the greatest dramatists (with the exception of Shakespeare), Aeschylus, Sophocles, and Euripides; the greatest general, Miltiades; and the "eagle among the poets," Homer.

As I stood amid those glorious ruins, I wondered, "Is the intellect the last word?" Looking across the space separating us from Mars Hill, I recalled that it was written of Paul and Silas, who had come to this city, that "then they went beyond Athens." That was the message of the hour for me, indeed, the message underlying our entire journey around the world. Having been for thirty-five years a college teacher I appreciated the need for the intellect; but in this hour of world crisis the intellect is not enough. Not only Paul and Silas, but all the rest of us must go "beyond Athens" if we would find the final solution to the problems of life.

There is indeed a strange partnership in those twin hills, the Acropolis and Mars Hill, standing there side by side. One is sacred to the intellect, the other sacred to the soul. Wherever Greek civilization went without Christianity it degenerated. Wherever Christianity went without the undergirding of Greek culture, it lapsed into superstition and barbarism. But wherever Christianity and Greek culture went side by side, great civilizations were the result. Matthew Arnold's essay on Hebraism and Hellenism, followed by his still greater essay on Sweetness and Light, points out the dynamic symmetry of these two influences, one furnishing leaven for the soul and one furnishing light for the mind, together invigorating the modern world.

Ten years ago Greece went through a terrible ordeal. In December 1944, a few months after her liberation from the German occupation, the Communist party withdrew from the Greek government and tried to seize it. They burned and looted villages, torturing prisoners, abducting men, women, and children by the thousands and forcibly recruiting them into the guerrilla army. Nearly 700,000 refugees from the hills fled to Athens, being fed by American friends while they waited for their home areas to be freed of guerrillas.

It was almost impossible to root out the Communists as they masqueraded as villagers by day and did their marauding by night, and when driven against the wall, they slipped across national boundaries into Communist lands, returning when the pressure was off. Field Marshal Alexander Papagos finally solved the problem, and he did it by concentrating on the inner preparation of his men instead of the outer.

The hardest, most valiant unit in Papagos' army was composed of eighteen thousand soldiers who two years before had been youngsters with pro-Communist leanings. The Greek government had sent all such young men to Macronisos Island off Athens for a democratic indoctrination course. Here they learned the glories of Greece, its history, its potential. They were taught the relationship between religion and the dignity of man. In this school they came to know the techniques of Soviet Communism and the designs of Russian aggression.

Large numbers graduated as vigorous exponents of a new Greek nationalism. Less than five per cent turned out to be incorrigibles or confirmed Marxists.

These young men saw a vision of a new Greece, the promise of a land of opportunity for all. They wanted to rededicate Greece to the ideals of political and religious freedom. Greece would be born anew. It would never be the tail to any kite—Russian, British, American. The problem was to find work and employment for the surplus population of 1,500,000 people. As soon as Macedonia was cleared of guerrillas, Greece, with American help, introduced vast hydroelectric projects. New industries were established. In time all of Greece's people were finding employment, the specter of starvation disappeared, and Greeks no longer were lured into the political slavery of a Russian satellite state. Soviet propaganda that only Communism guaranteed work and bread for all had been disproved. In the hearts of a long suffering people was born a dream of a new Greece.

Alexander Papagos, as premier, took great strides toward making this dream come true. We must remember that Greece, a country two-thirds barren mountain slope, has always been poor. Throughout history her people have been obliged to seek livelihood in foreign lands. Only since recent developments in agriculture, supported largely by United States financial and technical aid, has Greece reached rudimentary self-sufficiency in food and normal necessities.

Ten years ago the whole future of Greece was in peril. Following World War II, when the United States was pouring billions of dollars of aid into Italy and Greece to safeguard them against the inroads of Communism, the corruption and misuse of funds was scandalous. Most of it went into the hands of the reactionary rich who siphoned it off into foreign investments instead of using it to rebuild the homes of those who had suffered most in the war.

However, today the government of Field Marshal Alexander Papagos has achieved some remarkable results in spite of the fact that it is still indifferent toward labor and civil servants.

It has maintained political stability, and has introduced legislation providing for fundamental and far-reaching economic improvement. It has been able to float a successful $10,000,000 internal loan, decrease investments in gold to some extent, and it has succeeded in balancing the budget—a feat not achieved since before World War II.

At the beginning of 1955 it may be said that basic conditions for further improvement are sound. Hopes are not likely to be dashed unless the international situation deteriorates.

CHAPTER VI

ABOVE THE SUN IN EGYPT

IT WAS ON THE HOUR OF MIDNIGHT WHEN OUR GREAT FLYING BIRD descended on the sands of Egypt. A handsome young stranger who introduced himself as Rev. Wilbur Skagg of the Church of God met us at the Cairo airport and conducted us to a typical Egyptian inn which looked very foreign to our eyes but had the familiar-sounding name of Hotel Windsor.

The next day brought the most thrilling sightseeing experience of our trip. It was a day of national celebration of Egypt's liberation from King Farouk which had occurred on July 23, 1952. The fact that the Egyptians celebrate this liberation every half-year shows how thoroughly they rejoice over their freedom. We saw nearly fifty-thousand uniformed Egyptian young men, all volunteers, marching on parade, demonstrating their determination to remain free.

Our first destination was the Great Pyramid. Rev. Manis Abd-Elnoor (meaning "Slave of Light") together with Samuel Habib, who is now studying journalism in the United States in order to help Frank Laubach in his literary work, came to be our guides and companions in a car loaned them by Miss Davida Finney, head of the government literacy work of Egypt. This thoughtful lady, whom we had not even met as yet, also loaned us her Egyptian chauffeur. Our every need was being cared for. We crossed the great and famous Nile over a beautiful bridge, then crossed the smaller Nile and passed on through Geiza which adjoins Cairo as Minneapolis adjoins St. Paul. I expected it would be a half day's ride out to the Pyramids, but they were just outside Geiza—where the mysterious Sahara Desert begins.

We had to climb about thirty high steps up the outside of the Pyramid before we reached the entrance. I had often wondered how one climbed the dark inner corridor. How low would one have to bend to get through the low sections? Would there be air enough? Would one get claustrophobia? How would one feel? But I forgot all those apprehensions in the thrill of experiencing at last what I had so long dreamed of doing.

We started up that narrow, cleated, sixty-degree sloping passageway of the high-ceilinged section of the main corridor at a breathtaking pace, but soon slowed to a deliberate ascent. We paused at the landing where the long low passageway branched off, leading to the Queen's Chamber annunciating (according to certain symbolic interpretation) the introduction of an era where the love of Jesus would lift the meek, downtrodden, underprivileged, individual, nations, races, and sexes and set them free. I was glad we postponed going through that Queen's Corridor until our return trip, as it would have taxed my endurance to walk that distance stooping down. As we continued upward we reached the point where the high ceiling ended; from there on we did indeed climb "bending low"—so low it was almost like going on "all fours." Finally we reached the top where we could straighten up. On the level grade approaching the King's Chamber we first had to stoop under a low corridor, symbolizing, so the students of the Prophecies of the Great Pyramid tell us, the First World War. Then we could straighten up with plenty of head room for a few steps and then had to bend for a few more steps under the "depression of 1929," and then, Hallelujah, we were in the King's Chamber where in the center stands an open tomb about the size of an overgrown bathtub. This tomb represented the Second World War—a tomb where the last of all the world wars is supposed to be buried. A few steps beyond this tomb the corridor runs smack up against a stone wall which, according to a report in *Time Magazine* of August 31, 1953, "signifies the final collapse of aggressive military systems and the cleansing of the earth and humanity as God's sanctuary."

And so at last we stood in the King's Chamber. Let us hope that the prognostications are right and that the symbolism of this chamber proclaims the end of all wars with the implication that whatever nation takes the aggression in starting a war will be in danger of crushing itself into fragments against the implacable wall of destiny.

This tomb was used by Egyptian priests in their initiatory rites. They placed the novitiate in the tomb and gave him a drug that induced three days' sleep, at the close of which he was resurrected as a "new creation." This beautiful symbol of rebirth was later actually materialized by Jesus. Roland and I stepped into the tomb and, joining hands with Marcia, Menis Abd-Elnoor and Samuel Habib, who remained on the outside, we five stood in silent prayer, the Lord cooperating beautifully by keeping all other visitors out of the room. Then I prayed this prayer aloud:

"Heavenly Father, here in the King's Chamber where the 'corridor of prophecy' ends and the final prophecy of world peace begins, we join our hearts in a great and vital petition to Thee. On this day that Egypt is celebrating her liberation from tyranny, in a land where 6,000 years ago the Israelites also celebrated their liberation from an earlier tyranny, we pray that the entire world will be liberated from the greatest of all tyrannies, war and the causes of war. Here stand representatives of the oldest and newest civilizations, the eastern and western hemispheres, the old world and the new, uniting all the world today in a prayer for peace. Amen."

As I prayed these words I imagined that all the heart-yearnings of two billion people were flowing through me to God from all over the world!

Then down the passageway we went, detouring for a few moments in the Queen's Chamber and then out into the open air, carrying a memory that will never fade.

On camels we rode the half mile or less past the three pyramids to the low excavated plane where we looked into the face of the Sphinx. It has the face of a man, the head of a woman, and the body of a lion, symbolizing wisdom, beauty, and power. Later in the day in the Public Square of Cairo we saw a statue representing a stirring modern interpretation of the Sphinx, showing the lion body beginning to rise, forelegs straightened, and beside the Sphinx the figure of a standing woman, head uplifted, veil pulled back, and eyes open, symbolizing the awakening of the soul of Egypt, ready at last to step forward in all her wisdom, beauty, and power.

And it is about time that Egypt was awakening from her age-long slumber. Egypt represents the oldest known civilization in the world. For hundreds of years she was the ruler of the world, but for three milleniums she has been ruled by other nations, beginning with Babylon and ending with England.

The real power behind this present revolution is not Naguib but

Nasser, a young man of high character and outstanding ability, still in his thirties. He has directed the whole movement with a high selfless purpose trying to keep out of the spotlight himself. But the problem he faces is tremendous. The density of population is the highest in the world and the living standards the lowest. The average individual income is less than eighty-seven dollars a year, and 75 per cent of the people are illiterate. The physical condition of the people is low: the plagues the nation was visited with in the days of Moses can hardly vie with the plagues of amoebic dysentery and blindness that she is plagued with today. Only 4 per cent of Egypt is habitable; the twenty-two million inhabitants are confined to the narrow green strip of the Nile Valley, two and a half million of them living in Cairo, the largest city in the Moslem world.

Having taken a good look at this statue symbolizing the awakening of the new Egypt, we were conducted to the Museum where we were whisked back three thousand years to glimpse Egypt's opulent past as represented by the fabulous jewelry and relics belonging to the Prince! We were shown six immense gold caskets, of graduated sizes, each having been encased in the casket one size larger. The largest was the size of a good-sized room; the last the size of an immense coffin. This gigantic coffin in turn contained seven mummy cases, each of diminishing size and each of which had the reclining figure of Prince Tutankhamen carved in gold upon its top. The sixth and last case enclosed the mummy of the Prince himself. The ornate decorations, all gold, upon all these cases and caskets simply took our breath away. The jewelry and relics once sealed within these caskets filled nearly an entire wing of the Museum. All these riches of toil and treasure had been hidden away from the eyes of mankind, protected by a secret poison destined to "liquidate" all but one of the seven archeologists who penetrated the chamber where the great discovery was made in 1922. Immortality, according to Egyptian legends, was only for the rulers, and the more safely their physical bodies were preserved the more certain would be their eternal life.

A perfect modern parallel to this ancient royal selfishness and total disregard for the lives and the rights of others can be found in the last monarch of Egypt—King Farouk, himself. It was very appropriate that we should have been taken immediately from the

relics of the dead ancient monarch to the palace of the living ex-
monarch of the present.

King Farouk's palace, only a few hundred yards from the Great
Pyramid, is the most artistically ornate and expensively furnished
and decorated mansion I ever hope to see. Farouk was so selfish
that no one enjoyed this mansion but himself and favored guests.
He had many castles and entertained favored guests lavishly, but
not one bite of food left over from table-laden banquets would he
let the poor servants or starving peasants eat; all of it had to be
buried in the ground. He exacted terrific taxes from the poor.
When he was banished the whole nation rejoiced and almost immediately a law was passed allowing no land owner to own more
than two hundred acres. In contrast to the attitude of King Farouk,
Egypt's President Nagiub in his address that day announced that religion was the only true foundation of true governments and that
Egypt's new life would begin with a revitalization of religion.

We had come to Cairo to see the pyramids, not anticipating any
significant religious meetings for us to address as I did not know a
single religious leader in Cairo until I arrived. To our amazement
and joy we found the greatest spiritual response of our entire trip
in this city of two million. This city is filled with people of all
nationalities and each group preserves its own identity, but in the
Church of God Mission individuals from all groups come together
every Saturday evening for a "singspiration." And how they did
sing!

As if the Lord had arranged this meeting particularly for us it so
happened that only English-speaking folks came to these special
sing times, as all the songs were in the English language. So our
very first evening in this land of diverse tongues found us greeted by
a well blended group eager and ready to receive our message at
first-hand. Under such conditions no wonder Roland Brown's joyous
message brought a joyous response. And when I finished my talk,
instead of appearing wearied, they acted as if they were eager for
more! Afterwards, as in a country church or in my Bible Class back
home, everyone hung around visiting and showering love and appreciation upon us.

The next morning, Sunday, Roland spoke in Reverend Skagg's
Church of God, and I spoke in the Evangelical Church of Reverend

Ibrahim Said, the largest Protestant church in Cairo. Rev. Ibrahim Said fetched me an hour in advance and asked me to think my talk out loud as we sat in his study. He took careful notes. Later, after I finished my sermon to his huge congregation, he was able to give his translation in a solid piece, a method that fits my delivery better than being interpreted, line by line.

Ibrahim Said, who is the most eloquent preacher in Egypt, built this church from a hundred members to two thousand, the largest congregation in Egypt. He told me that the teaching of Christianity had not been allowed in the schools by King Farouk, but since liberation, permission has been given by the government and Ibrahim Said has been commissioned to write four books about Christianity to be used in the schools. The very first edition of these books will be 150,000 copies.

When I faced his congregation of fifteen hundred people I was amazed to see over one thousand men and less than five hundred women. The strange, fierce sounding Egyptian words sung to familiar American hymn tunes were thrilling but almost frightening. At times I felt as Moses must have when facing the Egyptians with Pharaoh and the dignitaries of his court all lined up before him. Half the men were wearing fezzes, hats like red inverted flower pots with tassels—a head-dress they never take off in churches or restaurants. And every minute I was inwardly thanking God for this opportunity. I talked on "Praying Above the Sun."

"In the book of Ecclesiastes," I told them, "the old preacher asserted that there was no new thing under the sun. He elaborated on this by repeating twenty-seven times, 'vanity, vanity; all is vanity under the sun.' I could agree with the dear old pessimist when it comes to drinking and betting and carousing. But when he included labor and learning and practically all the worthwhile activities of life, I was about to conclude that the old man had gone too far, until—

"And this was what stopped me—the sudden realization that in spite of our great increase in human intelligence and our vaunted progress there have been more people killed and more property destroyed, and more terrible things happened in the past fifty years than in the whole history of mankind from the days of Jesus until the last fifty years began. If we are progressing, it appears that in all ways except scientific inventions we have been progressing backward. And the cause of it all is that we have been doing too many things *under* the sun—that is to say with the intellect only, when the only things that count, that can never be destroyed are the things done *above* the sun—in the realm of the Spirit.

"Franklin Roosevelt had a Brain Trust. What calamities could have been prevented had he had a Prayer Trust! The Children of Israel didn't *think* their way out of captivity. A man-child was born and placed in the bulrushes, and without any skills in the realm of logic or oratory he led them into freedom. Hopeless alcoholics and fallen men and women don't think themselves into rebirth and rehabilitation. Another man-child was born and wrapped in swaddling clothes and laid in a manger. Not through thoughts in human minds but through the grace of this man-child are men saved.

"The world has tried to fight its way out of trouble, and found all its efforts were vanity, vanity under the sun. It has tried to *think* its way out and that too has bogged down to a mere weariness of the flesh. We should find an elevator to carry us above the sun. Yes, the time has come when we must turn to prayer and pray as no Christians have ever prayed before."

I was fascinated by the face of a white-haired woman in the audience, a face as responsive as the antenna of a radio. Afterwards she introduced herself as Miss Davida Finney, whose car and chauffeur had been serving us. She is head of the American Mission (Congregationalist) and leader of the literacy work in Egypt, and she announced she was to take me to dinner in the Mission. There I met an Egyptian woman, Miss Helena, who is to be Miss Finney's successor when she retires. These two have been a wonderful help to Dr. Laubach in his literacy work. "Literacy is the heart of the real Point Four Program," said Miss Finney. "Every village is crying for helpers to come to them and if we had a million dollars to send out enough Christian literacy teams we could 'literacize' and take a long forward step toward Christianizing Egypt in one year. Selfishness and fear are the blocks. Our government, out of fear, would rather spend sixty billion on armaments than one million for literacy; and the Egyptian government out of fear holds the work in check, as they are afraid of making the common peasants literate too fast. So they object to the 'Each one teach one' method which requires every learner to become a teacher and pass on what he has learned before he gets a second lesson, a method which enables literacy to spread like wildfire with little professional help. By the government's requiring that every teacher be paid the work is slowed up."

In the afternoon I addressed a gathering in the Church of God in the same hall in which we had met Saturday night and I sincerely hope that my talk on "The Prodigal Son" encouraged some prodigals to return to the Father. Then Wilbur Skagg took me in his station wagon over to the American Mission, where Roland was speaking. There for the first time I met Rev. Eldon, who had been the dynamic, yet unobtrusive, arranger of many of these meetings. It was there I also met Miss Martin, head of the American Mission College for girls, an outstanding college attended not only by the daughters of the leading families of Egypt but of all Africa. Miss Martin, through them, has had tremendous influence over the leaders of the nations of that part of the world. To my joy she invited me to speak at the college the next morning.

The next day, as I stood before those eight hundred girls I found myself looking into the future, for these young women may decide the destiny of Africa. Daughters of many of the influential men of Northern Africa were there, such as the daughters of Haile Selassie of Ethiopia, also many daughters of cultured Arabic refugees from Palestine. It was a typical, required chapel service, limited to twenty minutes, so I do not know how much of a dent my message made on them, but the large staff of teachers, most of them Americans, were certainly grateful. They seemed truly disappointed that I couldn't spend more time with them. Miss Martin told me it was against the law of the land for a Moslem to attend a Christian service but in spite of that fact the Moslem girls in the college constantly came to chapel. She said the wife of the Egyptian Ambassador in Washington, D. C. had been educated at this college and, although a Moslem, is a great influence for spiritual uplift.

Menis and Samuel arrived with Miss Finney's car to take the Browns and me on another fascinating tour. It was our only opportunity to get a systematic and intimate look at this picturesque city. First we went to the bazaars where we meandered through the narrow streets surveying an endless variety of wares, and pausing to watch the workers in ivory and brass and bronze busy at the entrances of their shops.

Then we went to the Citadel. Inside the grounds is a famous

mosque and, after seeing its palatial interior, at our request, the guards turned on the thousand lights long enough for Roland to take a picture. It was here that the grandfather of King Farouk invited all the rulers of Egypt, the meneleeks, to a love feast, and when they were assembled called in his soldiers and had them all killed. Thus he became the absolute ruler. The boomerang for a dynasty built on such treachery arrived two generations later, only two years before our visit, when King Farouk was cast off the throne. Should he return today from his exile, we have been told that every Egyptian would strive to be the first to strike a fatal blow.

In the courtyard of the mosque we watched Moslems wash themselves at the sacred fountain in preparation for prayer. First they washed their hands and forearms up to the elbows, then their feet, then their necks and faces, spending much time on their ears and nostrils. Some of the older men spent an unconscionable length of time on these ablutions. If they did this five times a day I don't see how they could get anything else done. When the hour appointed for prayer came the voice of the priest at the foot of the high tower rang out: "Let all good people come for prayer." They now knelt down on the matted floor and began their leaning back and forth, spending long periods prostrate with forehead touching the floor. If most of this prayer energy was released for the world, and not merely for personal well-being, what power for good would be poured forth! Women, I noticed, did not join in this public prayer.

Next we went to the oldest Christian church in Egypt built over the cave where Joseph and Mary brought the baby Jesus to escape the "Slaughter of the Innocents" by Herod in Bethlehem.

In the afternoon we were taken to the home of Ibrahim Said where the leading Christian ministers of Cairo had gathered, first for tea and then to listen to messages from us. This turned out to be a God-given opportunity to initiate them in the kind of "revival" they all said they needed, "worth the entire trip to Africa." The editor of their Christian magazine said he would write it up with pictures, which Roland and I were able to give him.

From there Professor Arthur Brown, head of the Department of Philosophy and Religion of the American University, took us to his home for a wonderful supper. His wife warned us against eating lettuce and raw vegetables lest we get amoebic dysentery which is so common in Cairo. We told her how careful we were about such things, and we then went into raptures over the fresh strawberries we had eaten the night before.

"Oh, never under any condition ever eat a strawberry!" she exclaimed. "When people eat strawberries they *always* get amoebic dysentery."

We recalled how Jesus said it was not what people took into their mouths that defiled them, but the kind of thoughts they entertained in their souls, so we took special pains to ask God to cleanse our souls that night.

We did not get amoebic dysentery!

At 8:30 p.m. we were taken to the home of Mr. Frank Elmore, the legal advisor for the Point Four Program of all Arabic speaking nations. One man was in charge of developing new water supplies so as to bring more desert land under cultivation; one was developing sheep so that the peasants could get ten pounds of wool instead of three from each sheep; another was breeding thousands of American poultry. All these men were sincerely interested in our messages. Instead of spending their evenings in cocktail parties as we had heard many Point Four people do, they are going all out to develop prayer groups of which Mrs. Arthur Brown will be the chief promoter.

The next morning Miss Martin took me to the church where the Presbytery, consisting of one hundred Presbyterian ministers (all wearing fezzes) were meeting. Here I was privileged to tell of my experience with prayer and why I feel that only God and prayer can save the world. They were glad to hear of how President Eisenhower leaned on prayer, and how we were building a belt of prayer around the globe. When I finished, a man who had been writing at something during my entire speech, instead of watching me, arose and began an eloquent address in Arabic on some theme which, of course, I could not understand. When I asked the man beside me what he was so eloquent about, he replied that he was giving, word for word, a translation of my talk.

The Rev. Ibrahim Said took me to his home where Roland and Marcia, who had spent the morning taking pictures of ancient Cairo, joined us for dinner. That evening we closed our stay in Egypt with a grand meeting in his great Evangelical Church. What an experience in Egypt! Hallelujah!

CHAPTER VII

PALESTINE

OUR LAST NIGHT IN CAIRO WE STARTED TO BED EXPECTING TO RISE AT four-thirty to catch the Air Jordan plane for Jerusalem when a phone call came saying engine trouble would prevent our leaving for twenty-four hours. We slept that night in perfect peace knowing when the Lord closes one door He opens a better one. The next morning around nine o'clock Wilbur Skaggs took us to Mid-East airlines and found the best of accommodations as far as Beirut. We knew that when we reached there the Lord would provide a way for us to continue on to Jerusalem. And He did! As Wilbur Skaggs watched us pocket our new plane tickets he commented that he wouldn't have sent his worst enemy via Air Jordan. I knew I wouldn't make my worst enemy rise at 4:30 a.m. So we all thanked the Lord. We had decided by this time on our journey that the Lord was an excellent tour manager. He had made changes in three out of our last four flights and every change had been to our advantage.

As the Red Sea parted for Moses and the Israelites four thousand years ago, so the clouds parted for us permitting us to get a good view of their route of flight as we were crossing the sea—in one regard just like the Israelites—without getting our feet wet. Again later the clouds parted to let us see Mt. Herman; and again as we were flying over Damascus. So many clouds accompanied us that we pondered their meaning. We remembered the Biblical account of the pillar of cloud that led the Israelites by day; the thick cloud on Mt. Sinai from which God spoke to Moses; and the overshadowing cloud at the Transfiguration. In those days the cloud symbolized the Holy Presence which was with them and we rejoiced at the assurance that the Presence was with us also.

The moment our feet touched the solid ground in Palestine, we drew in long breaths. We were on the same soil and drinking from the same air of Jesus in Palestine.

A Mid-Eastern limousine carried us the mile journey up to Old Jerusalem over a road Jesus had so often trod in his journey from Nazareth up to Jerusalem, and dropped us off at the American Colony Hotel. Mrs. Bertha Vester, the delightful owner of the hotel, has spent seventy years in Palestine. She explained that in the days before the partition of the Holy Land into the Arab and Jewish sections we could have used the Y.M.C.A. building for some really large meetings, but all the buildings of that type, as well as most of the people she could have drawn, were now on the "other side." This led to a discussion of the whole Jewish-Arabian problem. We were told that the United States government directly or indirectly through the United Nations has been guilty of considerable unfairness to the Arab states. The immense political pressure of the influential advocates of the Zionist movement, just before election, led to "selling the Arabs down the river" for the sake of the New York Jewish votes which could swing the election. The rich land of Palestine was allotted to the Jews, the stony land to the Arabs, and when the time for evictions came, the Arabs were driven out without homes, private belongings, or even the money invested in property or banks at home.

Mrs. Vester said that her friend Dr. Lambie, a medical missionary in charge of the Barace (Berachah) T. B. Hospital near Bethlehem, was our best hope of gathering a group together. She phoned him in Bethlehem and it was arranged that the following day he and Mr. Khoury, an Arabian Christian who had written us before we arrived, would meet with us in our hotel and make plans.

As they would not arrive until noon that gave us all morning for wandering about and a wonderful morning it was. With guide and taxi we went at once to the Mount of Olives. The secret of getting to the soul of the Holy Land is to strip off the elaborate outer trappings of temples and shrines erected through the centuries of Christendom over all the Holy places and to behold again the simple, uncluttered contour of the land which is essentially the same as in Jesus' day, thus letting the man-made structures not obscure, but mark more vividly, the places where Jesus' feet have trod. This I found it quite possible to do.

Within the ancient building known as the Chapel of the Ascension an uncovered stone in the floor marks the spot where Jesus is reputed to have stood at the time He ascended into Heaven.

So here Roland and I took turns standing as we asked the Lord to
draw us upward, always upward, and hold us always in the Heavenly Dimensions.

Then we went to the Garden of Gethsemane. They say olive
trees never die unless they are actually pulled up roots and all, so
when we found that four of the olive trees of Jesus' day are actually
still standing in the garden, we touched them lovingly and reverently as Jesus' disciples must have touched them two thousand
years ago. Those trees and the hills and the stones under our feet
brought Jesus very close to us. The Roman Catholics have built a
beautiful temple over the stone beside which Jesus is supposed to
have knelt when he prayed, "Not my will but Thine be done." We
three were alone in the Temple at the time so we, too, knelt there
and prayed that the wistfulness of Jesus for the saving of the world
that dark night would bear fruit now that two thousand years have
gone by. We timidly offered to make restitution for the three
disciples who were sound asleep during Jesus' agony in the garden
by being three disciples wide awake to act as channels for all Jesus'
dreams and desires to become manifest. The word AWAKE had
special meaning for us, because we represented an interdenominational movement that uses the letters of that word to call all Christians to promote "A War of Amazing Kindness Everywhere."

Next we went to a place locally known as Gordon's Garden. It
was here that General Gordon initiated some archeological dig-
gings that uncovered what many investigators believe was the true
Garden of Joseph of Arimathaea. And in the bordering hill of
solid rock they found a tomb. Mrs. Mattar, the lovely Arab-Chris-
tian lady, whose husband is the keeper of the garden, conducted
us through the garden, and left us alone at the tomb. It looked
exactly as I had expected, even to the carved-out trough so that the
"stone" could be rolled away from the entrance. Stooping down
we went inside and after a period of holy silence Roland seated
himself at the head and I at the foot of the tomb where the two
angels were seated when Mary Magdalene and the others looked
in and the angels announced to them, "He is not here, but is risen."
Then we all prayed in turn that Christians around the world might
no longer worship a Christ entombed in rituals and memorialized
in church windows and art galleries, but a living Christ manifesting
through us here and now. Whether or not the site was authentic,

the experience within of the living Christ was authentic, and that
is all that really counts.

Shortly after we reached the American Colony Hotel that noon
our two guests arrived, Dr. Lambi and Mr. Khoury, both from
Bethlehem. How refreshing it was to be with them. They were the
first two we had met in Palestine who were on fire to see the Christians of the Lord's land lifted from the spiritual lethargy into
which they seem to have fallen. Dr. Lambi, an old man at sixty-
eight, had expended himself in a remarkable missionary work
covering most of Africa and Asia before coming to Palestine to
direct the hospital work. He had to leave before lunch but not
until after he had invited us to come to his home the next day,
when we could continue to plan some way of reaching the people
of Jordan. Mr. Khoury stayed in our hotel for lunch. He was born
in Samaria; his ancestors were Arab Christians from the days of the
Apostle Philip's ministry. He was a clergyman, had three degrees
from American Universities and was then working for the United
Nations. He invited us to spend Saturday with him on an all-day
trip to Samaria where he could show us many Bible landmarks.
For Sunday he and Dr. Lambi could arrange initial meetings in
Bethlehem, after which we could see what would open up. Trusting utterly to God's guidance, our hearts were in a constant state of
wonder and gratitude over the way He was making every path
clear.

After Mr. Khoury left we summoned our guide again and selected
the winding road that led from Jerusalem down to Jericho. *Down*
is the correct word, for the descent within those eighteen miles
drops from twenty-five hundred feet *above* sea level at Jerusalem
to the Dead Sea, eight hundred feet *below* sea level. We paused at
the brook Cherith where Elijah had fled and where he was fed by
the ravens; we saw the wilderness hills where Jesus was tempted
of the devil; and finally we crossed the Jordan upstream from the
place where John the Baptist baptised thousands.

Along the way we saw flocks of sheep, many flocks mixed together, grazing where nothing but sheep could gather nourishment
from these rocky hills. On our return at dusk we saw the shepherds
calling their sheep out of the mingling flocks, and watched as each
sheep responded to its master's voice. Jericho is so deep in a valley
that it is always warm, and is therefore a popular winter resort for

the citizens of Palestine. All permanent buildings in Jericho are built of stone but outside the city we found hundreds of mud huts belonging to hordes of refugees. We went on till we reached the Dead Sea, as smooth as glass this day as there was no wind, and so clear and transparent that we could see every pebble at its bottom. But to touch the tongue with a finger wet with its briny water was to taste something as bitter as quinine. Beyond the sea loomed the hills of Moab where Moses stood and looked down upon this well-watered valley of the Jordan and called it a land flowing with milk and honey. With the mountains in the background fading into soft blues because of a slight haze, in contrast to the brilliant crispness of the transparent water, this view of the Dead Sea would tempt any artist.

On our return to Jericho we stopped to watch the English archeologists excavating *ancient* Jericho, the Canaanite city where Joshua sent his spies to spy out the land. Here at a dozen different levels deep down in the earth we saw English experts kneeling with trowel and brush carefully uncovering the precious relics of the past while around them Arab helpers with pick, shovel, and bucket, under careful supervision, were removing at a little faster rate the worthless "fill" from areas where nothing precious was being uncovered. A whole day of excavating would often go by with less than one foot of progress. Such work requires faith, fortitude, and patience. They started this work in 1910, and it may be the year 2,000 A.D. before the job is finished. "This stratum," one English archeologist pointed with his finger to a level far below the surface, "belongs to a civilization two thousand years ago and that deeper stratum three thousand years ago. The deepest level down there is five thousand years old. Way down there we are uncovering the oldest known city that existed centuries before Joshua came." One city upon another; one civilization built upon another!

Below us, at the side of the road that extended miles northward toward Galilee, was Elijah's well and hundreds of women with empty jars on their heads were coming in a steady stream and hundreds more were returning with the filled jars on their heads. It was in the late afternoon and a thousand women must have passed by before we left. I could imagine the calendar had been turned back two or three thousand years and that these were Biblical times. Riding back to Jerusalem the hills looked like backs of swine exactly as I had described them in my book, *Come Follow Me*. And so ended our first full day in Palestine!

The next day we travelled the road to Bethlehem, part of it by way of a long detour because the barbed wire that marks off the Jewish sector cut across the good road. Dr. Tom Lambi showed us through his hospital and then took us to his home. For years, before coming to Palestine, he had been a typical David Livingstone for the natives of Africa. In his aging years he and Mrs. Vester of the American Colony Hotel raised money for a desperately needed T. B. hospital for the Jordan sector, which he was running very efficiently, but with a mournful wistfulness, for all the patients were Moslems, and how he yearned that the inhabitants of the Holy Land might know Jesus!

After dinner he read aloud from the twentieth chapter of 2nd Chronicles how the Lord told the Israelites to leave the battle to Him, and so instead of fighting they sent forth singers of praise to God while the attacking nations, each failing to recognize the other in the heavy mists, fell upon each other and all were destroyed. It required three days for the Israelites to gather up the spoils, after which they assembled in the valley of Berachah to thank the Lord. Dr. Lambi pointed from the window of his house and said, "That is the valley of Berachah, the place of thanksgiving." So at this place of thanksgiving we stood for a time counting our own blessings. That was the last time we ever saw Dr. Lambi. Before the year rolled round while he was delivering a talk at the Gordon Tomb his spirit took wing and his body fell near where the body of Jesus had lain. So ended the second day.

The third day Mr. Khoury took us down another winding road, the one that Jesus took whenever he went through Samaria to Galilee. We saw sowers in the fields casting seed; some, apparently, was falling on good ground, but so much seemed to fall on stony ground. Mr. Khoury told us of the legend in which God gave each of two angels a sack of rocks to scatter over the face of the world. One dropped his entire bagful on Palestine, scattering enough rocks in that one country to build all the buildings in the world, with plenty left over. Here and there we saw oxen, often yoked with a mule, pulling a single bladed wooden plough, the only kind of a plough that could possibly fit between, and survive, the stones. When we saw fields with wheat and barley coming up in February, to be followed in the summer with a crop of vegetables, we realized the situation for food is not altogether hopeless.

Every turn in the road brought vivid reminders of the days of the Scriptures. All along the way we became increasingly aware of Jesus' mantled figure and the twelve mantled men with staves in their hands walking ahead of us. Finally we caught up with the invisible Jesus at Jacob's well, the most genuinely authenticated site in all Palestine. We saw Him requesting the woman to draw water for Him. As we drank water from the same well we contemplated the three levels through which Jesus drew this woman— from the sewer level to the street level to the sky level.

There are three levels of worship, Jesus told the Samaritan woman: "Ye worship that which ye know not." Hers was ignorant worship. The Jews said, "We worship that which we know." Theirs was intelligent worship. But the highest level of worship was introduced by Jesus Christ: "The hour cometh and now is, when the true worshippers shall worship the Father in spirit and in truth."

Hardly the length of a football field away stands the site of the village of Sychar from which the crowd came to hear this Man.

Mr. Khoury, our Arab friend and guide who was born and brought up in Samaria, took us to the temple of the Samaritans, a dwindling race belonging to three tribes, of whom there are only three hundred and three survivors now living. But, as they consistently inter-marry, they are all "pure Samaritan." Three bearded priests, each of a separate tribe, had to be summoned to let us into the temple as all have keys of different shape and the door will not open till all three locks are unbolted. Inside was their famous thirty-five hundred year old scroll of the Pentateuch, hand-engraved on ancient sheep parchment, which if unrolled would extend seventy-five feet. Ten million dollars could not buy this parchment.

Then the three priests took us to the High Priest who is a direct descendant of Aaron. As in the past, the Samaritans follow the first five books of the Bible and nothing more. They still fanatically maintain that the only place God is to be found is on Mt. Gerizim, and the High Priest told us how the real Ark of the Covenant is hidden in that mountain and not in Jerusalem. They observe the Sabbath, Saturday, allowing no cooking, no work of any kind on that day: only prayer and meditation. They even refused to allow Roland to photograph them on the Sabbath as that would be "work."

We found how very intense is this conflict between Jews and Samaritans over the proper place to worship God—in the Temple or on the Mount. That point of dispute is the real reason the Samaritans broke off from the Jews, and it has remained the grounds for their antagonism through the years. How vivid according to the fourth chapter of John this contention made the conversation of Jesus with the Samaritan woman by the well. Jesus directed her, "Neither in this mountain, nor in Jerusalem," but in the secret place of your heart ye shall "worship God in spirit and in truth." But her descendants still hug their mountain worship and still sacrifice sheep there once a year.

We also saw the excavated city of Samaria which was the capital of Israel for hundreds of years, with its forum built during the Romans' rule, and its coliseum as big as the Yankee Stadium with a great road, like a four lane highway, running between the pillars, through which the chariots entered in triumph.

Rev. Sarah, the young Arab Christian minister of the only Protestant church in Samaria, arranged a meeting of nurses and visitors in Samaria's famous hospital, and Roland and I had a very vital meeting with them ending with a zealous desire by all to start prayer cells. We had been told that the Christian Churches of Palestine are asleep, but it heartened us to find that the ministers we met at least admitted they were asleep, for in this humility and honesty lies the hope of the nation. When a pastor, such as Rev. Sarah, begs us to waken his church, "beginning with me, the minister," then we know that a real awakening will come. On returning to Jerusalem that evening we went to see the Canon of the Episcopal Church and he begged Roland to address his Arab Anglican congregation on Sunday morning, exclaiming in almost identical words of Rev. Sarah, "I need awakening myself." We were sure that great blessing would come to this minister and his church.

On Sunday while Roland addressed the Episcopal church in Jerusalem, I addressed the only Protestant church in Bethlehem, a church which holds around one hundred and fifty people. Some twenty-five in my morning congregation were blind and they sang, as a choir, the hymn, "Jesus Is Coming Again." I told the audience,

"Jesus is coming every day in our hearts but we don't all know it. The Shepherds *heard* the angels announce it, but they didn't *see* the star. The wise men *saw* the star but didn't *hear* the angels. These blind friends can't see but they can hear and today they enabled us to *hear* a beautiful song of hope while we *saw* their faith."

After our morning services in Bethlehem and Jerusalem we gathered in the Khoury home for a delicious native meal in fellowship with this delightful family and then were guided by Khoury to the cave of the Nativity where we prayed for Jesus to be born in the hearts of people everywhere.

We three had meetings with various youth groups on Sunday afternoon. Roland met with young men in Jerusalem assembled in the grounds of the Gordon Tomb; Marcia led a large group of girls in Bethlehem; while in the same sacred city I led the sixty boy Crusaders, a strange title for descendants of the very Arabs the ancient Crusaders had fought in the past. So ended that Lord's day.

Many of our good friends begged us to return for a month in Palestine next year. They agree that there is a spiritual heaviness that fills the air in Palestine. "Truly without a vision the people perish," said one of them. "Jesus' vision has too long been absent from the inheritors of His homeland," said another.

In 1956 Roland Brown will give them that month, giving two full weeks to each side of the present political controversy—the Arab and the Jewish.

Bless the Lord! Praise the Lord! Thank the Lord! In the closing days of our Palestine sojourn He brought my fondest dream into fulfillment in ways beyond my powers to ask or think. My dream was that our little team of "Paul, Silas, and Lydia" might find twelve individuals in Palestine with whom we could have vital prayer fellowship and that these twelve might be set on fire as a praying band, somewhat as the twelve disciples were in Jesus' time. The last night the dream came true. R. N. Dawson, vice-consul of the British Consulate-General, invited twelve to meet with us in his home. Among these friends was Lady Glubb, mother of General Glubb, the most influential man in Palestine, organizer and leader of the famous *Arab Legion*. Lady Glubb told me she had been reading *Song of the Souls of Men* every day for years until it was almost worn out, and her soul's sincere desire was to meet its author. Other guests included the sub-agent for Jordan of the British Foreign and American Bible Society; the honorary treasurer of Missions to the Blind; a representative of the World Baptist Fellowship; a member of the National Association of Evangelicals in the Middle East representing the churches and Missionary Alliance; and a missionary of the Defender Mission. Two of the most interesting and most dedicated souls present were Mr. and Mrs. Mattar, wardens of the Garden Tomb of Jesus, a place where prayer groups meet every day. The twelve came from Jerusalem, Hebron, Amman and Beirut, and when we add Mr. Khoury, Dr. Lambi, Rev. Sarah, and the Canon, and others whom we met in Bethlehem and Samaria, plus the Christian priest from Nazareth we were to meet later, we have truly fellowshipped with representatives from all over Palestine.

As this book goes to press word comes to us that Mr. Mattar, while making inspection of a deep cistern that had gone dry, came upon an underground church that bears evidence that it might have been the sanctuary of the disciples after Jesus left—the first Christian Church in history.

CHAPTER VIII

WITH JESUS IN JESUS-LAND

OUR TRIP TO THE AIRPORT TO LEAVE PALESTINE WAS ACCOMPANIED by a mighty wind sweeping out of the north with such perilous force that no plane could land or take off. The Mid-East Airlines very graciously paid our way back to the American Colony Hotel, paid for our lodgings, supper, breakfast, and promised free transportation back to the airport the next day—so we had one more night in the land of Jesus.

As I rode back to the hotel with the tempest raging all around me, I couldn't help but think of the tempest of bitterness and hate sweeping over the little land of Palestine. One half of the land is in the possession of the Jews, one half in possession of the Arabs, neither group of which has Christ, and separating the two is a buffer "no man's land"—a ghostly area peopled only with resentment, suspicion, hopes of revenge, fear of ambushing groups moving under cover of darkness—an area no one dares cross. But neither of these possessive groups possesses the spirit of Jesus relative to the solving of their international deadlock. Had the Jews returned to Palestine in the Love Way, the Jesus Way, all would have been well. If the United Nations had thought out a Love Way which was Love ALL THE WAY in accomplishing the partition, or if the Arabs had become forgiving, to a near superhuman point, the situation today would be different.

It is true that arrangements for the first return of the Jewish people "to Jerusalem" since the time of their dispersal in 70 A.D. were made by the United Nations. It is true that, according to the Balfour Agreement, Palestine was to be partitioned and the fertile and modern coastal section was to be given as the uncontested homeland of the Jews, and the Arabs who were living in that section were to be vacated to the arid, mountainous, rock-invested area to the east—to be known as Jordan.

71

But bad means never achieve good ends. The Arabs consider themselves tricked and cheated by the way in which the segregation took place. Eight hundred and seventy thousand of them were pushed out of their homes on "the other side" without the privilege of taking any of their possessions with them and were placed in sixty-one refugee colonies on the Jordan side. Today, after seven years, they are still living in tents and mud huts with no security of work, adequate housing, education, or hospitals. An account of their complaints would make an endless tale.

We were well aware that we were hearing only the Arab side of the dilemma, since Jordan was the nation we were visiting. We are certain that the Jewish people would have presented a different angle of it. But there is no question that great injustice has been done to the Arab people.

The Arabs could escape from their poverty and misery if they would consent to be moved to Syria where tillable land could be found and adequate homes could be built, but they are so filled with hate and resentment that they won't budge from their tents and caves until they can return and recapture their old homeland. Vengeance contaminates the very air. It may be that this poison of mutual hate that broods over all of Palestine is the blight smothering the life of the churches in the Holy Land!

There is one statesman whose insight, had it been followed, could have prevented all this tragedy. And that statesman is Jesus. Christendom has never properly recognized the statesmanship of the Man of Nazareth. When the five thousand men tried to make Him King it was not in tribute to his power of love but to his power of "magic." The crowd desiring to crown him was largely made up of the "zealot party." They were revolutionists beginning to see in this popular "miracle worker," this "master of magic," their readymade solution for throwing off the yoke of Rome. His compassion for the people which led to his multiplying the loaves and fishes merely added fuel to their determination to make him their leader. It gave undebatable proof before the whole throng that he was a leader of power, so they rose as one man and proclaimed that he alone could be their savior from the Roman yoke. In answer he turned and fled across the Sea of Galilee.

Discomfited and disappointed with this first refusal to be their leader, they gave him a second chance at the next Passover. Standing as we did on two occasions before the sealed "Golden Gate" through which Jesus had made his triumphal entry into Jerusalem, I could see in my mind's eye that foal of an ass carrying the Master up that steep road strewn with olive branches as the vast mob of people who wanted him to be King acclaimed his arrival at the capital city. After he ignored that second offer the mob turned against him and made a bargain with Pilate to unloose a more militant leader named Barabas in whom they could expect better cooperation than from this disappointing pacifist, Jesus of Nazareth.

Had the Jews obeyed the laws of love that Jesus laid down, of turning the other cheek and forgiving their enemies, and continued to render unto Caesar the things that were Caesar's for another century or two, there would not be a "Palestine problem" today. Following the siege of Jerusalem, the Romans sold the citizenry into slavery, banished the rest of the inhabitants of Palestine from the land, and invited in the Arabs to take over. Had the Jews bided their time, as the other conquered provinces did (the Franks and Germans) until Rome fell by its own weight, Palestine today might be one of the great powers, along with France, Germany, Britain, Russia, and the United States. Had the Jews listened to their own Countryman and practiced "The meek shall inherit the earth" as Gandhi, a devotee of the Sermon on the Mount, practiced it two thousand years later, the land would happily now be in their hands.

As the Jews carried this great statesman to Calvary, the One who could have been the Savior of their nation, as well as the Savior of mankind, they scorned the warning which he gave them as he walked along the way, "One stone will not remain upon another. Weep not for me but for yourselves and your children."

Today the untried doctrine announced in the Sermon on the Mount remains the only panacea that will usher in the age of Peace and Brotherhood. Had the leaders of the Jews accepted Jesus and his Twelve as a Spiritual Trust, instead of depending upon the Brain Trust of the Sanhedrin, Israel today would have been a great and powerful nation. By the same token, had Franklin Roosevelt accepted a Spiritual Trust at the time he appointed a Brain Trust, he could very probably have prevented the Second World War and the resulting crises, including the mistakes at

Yalta, and the part we had in the dilemma in Palestine. Only if Eisenhower appoints (as I trust he already has) a Spiritual Trust will he be able to prevent a Third World War. Only when all groups who profess to believe in Jesus Christ follow the teachings of the Sermon on the Mount will we have permanent peace on earth.

"This is probably the last night I shall sleep in your native land, Jesus," I whispered as I was falling asleep that night. "So hold me very close, dear Savior."

If we have a right to select our own guardian spirits I have already selected John, the beloved disciple, as mine. So I turned to him in fancy and whispered, "Do you think I would have the right, before I leave this Holy Land, to go back two thousand years in time and find Jesus as He walked in Palestine and ask him for special advice for my age?"

"I will myself take you to him," he seemed to reply. "When the time is ripe I will tell you."

Those of you who have read my book, *Come Follow Me,* may recall the experiences there related—half dream, half vision—but all tremendously real to me. That night all those dreams and visions focused into this experience:

The night was far spent when I felt John shaking my arm vigorously. Oh, how hard it was to get my eyes open! Never had I seemed so heavy with sleep!

"Now is the time," he whispered.

"Now is the time?" I whispered back. "What time?" It was as though the weight of centuries were holding me down.

"I could awaken two thousand people easier than I can waken you," gasped John. "What is the matter? Are you drugged?"

"Yes," I replied, "drugged with the sophistication and materialism of an entire age. When you shake me you are shaking the inertia of two billion human souls. No wonder I am hard to waken."

"Get up at once. The Master is awaiting you—on the mountain. Now is the time for you to speak to Him. Now is the time to ask for that blessing."

Five seconds later my hands were moving like fans on a July day, lacing my sandals and throwing my mantle about my shoulders. Oh, with what speed one can dress for a blessing like this! In a moment we were outside leaving the other disciples asleep within.

"Where is He?" I panted.

"Follow me."

We walked in silence through the town, around the bend of the road leading to the east, and on up to the crest of the Mount of Olives. And there at the highest point, seated on a stone and facing east, was Jesus. When I turned to thank my guide, John was gone.

Without a word I dropped at the Master's feet and let my eyes, like His, seek the dawn along the eastern horizon.

We sat in silence for a long, long time. Then as the gold of the sun's rim threw slanting gleams across the countryside, I heard His voice speaking behind and above me.

"You have come from a time far off. It is a time when much that I have prophesied will be coming true. Otherwise you would not be able to be here. A ribbon of eternity connects this age with yours, just as that ribbon of sunlight ties all these fields and meadows together as one. As the sun bridges Space, so the Son of Man bridges Time. There is no Time to one who is born again—everything to him is Eternal—and in Eternity all is one. . . . Before Abraham was, I am. After all your woes and wars, I shall still be." He paused. Then, as the sun began to flood the Jordan valley, He continued, "And now, my friend, what blessing would you ask for your age?"

"O Master Jesus, I would bring to you in my hands, in my full heart, all the people of my Time, yes the Time itself, and kneeling, lay them at your feet to be blessed."

"And what special wish do you make when seeking this blessing?"

"My special wish is for the entire age to be reborn, for everyone living to be born again. For what is life, if it be merely to eat and drink and reproduce one's kind, if our hearts are filled with hate and pride and greed?"

"You ask wisely, my son," He answered, and by now the voice was so clear *I knew this could not be a dream*. It was *real;* I was in the presence of the Christ Himself.

"You ask wisely because *one cannot live* unreborn in an age where people talk across continents and fly across oceans—where time and space no longer control, where only Eternity exists. A man in that world must be reborn into Infinity. He cannot live

safely beyond time and space unless he has found the secrets of
Eternity. In such an age the man who limits himself kills himself.
Many men in your time will die beneath the wheels of the chariots
of war or by the arrows of hate because your leaders have not been
reborn. Unless your people can find the doorways of love and
prayer, and throw them wide open—as wide as you open the doors
to invention and discovery and through repentance and surrender
die unto the little self and be reborn to the Great Self, the doors
of death will yawn wide for entire nations. Unless you be born
again in Love you shall die and find rebirth in Suffering."

"And how can the evil days be shortened?" I cried.

"Only through turning to the Father in love and devotion, with
all your heart, mind, soul, and strength, and to the neighbor at your
gates with forgiveness, tolerance, and good will. When pride and
discrimination have vanished, when greed after gold has disappeared, when slavery to the cravings of the flesh is surmounted—
then will you see the Kingdom coming to earth as it is in heaven."

"And will that come in my day?"

"What is that to thee? Follow thou me."

The next morning I was filled with this dream, if one wishes to
call it a dream, as with the Browns I went to the Jerusalem airport
—a flimsy little building where we almost froze while awaiting the
arrival of the airplane. A new landing field was being constructed
and seven hundred Arabs, with picks and shovels, were digging up
stones, breaking them with sledge hammers, and spreading them
as a foundation upon which later to pour and smooth the carpet
of cement where airplanes could land. I was watching them carefully, meditatively.

These were men who had been ruthlessly exiled from their homes
and firesides through no fault of their own. To me they represented all the dispossessed persons of the world. Compassion filled
my heart. That moment I became a focal point through which the
compassion of Christ himself flowed through me upon all the
suffering ones of the whole world. I had the impression of being
bathed in a great blinding light. The presence of Jesus I had experienced the night before was now with me in overwhelming
power. I could feel the prayers of all the praying people of the
world praying through me.

Suddenly the most distinguished looking Arab of them all raised his head and stared at me. His eyes widened as though he were seeing something. He dropped his pickax and approached me with dignified step. He did not stop till he stood right before me. Then, as one performing a rite, he took my gloved hand in his, bowed reverently, and touched his forehead to my hand, then kissed it, then the forehead again, and then a second kiss. In amazement I laid a silent blessing upon him as I felt the love and prayers of all the praying people of the world flowing through me and I knew as positively as if he were standing there in person that Jesus was placing his benediction upon us both.

That was my last experience in Jesus-land, my last memory of Palestine, a memory that I will carry with me forever.

CHAPTER IX

FROM THE NEAR EAST
TO THE FAR EAST

THE RETURN FLIGHT FROM JERUSALEM TO BEIRUT WAS ACCOMPLISHED in one hour and fifteen minutes and yet we passed over three countries, Jordan, Syria, and Lebanon, and spanned four thousand years of history. We started our flight from Jerusalem, with its "Dome of the Rock Temple" erected over the great stone which is the site of the altar on Mt. Moriah, where Abraham took Isaac 2000 B.C., and landed in Beirut where we had reservations in a beautiful modern hotel. How thrilling to see from the air places we had visited while on the ground: the Dead Sea, the Jordan, Jericho. But for the major part of the trip we were again among the clouds, breaking through them as we circled out over the Mediterranean and then came in for landing. For the first time we found spring-like, almost summer weather.

The American Colony Hotel in Jerusalem was the first place in which we had had central heating since we left America, and that only during morning and evening hours. In many places we had slept in underwear as well as pajamas, and for a solid month in Europe and Egypt we had worn our sweaters under our vests by day. For so long we had been shivering inside buildings where the temperature was the same as the temperature out of doors, forty, fifty, or sixty degrees, that we were more than ready to enjoy some heat.

We took a taxi to Palm Beach Hotel, fronting on the beautiful Mediterranean.

Although we knew no one in Beirut we had been given the name of Dr. Stolfus, President of the College for Women, so before going to our noon meal Roland phoned President Stolfus, explained who we were and told him about our mission on this world journey, adding that we would like to meet him and some of his faculty if that were possible. The president's response was indeed astonishing. He said his wife was "devoted to Glenn Clark," and, after consulting her, assured us that she would come over to the hotel immediately after lunch. She proved to be a former Macalester College student of the class of 1917. Her name had been Ethel Leck. I remembered her very well. She had been engaged to Irving Roth, my star long distance runner as well as my star debater, who was killed in the First World War. She had also been in my short story class. Her father was the contractor who built several of our college buildings: Wallace Hall, the Men's and the Women's Dormitories, and the famous Gymnasium I have mentioned often in my talks. She had even attended the Camp Farthest Out at Koronis when home on furlough in 1942. She has lived in Beirut since 1919, thirty-five years, and eagerly told us about places where we should go and people we should meet.

This is the amazing way God takes over: although it was examination week so that there were no chapel services at which we might address the students (a situation she deeply regretted) there was to be a reception from 4:30 to 6:00 that very afternoon in honor of Miss Orne, their Dean of Women, who had just returned from a year's furlough. Mrs. Stolfus said that occasion would provide a wonderful opportunity to meet the faculty and students and it would permit them to have informal fellowship with us.

Two hours later at this reception when I was introduced to Miss Orne, she embarrassed me by exclaiming, "Not the famous Glenn Clark!" We found ourselves meeting President Leavit, president of the American College, open to both boys and girls, and his lovely wife, who proved to be the sister of a co-founder of the New England Camps Farthest Out, Rev. Dan Bliss. Both seemed as thrilled to visit with us as we with them. Then there was Pastor Eide of the Union Church and his wife who had read my books and wished I could be there to address their congregation the next Sunday; and Dr. Ead, pastor of the Irish Presbyterian Church. Most of the professors of the college were also present all of whom we were very happy to meet. They arranged for a group of people to meet with us the following evening. Then Professor Willouby and Professor Fisher took us to the Seminary where we met a third college president and then to the home of the Arab pastor of the Arab Christian Church. He is Rev. Farid Audeh of the National

Evangelical Church, President of the Supreme Council of the Evangelical Churches of Syria, Chairman of the Near East Christian Council.

That afternoon was providentially the very afternoon Rev. Audeh had set aside for receiving guests so we had a splendid visit with a number of interesting people, as well as with this great and modest man. A year previous he had attended the Presbyterian General Assembly in Minneapolis, and regularly acts as the representative of Lebanon on the Near East Council at nearly all international assemblies, whether in Sweden or India, including the World Council of Churches that was to meet in Evanston in 1954. My heart leapt with joy when he asked me to pray before we left.

When we returned to the hotel, in time for a late supper, Marcia Brown said, "Who would have dreamed that the first afternoon in Beirut, a city where we thought we knew no one, we would meet so many wonderful people in such a vital way!" Constantly we were astonished at the amazing ways of God.

We set aside the next day, Friday, to rest, read, and pray and then in the evening we were taken to the home of Professor Willouby at the American Mission. Gathered there we found again exactly the people we wanted to meet: Rev. Dewey Eder, pastor of the Community Church, and his wife, who in twenty-four hours time had become our very close friends in the spirit, Rev. Stolfus, President of Beirut College for Women and his wife Ethel, who were now like members of my own family, and about forty professors, divinity students, and other interested persons. We sat in a homey circle and Roland and I were kept talking informally for two hours, followed by a period of answering questions extending into the refreshment time, and everyone seemed loath to leave. To our great joy a Jewish editor and his wife from Nazareth were present, both Christians of influence in Nazareth, the one city we had especially wanted to visit, and they happily completed the Palestine contacts for us.

The next day, Saturday, we drove up and over the snow covered mountain of Lebanon, crossed the Lebanon-Syrian border, taking a short trip northward to Baalbek and then back to our highway and on eastward to Damascus. At Baalbek we saw the famous Roman Temples of Venus, of Jupiter, and of Bacchus, remarkable edifices now chiefly ruins due to a disastrous earthquake two hundred years ago.

At Damascus we were eager to follow some of the footsteps of Paul. We intentionally walked part of the way down the street called Straight and later, of necessity, walked down the *very narrow* Ananias Street in order to enter the house of Ananias where we climbed down the stairs into the room, seventeen feet below the present street level, where Paul stayed following his conversion experience. We knelt in that sacred place in close communion with the man whose name was selected by the city founders to be given to my "home town" in Minnesota—St. Paul.

In Beirut one-fourth of the people are Moslems, three-fourths Christian, whereas in Damascus the proportion is the reverse. In Damascus we went to the largest mosque in the world, carpeted with hundreds of fabulous Turkish rugs, upon which we saw scores of men kneeling and praying, facing Mecca. The vast amount of time they give to these prayers should make us Christians ashamed. We were told that with many Moslems much of the praying was mechanical (as I am sorry to say is also true of many of us Christians) but nevertheless the expression on their faces was so devout and their manner so serious that we could not quickly forget them.

Back in Beirut the airline bus picked us up at midnight and carried us to the airport where, at 2:30 a.m. Sunday, February the 7th, we boarded the plane for Delhi. Flying toward the sun, we descended at Madan in Mesopotamia at 6:30 a.m. (clock moved forward) and at Karachi in Pakistan about noon. While waiting in the wire enclosure outside the Karachi airport, drinking in the delicious warm air, I fell into conversation with a handsome, refined gentleman who proved to be Mr. K. M. I. Ullah on the staff of Pakistan's leading newspaper, the *Dawn*. I talked with him about the trouble between Pakistan and India. He replied that it stemmed from the rivalry over the proposed plebiscite in Kashmir. Kashmir really wanted to join Pakistan, he said, as by race and religion (Islam) it was completely in tune with them, but Nehru's family had come from Kashmir and chiefly for sentimental reasons he wanted it for India and therefore wouldn't allow the plebiscite to take place.

"The rivers that Pakistan depends on for irrigation," I remarked, "pass through the edge of India, and they could cut off your water supply if they wished. Is that true?"

"Yes," he replied, "the rivers pass through land that India can't use for agriculture and she doesn't need the water, but she holds her control of the rivers as a threat over us."

"Why did this partition between India and Pakistan come about?" I asked.

"While there had been tensions for centuries between the Moslems and Hindus in India," he replied, "things were going very well until the Hindus took unfair advantage of their numerical strength in Congress. Up to that time Jinnah had been a very tolerant and cooperative person, a warm supporter of Gandhi in many respects. When Congress refused demands of the Moslems for a redistribution or some other way of achieving a proportionate representation based on numerical strength Jinnah began to demand partition. In a district which had 225,000 Hindus and 175,-000 Moslems the Hindus could elect a Hindu representative and leave the minority without a voice. It was a similar unfairness that led your American colonies to seek partition from Britain: 'Taxation without representation is unjust.' Bitterness increased until partition became inevitable. Unfortunately there were many Moslems in India and many Hindus in Pakistan. Therein lay the tragedy. Mass migrations began, emotions got out of control, and over half a million lives were sacrificed."

And so I was introduced to the Pakistan problem from the point of view of a very fair-minded Moslem in Pakistan. In a few days I would be able to hear the Indian version. We climbed aboard our plane and took off for the next stop—India!

CHAPTER X

WE ENTER INDIA

DELHI WAS THE OLD CAPITAL OF THE MOGUL EMPIRE IN INDIA, AND hardly an acre between Old and New Delhi but carries some relic of the historic past. The present city, the seventh of the series, was reconstructed by Emperor Shah Jahan, and the greater part of it is still confined within his walls. The Chandin Chank ("silver street") which was once supposed to be the richest street in the world, has fallen from its high estate, though it is still a broad and imposing avenue with a double row of trees running down the center.

A short distance south of this "silver street" the Great Mosque rises boldly from a small rocky eminence. Large as it was before the partition, it was too small to hold its 15,000 congregation. I wondered how many worshippers dare come there now.

While in New Delhi we were the guests of Mr. N. J. Cornelius, the secretary of the Young Men's Christian Association. As I was eager to get at the heart of this India-Pakistan problem of partition I asked him while we were eating dinner if he had any first hand experience in the matter. "I certainly did!" he exclaimed. "It was a nightmare. Yes, one of the tragedies of history, and it took place only seven years ago. When reports came out of the part of the Punjab assigned to Pakistan that the Moslems were murdering and forcibly converting the Hindus and raping their wives and daughters, the Sikhs and Hindus in Delhi began a similar orgy of slaughter of the Moslems. It was terrible to look out my window here and see neighbors killing neighbors right in our front yard—neighbors who had been friends the very day before."

Later, as Mr. Cornelius drove us around the city, he pointed out the camps which the Nehru government has now set up outside Delhi to catch the hordes of immigrants before they inundate the city. He recalled how during the height of the exodus fifteen million unhappy, fearful human refugees in fifty-seven mile convoys trekked for hundreds of miles away from their homes toward distress, disease, and death. It was a two way flight. Out of the part of the Punjab assigned to Pakistan, moving toward Delhi, came millions of Hindus and Sikhs fleeing the knives and clubs of Moslems. Out of the Indian Union moving toward Pakistan went millions of Moslems fearing the daggers and lathis of Hindus and Sikhs. Cholera, smallpox, and similar killers scourged the migrant hordes. The dead and dying strewed the roadsides while the vultures circled overhead.

The two dramatic figures in this tragedy were Jinnah and Gandhi. Here is Louis Fisher's description of this great Moslem. "Mohammed Ali Jinnah was an extraordinary figure. Very tall, very thin, very well dressed, his long silver-gray hair brushed straight back, black patent leather pumps and a monocle on a black cord—one of the best dressed men in the British Empire—he was the perfect antithesis of Gandhi. In personality and character the contrast was even greater. Gandhi's outlook was broad, Jinnah's was narrow. Gandhi was humble and loving, Jinnah was conceited and filled with hate. Jinnah was a Moslem but not a devout one. He infringed the Islamic code by drinking alcohol, eating pork, and seldom going to mosque. Yet the irreligious Jinnah insisted on dividing India into two religious states, while the religious Gandhi insisted on a united secular state."

This may be an unfair viewpoint of Jinnah, but if Louis Fisher makes Jinnah the villain in the drama, he makes out Churchill as the arch-villain.

"Churchill fought the Second World War to preserve the heritage of Britain. Would he permit a half-naked fakir to rob her of that heritage? 'We mean to hold our own,' Churchill said. India was England's property. He refused to relinquish it. From the time he became the King's First Minister in 1940, to the day in 1945 when he was ousted from office, Churchill waged war with Mahatma Gandhi. It was a contest between the past of England and the future of India.

"To Churchill power was poetry. He was a Byronic Napoleon. He passionately hated the foreign tyrannies which threatened England and directed against them all the moral fervor his genius could generate but had no sympathy for Gandhi's moral struggle against British domination. He would have died to keep England free but detested those who wanted India free. To him India was the pedestal of a throne.

"This explains the failure of the mission undertaken by Sir Stafford Cripps on behalf of the British government in the middle of 1942. Cripps, the thin, austere, rich, ascetic, vegetarian Labourite, could have come to an agreement with the Congress party, indeed held it within his grasp, but Churchill had visions of Gandhi striding up the steps of the Viceroy's palace to share power with the King-Emperor and would have none of that.

"In the historic perspective of subsequent events it is clear that 1942 would have been the best time to take Patel, Nehru, Rajagopalachari, Azad, and their colleagues up those steps, past the superbly handsome, statuesque, motionless, colorful Indian guards with their lances, into the inner chambers of power and thus prepare the way for an independent India voluntarily associated, as now, in the Commonwealth. The British army and police, then in full control, would have guaranteed a peaceful transition and obviated the vivisection of India into the Indian Republic and Pakistan with all the enormous expense in lives, hatreds, economic deterioration, and political tensions which both are paying and may continue to pay for decades. But the same gloriously indomitable will which enabled Churchill to stand unflinching in the face of what seemed inevitable defeat at Hitler's hands made him an unyielding block on India's road to her inevitable freedom. He would not be the instrument of liquidating the Empire." *

Had Attlee been premier at that stage, the tragedy in India might have been averted.

Flying into New Delhi from Pakistan I found myself in the midst of present day hatreds, economic deterioration, and political tensions. Then it was that I realized how great Gandhi had been in days even more tense.

In that crisis Gandhi had risen to his greatest heights. In the fall of 1947, he came to Delhi and planted himself athwart the torrent of boiling passion, preaching his message of love. "There is no gain in returning evil for evil," he cried. Whenever he heard that bloodthirsty mobs were gathering he rushed into their midst. The angry human sea parted as he walked among them, face smiling, palms

---

* Louis Fischer, *Gandhi*. Signet Key Books, New York. Copyright by Louis Fischer.

touching in the traditional blessing. The waves of anger subsided. He attended a gathering of one hundred thousand bearded Sikhs and condemned their violence against the Moslems. "Keep your hearts clean," he said, "and you will find all other communities will follow you."

To put a final end to the riots and bloodshed he decided to fast. "It came to me in a flash," he said. He began this fast on the morning of January 13, 1948. He called it an "all-in-all fast to the death if need be, directed at the conscience of all—Hindus and Moslems. Death for me would be a glorious deliverance rather than that I should be a helpless witness to the destruction of India. I am in God's hands." That was his last fast, and the quality of courage, humility, and love that surrounded it has put a stamp upon India that will never fade.

The fast was finished. Gandhi began holding daily prayer meetings on the lawn of Birla House, Calcutta. Sunday, January 25, 1948, the prayer meeting attendance was especially large. Gandhi said that it gladdened his heart that Hindus and Moslems were experiencing "a reunion of hearts." He begged all the Hindus and Sikhs present to each bring along "at least one Moslem" to prayers hereafter, as a concrete manifestation of brotherhood.

Five days later, as Gandhi came to the prayer meeting, three shots sounded, Gandhi's arms dropped to his sides. "Oh God," he murmured and was instantly dead.

Mr. Cornelius drove us to the memorial erected on the spot where the body of Gandhi was cremated. We saw the streams of native Indians coming down the walk to this simplest of shrines and with heads bowed, palms touching in reverence, reading the last words of the Mahatma engraved on the memorial, "Oh God!"

Gandhi-ji, as we heard him so lovingly referred to by missionaries, is loved and revered even today by no telling how many millions of Indians as well as by numberless Christian leaders and lay people the world around. Men whose spirits were fired by him are treading faithfully and victoriously in his footsteps. As I watched the throngs coming to this memorial erected to a "glorious way of life," I prayed that the whole world might come like streams, rivers, floods with words engraved deep in their souls, "Oh God! Our Father, hallowed be Thy name," and more words trembling on their lips. "Thy kingdom come. Thy will be done on earth as it is in heaven."

Since we had arrived in Delhi a day before we were expected, we felt that this extra time could be appropriated for our coveted trip to see the Taj Mahal. From Delhi the town of Agra can be reached quickest by bus or car, but it requires a full twelve hours to make the trip and return by bus. So we hired a taxi and took off on the one hundred and thirty mile ride to Agra, which was itself an experience in *seeing* and *feeling* India. Punjab means "five rivers," so our expedition took us past the most fertile fields of India. A single-lane, black-top road the entire distance meant that we must run one wheel onto the dusty shoulder whenever we were meeting or overtaking another vehicle and we were passing something all the time. As in England we kept to the left and passed, or tried to pass, slow moving cars, cattle, camels, pedestrians, cattle, bicycles, trucks, cattle, more pedestrians, more cattle, pushcarts, donkeys, cattle. Monkeys sat along the roadside watching us. People and animals filled the village streets, our highway, and only stepped aside as the car threatened to mow them down. Our siren was screaming the whole one hundred and thirty miles, and it was a miracle the way the whiskered, turbaned Sikh, driving our car, failed to kill anyone.

This fertile portion of India—the Punjab with its five rivers—did not look especially fertile to me. The nephew of Cornelius accompanied us—a brilliant young man who will have a brilliant future, probably in government service as well as in Christian endeavors. He pointed out some of the terrific problems existing in India. One of the reasons the land is so unproductive is because the cattle manure is not ploughed back into the soil but, as with the "buffalo chips" of our own western plains, is used for fuel; long hours are spent collecting it, shaping it into flat "cakes," drying it. The people have no other fuel.

Another problem is the cattle, the sacred cows which we passed in immense herds, or observed leisurely resting as they lay in the middle of the street, forcing traffic to detour around them. "They cannot be killed! They cannot be eaten! But they can devour food desperately needed for human consumption," said our young guide. To be sure, their milk is treasured for food, but even when the cows eat the best the land can produce, they are still so underfed or so old that they give less than two pints of milk a day (in contrast to Brocade, my father's Jersey that gave eight gallons a day). "If the unproductive cows could be slaughtered for meat, removing half the cattle from the land, the starvation in India would end; but anyone who might suggest such an economic reform in this predominantly Hindu country would be ostracized from the community."

Another problem is the land inheritance law; when a small landowner dies, his land is equally portioned among his children. "After centuries of this subdividing, many farms consist of plots no more than ten by twenty feet in size, too small for efficient farming and totally inadequate to produce food enough for large undernourished families."

At last we stood before the Taj Mahal, a masterpiece in architecture, erected in honor of a woman! Muntaj Mahal was the favorite wife of Emperor Shah Jahan, noted for her beauty, accomplishments, and tender-hearted sympathy for the poor and distressed. Indeed, her intercession saved many condemned to death. She was married at the age of nineteen, bore her husband six daughters and eight sons, and accompanied her husband on his campaigns. After seventeen years of married life she died giving birth to her fourteenth child during one of these campaigns. Shah Jahan's grief was intense. For several weeks he refused to see any courtiers; no music or festivities were allowed. In two years his hair turned gray. Then he started the building of one of the wonders of the world in memory of his wife. The memorial was seventeen years under construction, employing the services of twenty thousand workmen and costing twenty million dollars.

The contrast between this memorial and the tomb of Tutankhamen is notable. The gold caskets within caskets entombing the Egyptian king almost equaled in cost the Taj Mahal. But in the former all the beauty and splendor were locked away from human eyes, and an evil spell was added to destroy anyone who dared to enter and witness its splendor. The Taj, on the other hand, was erected for the eyes of all mankind to see. But in each case the millions of dollars spent for precious stones, gold, and marble could have bought food and blessings for thousands—even for the thousands of slave-laborers who received little more than sweat, torture, and tears for doing the work.

Perhaps because of the oppression of the laborers, an evil spell lurked around the Taj too. The eldest son murdered all of his brothers and locked his father, who built the memorial, as a prisoner in a castle overlooking the Taj Mahal. In his old age this son, out of remorse for his evil deeds, committed suicide.

Again, this memorial of perfect workmanship might be compared to the memorial of perfect workmanship that Dante erected to the memory of Beatrice in the form of the *Divine Comedy*. Both were memorials to women and both were the greatest of masterpieces in their respective fields. The *Divine Comedy* is probably the finest work of literature ever produced and, like the Taj Mahal, is as perfectly constructed as a mosaic window, every piece in its place. For instance, it has three parts, one hundred cantos, one preliminary canto, and thirty-three cantos in each of the three parts. Three women intercede for Dante in heaven, three guides conduct him on his journey, he spends three days in each section, and each of the three parts ends with the word "Stars." The number nine is woven into every part: nine chambers of hell, nine ledges of purgatory, nine circles of heaven. Dante met Beatrice first as she entered her ninth year and he was leaving his ninth year. Every multiple of nine, when added together equals nine, the sign of perfection.

I, who have taught the *Divine Comedy* to students for thirty years, was especially interested in the way the Taj Mahal was put together with equally perfect symmetry. I personally prefer a balanced variety of different designs, as is found in each of the intricately beautiful stained glass windows in the famous mosque at Damascus. However, the perfect repetition of perfect design on each side of the Taj Mahal is without flaw and leaves nothing to be desired, and the fact that the pattern is not painted on and thus cannot fade away, but is carved out of and inlaid into marble, gives it a quality of permanent beauty not equaled in the world. It represents the most highly elaborate ornamentation that architecture has ever known—indeed it represents the stage where the work of the architect ends and the work of the jeweler begins. The *Pietra dura* adorning the mausoleum is said to be the finest in the world. However, to stand back far enough to get a full view of the whole structure, even back far enough to catch its full reflection in the pool, and then to look at it, not through the outer eyes which grasp things "but darkly," but through the eyes of the heart which see more and more of entrancing beauty in the majesty of wholeness, in the perfectness of detail, in the reverence of the priceless: that is the way to really see it so you can "take it with you."

Even so, as we rode home dodging pedestrians and animals, my thoughts were not on the Taj Mahal, the marvelous masterpiece of man, but upon Gandhi, the excelling masterpiece of God.

CHAPTER XI

NEW DELHI:
I BEGIN TO UNDERSTAND INDIA

THE EVENING AFTER OUR WONDERFUL DAY AT THE TAJ MAHAL WE had part in a most interesting meeting held in New Delhi. A splendid group had convened, half Christian, half non-Christian; a typical group of cultured Indians. Fortunately all could understand English.

As this was our first meeting in India, and as I was to be the first speaker, it was with considerable trepidation that I began my talk, but I sent up a silent prayer for the Lord to speak the message through me. Thereafter I felt a great inner surge of power and the words simply flowed.

"We three are on a trip to build a Belt of Prayer around the world, and the chief purpose of that journey is not to see the outside of things, but to find the inner spirit of every country we visit. As I look at you I am impressed by the singular beauty and charm of both men and women, age and youth, and I feel deeply that I am looking through your open faces into the inner sanctuary of your hearts."

The Lord had put the words on my lips and I was amazed at the responsive chord they struck, for I watched the lights "turn on" in the faces.

"It gives me great joy," I continued, "to speak a message from the heart of America. As you know, you and I, your race and my race, were once one. Our common ancestors came down out of the Himalayas, the birthplace of the world, and you sat down and meditated while we nervous, aggressive folk went on west. A study of the beginnings of our languages shows something about the point at which we parted company. There are certain words, such as 'mother,' 'star,' 'sky,' that are the same in your language as in ours, but when it comes to 'sea,' they are different—showing that we separated before we reached the ocean. Our part of the family traveled on and on, always westward; and under the great Baltic clouds we stayed so long that our skins got white, while you sat under the sun and your skins took on the color of the sun. Our people went on, growing more mechanically minded and materialistic in spirit as we mastered and brought under control a vast continent. Today we look across the great Pacific and we see you, brothers of ours, emerging from years of suppression into your new age of independence and greatness. Today we stand forth as the two greatest republics of the world.

"Now is the time for us to exchange our philosophies and achieve the united best of both. We are sending people to India to learn how to think and to meditate; the 'psychologies' in our colleges are but primers when compared to the old Masters of India; you are far ahead of us in the study of man's mind and spirit. Back in ancient days you had a love for wisdom and a hunger to find it while our ancestors were still carrying clubs, almost like cave men, in the northern forests of Saxony and Burgundy.

"But you are now sending your people to America to learn the sciences, just as we are sending our people to India to become philosophers. So let us trade; you give us a proper evaluation of the search for wisdom and knowledge that will lead to 'quietness and confidence' and we will give you the best we've learned of how to accomplish feats bordering on the miraculous. Let's become partners to bless the world; one in impact, if not in compact. You still have the dark skin, we have the white skin; but our souls are all the same color before God. Your religion, although somewhat different from ours, moves steadily toward the same Truth, the same God. We use different doors, that is all. But we can share those doors and I, as a Christian, would like to open to you the love door of Jesus.

"We admit that your religion takes you far into the mysteries of prayer and meditation, but we take joy in interpreting to you the life-giving mysteries of the infinite love of Jesus—the vital key to effective praying and fullness of joy. We admit that most of us Westerners have failed miserably to live up to Jesus' mandates of love. Your great Gandhi had a deeper understanding of the power of compassion to which Jesus gave such remarkable expression, than most so-called Christians. He went about India carrying the

Sermon on the Mount in one hand and the Bhagavad-Gita in the other and without the firing of a gun he liberated a great nation, one-fifth of the human race, from the most powerful Empire that ever existed. As we are learning from him who was one of you, we want you to learn from us, and so I close this message I am giving you with a prayer in which I use the blessed name of Jesus:

"Our Heavenly Father, Jesus' last prayer was 'that ye shall become one as I and the Father are one.' My prayer is that we nations shall become one. And so I am offering this prayer that India and the United States (the right hand and the left hand of the ends of this earth) may encompass and clasp this earth, this little round globe, in their own loving hands, and lift it up and give it to Thee, for Thine is the Kingdom and the Power and the Glory for ever and ever. In Jesus' name. Amen."

This talk seemed to open a way for all our future talks in India. Roland's talk that followed mine was completely Christ-centered, and to our delight the non-Christians seemed to welcome it.

Mrs. Welthy Fisher, widow of Bishop Fisher, and Director of Literacy work in the Allahabad Center, had come all the way to Delhi to be present that night. She was radiant in her conviction that the meeting had been led of God.

The next day we spent the morning in the police office getting all our visas extended and all other necessary red tape taken care of, and at 5:00 p.m. we met with many leading religious workers from the entire area gathered in the Y.M.C.A. parlors for a tea, wherein I quickly discovered we were all rapidly becoming friends. Then with a large audience—every seat filled—in the assembly hall of the Y.M.C.A., with Mrs. Fisher again presiding, we had a Spirit-empowered meeting from 6:30 till 8:00. Roland gave a masterly address in exactly thirty minutes. Marcia painted a picture while the audience sang an accompaniment and then she had them all stand and repeat and enact the story of the Good Samaritan. Cornelius was delighted to see John R. Mott's daughter participating whole-heartedly. My talk closed the meeting.

After the meeting several of us were invited for supper to the home of Miss Hersey, a remarkable social worker formerly with the U. S. Embassy, not with Point Four. Welthy Fisher and Charlotte Clough, a former student of mine and editor of the CIHU books, related their recent experience at Benares when they went to the confluence of the Ganges and two other rivers to witness the famous bathing festival and attendant religious rituals that occur every twelve years. They told how four million people converged upon this little point of land (the same place from which Gandhi's ashes were cast into the Ganges) and Charlotte and Welthy found themselves in the very center of the eager millions. "For a while," said Charlotte, "it gave us a glorious feeling of all moving together. Then the two converging streams of humanity pressed in closer and closer until four hundred persons were crushed to death. We were saved by following in the wake of a horseman who offered us a path to security. No one will ever know how many were drowned and swept downstream in the relentless push of that irresistible sea of humanity intent upon reaching the sacred spot and bathing in the sacred waters and participating in the sacred ceremonies."

Pearl Palmer, a missionary and former student of mine, was also at the supper, and a Mr. and Mrs. Sill, a young couple who are transforming a village where they and Pearl are working. They started this work with a literacy campaign. First they had to divide the people by castes, as they would be willing to "each one teach one" only if they were in the same caste. The villagers voted, in order to determine the director of the movement, and since outcasts outnumbered and outvoted the rest, one of them, an outcast and a near-saint, was selected. The high caste numbered only twelve families, all poorer than the outcasts, so this village represents India-in-reverse—the outcasts leading and lifting the higher castes. This demonstration is a revelation of what this new Republic in a new era may bring forth. Pearl and the Sills told eagerly of the warm spiritual atmosphere that pervades this village. Because the bulk of the population in India live in small villages, and there are thousands upon thousands of these villages, the need and hope of India today is for thousands of men and women who can bring light to the villages as these young people have done.

The next morning we went to visit Swami Ranganananda at Rama Krishna Mission. Mr. Cornelius, our outstanding Christian host, referred to him as probably the finest of the Swami. He includes both the Bhagavad-Gita and the Sermon on the Mount in his teaching, and he was so in accord with us that our conversation together was a mountain-top experience for us all. Every Sunday he addresses in English over one thousand people of all races and religions in the open air court before his place.

We made an interesting call upon Bishop Picket, a friend whom Dr. Laubach wanted us to meet. He invited us to tea, and we found in him a wise man whose wisdom and judgment and influence in the Christian field is outstanding. He is a friend of Nehru, but Nehru was not in the city so it was not possible for us to meet him. He praised the excellent work of Chester Bowles who made himself so much a part of the Indian life and whose removal from the ambassadorship with the change of administration was a real loss.

Our last meeting was held in a Baptist church amazingly well filled. Just before the evening meeting we went again to the simple but inspiring memorial on the spot where Gandhi's body was cremated—the shrine of modern India. After the evening meeting we had a small but power-filled meeting at the Y.M.C.A. to bless the members of the staff. Thus ended another great day and a great crusade in Delhi.

Before we can understand a nation we must be able to see the good in established institutions which to outsiders might at first sight seem anything but good. We Americans sometimes scoff at England and Holland for still clinging to the ancient institution of kings and queens. Dictatorships may scoff at the way in which our own nation's policy is shaped by the ballot, never four years the same. And we in America have been amazed that a nation like India should be bound hand and foot by such an out-moded custom as the caste system. However, knowing that every evil has its germ of good, one of the first things I undertook when I reached India was to find the germ of good in the caste system. At one of the teas in Delhi I found myself sitting beside a very scholarly Indian, undoubtedly a member of the Brahman Caste.

I asked him, "Can you tell me what is the germ of good in your caste system?"

"I don't know whether the caste system would serve as well in other lands," he replied, "but for us it has provided the solution to social conflicts."

"What!" I exclaimed. "I thought it was the cause of social conflicts."

"No," he assured me, "just the reverse. It explains why India, as a nation, has experienced such long centuries of peace. If you are a student of history—"

"I am. I majored in history while at college, and my interest has never waned."

"Then you will agree that the history of the world has been a history of conflicts. Every national story is full of such tales. Recall the story of the Israelites wandering in the desert under Moses and Joshua. What did they do when they captured a city?"

"Exterminated the people," I replied.

"That is one solution of social conflict—extermination," he said. "The Israelites chose that method. City after city they conquered and solved the problem of keeping their own race pure by exterminating those whom they conquered. Now it so happened that the inhabitants of Gibeon knowing how the Israelites treated the vanquished, and hearing that the Israelites were only a few miles away, resorted to a clever stratagem. They sent forth a committee with soiled garments and worn sandals, as if they had traveled hundreds of miles and, entering the Camp of Israel, begged mercy for their city which they pretended was a great distance away. After extracting a promise that none of their people should be slaughtered they left. Three days later when the Israelites found the city just over the hill they were so enraged they were eager to slaughter everyone. But remembering their covenant they substituted slavery for slaughter and led their captives away to be 'hewers of wood and drawers of water.' Thus slavery came into the stream of Hebrew culture, not a back-step but an actual forward step in human progress. That is, slavery was a step above extermination."

"The Greeks and Romans also utilized slavery as a solution of racial conflicts," I ventured.

"And the Nazis and the Communists in modern times used both slavery and extermination. For instance, in the Second World War the Germans tried extermination on the Jews and slave labor camps for the French. Russia has since followed the same lead, making use of both slaughter and slavery. China, centuries ago, added a third method: identification. She quietly absorbed conquerors and conquered alike.

"India, alone of all the nations, experiencing a larger inflow of divergent races than any other nation, did not resort to any of these solutions. She adopted a fourth method that might be called 'Harmonization.' The Aryans came first, followed by the Parsees, Mongols, Sikhs and so on. Should the Aryans exterminate the others as fast as they arrived? Should they enslave them as the Romans and Greeks had done? Should they absorb them until all trace of tribal differences disappeared as the Chinese had done? Instead, they permitted each group, whether racial or religious, to live in the land in peace, but in order to discourage intermarriage and the loss of their own group identity they established castes. As most of the incoming races specialized in some specific service or activity, the caste system gave each group a monopoly of its particular field, an arrangement which advantaged every group. There was no intention originally to make one caste superior to another, as the functions of all the castes were regarded as important to the well-being of the whole. The serenity of the teacher, the heroism of the warrior, the honesty of the businessman, and the patience and energy of the worker all contributed to social growth. But as privilege became equated with certain services and education became a restricted prerogative, gradually the sense of equality faded out. Yet it is amazing how pride in his work gives even the so-called lower caste Indians a dignity of their own."

Mr. Cornelius, Secretary of the Y.M.C.A. at Delhi, spoke up, "That is true. In spite of the fact that my family have been Christians for several hundred years, I would never think of marrying outside my own caste, so strong is the power of tradition in us Indians."

My final remark was, "I can see in the past history of nations that India used a far better method of solving the racial problem than the cruel methods of extermination and slavery. But isn't the world enlightened enough now to drop all these old methods—including caste systems as well?"

"Gandhi thought so," he replied, "and your Supreme Court, in passing judgment on segregation, evidently thought so, too. Let us hope that some day that time will come."

CHAPTER XII

COLORFUL EXPERIENCES IN LUCKNOW AND CALCUTTA

IN THE CITY OF LUCKNOW WE WERE GUESTS OF RAJA AND RONI Maharaja Singh, which translated into modern English would be King and Queen Singh. They lived in a palatial home with twelve servants and an immense yard filled with the most beautiful of flowers. Raja Maharaja Singh is the son of a Sikh and was in line to become King or Maharaja of a state in India, but he became a Christian instead and let the Kingship go to another. While he gave up the Kingship the title remained with him. He had been Governor of Bombay for six years and President of the National Y.M.C.A. Board. His wife is active in religious work and is today President of the Y.W.C.A. Board of India. She proved to be one of the most spiritual and charming women we met on our entire trip.

Our first afternoon in Lucknow we were taken to address the College for men, after which Roni Singh took us to tea at the home of her sister, the former President of Thorburn College. It was sheer delight to be escorted through the college by these two outstanding, humble women. It was the Play Day or they would have had us address the girls. This was the first college for women in the Orient, founded in 1870 by Isabel Thorburn who was its president until she died in 1901.

At Rev. John Hunt's church we had a splendid meeting at 6:30 followed by a fine supper at 9:00 p.m. at the Hunts' home. It took us some time to get adjusted to the hours people keep in India. Breakfast and lunch hours are similar to American customs, but in the afternoon there is usually tea at four or five, meetings at six or six-thirty and dinner at eight-thirty or nine.

I asked Mrs. Hunt why she seemed so free of household duties. She said they had a servant who came at six o'clock in the morning and stayed till eight-thirty in the evening with a few hours off in the afternoon. He did the marketing, bought the groceries, cooked the meals, washed the dishes, cleaned the house, and even planned the menus. His wages were $11.00 a month. "And his board," I added. "No, he keeps his family of five in a shack on the grounds, so he has no house rent, but he buys all of their food and clothes with that $11.00. That is good pay for India as many of the servants are paid only $7.00 a month."

The next noon Roni Singh entertained a half dozen distinguished guests at lunch and in the afternoon took us to the annual Flower Show. I had not dreamed such variety of beauty could exist—it was as if men and angels had gathered all the flowers of earth and heaven and fashioned them into exquisite arrangements. Competing with the flowers for our attention were two Indian military bands dressed in as colorful costumes as the flowers, playing very colorful music with bagpipes, drums, and twirling batons in a *most* colorful manner. We enjoyed the afternoon immensely, and not the least part of our delight lay in watching the rapt expression of the little brown-skinned boys as they listened, with their eyes popping out, to the bagpipes.

On the way back we stopped at the Psychiatric Hospital founded by Stanley Jones. The entire staff enthusiastically took us on a conducted tour of the institution. The place was Jones' original Ashram where people lived together from September to April. It is now used entirely as a clinic, Stanley Jones having moved his Ashram meetings to the hills where people love to withdraw during the hot season in April and May. Ashram originally meant colony—not a camp. Considering all the frustrations India presents we were surprised that there were so few patients in the hospital, and none of a serious nature.

Our second evening was given over to a meeting of leaders, ministers, and selected lay people. All of our meetings in Lucknow were conducted in English.

One of the strange observations that impressed us more and more was this: No English-speaking country is Communistic. Not only is this true of Australia, New Zealand, South Africa, and Canada, but even where English has been the second language, as in India and the Philippines. It might give us ground for hope to know that with the exception of China and Formosa English is now the second language of almost every Asian country.

A powerful undercurrent in Indian history is the tremendous reverence for life—not only human life but life of all kinds. To the Indian, life is sacred no matter what form it takes. The only Occidental I know of who follows this creed with equal reverence is the man the world is acclaiming today as the greatest of all modern saints—Albert Schweitzer. In India, if ants are in the house they are swept out carefully lest a single one be destroyed. Even to step on a worm is taboo.

Moses laid down rules in the book of Leviticus that no Jew must ever eat blood. Not till it is all drained from the flesh can the meat be eaten. For blood is life—and it is a crime to eat life. The Hindu goes a step further—not only is the blood to be abstained from but no creature that ever had life must be eaten.

While this deep reverence for life should hold our respect and not be treated lightly, it becomes perverted when the life of an animal is reverenced more than the life of a human being. And the practice presents some serious problems for the well being of the nation.

Considering this negative aspect, one can readily see how some atheists and many Communists get the impression that religion might become a curse and blight upon a people. Nehru, who is not religious, calls this reverence for all life a superstition. He claims that India's superstitions are the "Jonah" that is bringing her shipwreck upon her. For example one-fifth of the cattle of the world are in India and nine-tenths of them are totally unproductive. The cows are literally eating India into starvation. If three-fourths of them were slaughtered one-half of India's problems would be solved, but for a responsible statesman even to suggest such a course would bring immediate ostracism.

While we were enjoying watching the mischievous monkeys using trees as trapezes, and cavorting over the lawns and fields with fascinating antics, we noticed our companions were not so amused. "These little creatures are very destructive and we can do nothing about it." And then they told of a railway station further south where the monkeys greet incoming travelers by snatching their hats, purses, or packages—anything they can grab—and scamper up into the rafters with their loot; then the only way the passengers can retrieve their belongings is to buy a bunch of bananas and hold them out until the mischievous rascals bring back their property and make a polite exchange. However, these monkeys, which are so destructive they drive people frantic, cannot be killed. Roni Singh said her brother was a Christian and a great hunter. He went to a village and all the villagers signed a request that he kill all the monkeys, which he did. He was the only one who wasn't afraid of the "Karma" that was certain to follow. If the whole nation turned to atheistic communism the animals could be destroyed but people would become enslaved like animals. If the whole nation turned to Christ, on the other hand, the enslavement to animal worship could be rooted out and the people set free.

Reference to Karma brings up another of the creeds of India which I found had its good as well as its bad side. Hindus and Buddhists do not believe in a Savior who died for our sins. They believe every mistake in this life must be paid for in a subsequent incarnation. This fosters a universal callousness to human suffering. To alleviate a sick or suffering person is interfering with the course of his Karma. If one is relieved of pain in this life which has been meted out to him for sins in a former life he is merely postponing the suffering till his next sojourn on this earth. This faith in Karma accounts for the vast patience with which millions of underfed, overworked folk born into the lower castes in India accept with patience their lot.

When we left Lucknow Roni Singh promised to join us at our First Camp Farthest Out in India. We felt honored to be the guest of this woman who was loved and respected by all. When we rode with her to the Flower Show all the soldiers and policemen saluted the car. When the Browns and I flew to Calcutta the next day the plane went out of its way to carry us over Benares so that we three could see where the faithful bathed in the Ganges. When I asked why the pilot did this for us, I was told that Roni Singh had requested it.

When we reached Calcutta we found teeming and steaming humanity—seven million of them, a city as large as London or New York. Rev. Das and Mr. Griffith met us at the plane and drove us to the Lee Memorial Mission where we were given rooms on the third floor. No doors—only curtains—electric fans, mosquito cages over us at night, and no hot water. But at last the weather was warm!!

In Europe I had worn long underwear, winter weight suit,

sweater, and topcoat constantly wherever I went, indoors and out. In Greece and Rome I dispensed with the overcoat. In Cairo I even discarded the sweater. In Jerusalem I left off the sweater but often wore my overcoat when outside, for there, for the first time, we had inside heat. In Delhi and Lucknow I laid both overcoat and sweater aside. In Delhi I daringly packed away my winter suit, to remain packed until I reached Japan in April, and stepped into my blue summer suit. And now in the midsummer heat of Calcutta I finally laid aside my long underwear and donned my B.V.D.'s. From here on we anticipated that the weather would grow hotter and hotter. It did!

That first afternoon in Calcutta on our way to our first appointment where Roland was to address three hundred Hindus through an interpreter, we were detained on a main street by a procession of Communists carrying red flags with hammer and sickle emblem. As is so often the case with Communist parades, these were sympathizers of the unemployed. I had been wondering for some time how the employed fed their families on $7.00 or $11.00 a month! Now I wondered how the *unemployed* fed their families at all. Teachers, all through India, many of whom receive only $6.00 a month, were on a strike for better pay, which all agree they deserved, and Communists by "sympathizing" with them were fast winning converts.

We in America are not totally without blame in this matter. Only by increased world trade will India be able to raise her standard of living, but unless we lower our tariff barriers lower wages is the price India must pay for production at a competitive level. India must compete, for instance, with British cotton goods, and yet she has to import all her heavy machinery. Hence she must pay low wages. Indian Christians are often put on the spot because it is the so-called Christian nations which force down Indian prices.

Early that evening I addressed three to four hundred people in church; and later, at the Y.M.C.A. Roland and I both spoke. Between our talks, while the group stood and sang, Marcia painted a picture. Between the two meetings, we dined with thirty guests at the Lee Mission.

We found we had to be careful not to say anything in Calcutta that could be construed to sound like politics. Many Indians think that all missionaries and evangelists from the United States are subsidized by the United States government, and are in India to propagandize for the capitalist side in the impending world struggle. Surely these "thoughts" are Communist-inspired.

Our last day in Calcutta was rich in fulfilled dreams. In the morning we conducted a laboratory in prayer in a Methodist church, and then after a luncheon at the Y.W.C.A. we met a group of the Christian leaders for a profound and intimate discussion on prayer groups and how to lead them. Seed sown in this meeting was taking root, for the leaders decided to meet on the first Friday of every month as a monthly Camp Farthest Out class in prayer for the purpose of inspiring and stimulating prayer groups in other sections. In the afternoon Roland conducted a healing service in the big Methodist Church and we were amazed to see a whole school full of little boys march in. Not infrequently schools are closed when a healing service is planned, so curious and eager are the people concerning anything that borders on the miraculous. Roland conducted the meeting in a dignified and impressive manner, avoiding showmanship and sensational methods. I pray that numbers of the ill and maimed were healed. Everyone seemed happy and appreciative when they went out, and all wanted to shake Roland's hand.

An engineer returned to the Mission with me. He was troubled because prayer to him was a hard, dry, unhappy task. "How do you put joy into it?" I told him that after he prayed, "Thy Kingdom come on earth as it is in heaven," to step forth expecting to see the joys of heaven all around him, the right persons at the right time, the right ideas at the right time, and the right supply for the right need. "Not only pray for the Kingdom," I concluded, "but *expect* the Kingdom. Pray with joy and expectancy." He dropped on his knees before me, and begged me to bless him and pray that the joy of Jesus' fellowship would henceforth be his.

Later he told me the sad story about the six oldest children of the Lees' who founded this Mission—all of them were killed in an avalanche. That led to a deeper discussion on the way in which seeming tragedies can be turned into blessings. I read the story of the Lees' great loss that night and found great inspiration in the way the parents accepted this terrible bereavement. It reminded me of the four little sisters of Bertha Vester of the American Colony Hotel in Jerusalem who had been drowned in a shipwreck when her parents sailed for Palestine. I could fill a book with the tragedies told me on this world journey. Life is not a holiday where all our personal desires are instantly gratified. It is a hard school that challenges all our capacities for courage, patience, fortitude and forgiving grace. There is no home but has had its hour of tragedy, and no individual who has not had his share of trouble. Ask any saint where he got his glow and invariably he will relate the hardest experience that ever came to him. In the *Soul's Sincere Desire* I wrote, "Trouble is the best thing that can come to one, next to God Himself, if it turns one to God." Only when trouble turns one away from God does it become tragedy.

At six o'clock that evening we led a Youth Rally made up of two hundred college boys and girls. I spoke first, then Marcia painted the Old Rugged Cross as a trio of boys sang the fine old hymn. She had wanted to paint that particular picture for them but the song was not in the hymnal, so imagine her thrill when these young men, not aware of her wish, asked permission to sing this song at this very meeting. Thus all things worked together for good for those that love the Lord. Our speaking time was shortened so the choir could sing some Bengalese hymns. This did not disturb Roland and me as we enjoyed the singing, and we were filled with thanksgiving at the way the Lord at such times helped us adapt our messages so His power flowed through in wonderful ways whether we talked fifteen minutes or an hour. Roland's closing address was a masterpiece of condensing a big idea into a few words and swept everyone up to the heights.

We all got husky throats, and the Griffiths, who ran the Mission, explained the reason. No soloist ever sings in Calcutta. A few do book engagements there, but the dust in the air hoarsens their throats so terribly that nearly every concert has to be canceled. Bombay is the place where throats clear up, so we looked forward to having our throats improve on the morrow.

The next stops were Bombay, Poona, and Nasrapur. We had heard so much about the excellent scenery and quietness of Nasrapur that we could hardly wait to get there.

CHAPTER XIII

WE FIND THE KEY TO ALL RELIGIONS IN BOMBAY AND POONA

THERE ARE FEW MORE BEAUTIFUL AND IMPRESSIVE SIGHTS THAN THE approach to Bombay as the plane flies up the noble waterway that separates this island city, with its stately buildings on the left, from the palm-fringed shore of the mainland to the right. No city in the world has a finer water front than Bombay. The great public office buildings looking over Boell Bay are not individually distinguished for architectural beauty, but they have a cumulative effect of great dignity. Bombay's position as the gateway of India, its magnificent natural harbor, and the enterprise of its inhabitants have made it one of the first cities of the world. The commercial buildings will compare with those in most other cities, and as one rides through its fine wide thoroughfares he finds himself in a regular beehive of industry. Of really outstanding merit is the immense railway terminus, the post office, the museum, and the Royal Institute of Science.

However, we had not come to see buildings but men. It was not the outer scenery but the inner spirit we were seeking to find, and that we found in Rev. Ross Thomas and his lovely wife who met us at the airfield. They took us to the home of the Bishop of this area whose name I didn't catch, but whose lovely, humble spirit I sensed the moment I met him. We had no speaking engagement that first evening in Bombay, due to a mix-up in dates which I shall explain later. But that was a good thing since it gave our sore throats time to throw off the effects of the Calcutta dust.

The Bishop suggested we use that evening for a ride through the millionaire section of the city. One of the first things he showed us in that ride was the palatial governor's mansion that had been the residence of Raja and Roni Singh during the six years he had been governor of Bombay. Next he took us to the residential section of the Parsees, who derive their religion from Zoroaster who lived one thousand years before Jesus. Zoroaster was famous in antiquity as the founder of the wisdom of the Magi. It is possible that the three Magi who followed the star from the far east to the manger of the baby Jesus had derived their inspiration from the prophecies of this great Persian Sage. The followers of Zoroaster are called Parsees. They number only a hundred thousand but their influence far outweighs their numbers as they are endowed with great natural ability, combined with a thoroughly western initiative and progressiveness. They are a dedicated, sincerely religious sect, outstanding for their integrity and benevolence. They consider Zoroaster the first of the prophets. He taught them not to kill, to love one another, and that God is love. The books of Zoroaster in many ways remind us of the Psalms and Proverbs and books of the minor prophets.

They have temples where they can go and pray whenever they wish, but have no regular services, no Sundays or Sabbaths. Their high standard of ethics has made them so efficient and trustworthy that they are nearly all rich or at least well-to-do. Because of their regard for fire as the emblem of purity they are known as fire worshippers.

We skirted the Parsee Cemetery, concealed from the eyes of the curious by a wall of trees. No visitors are allowed to enter. I remembered their custom of exposing their dead on iron gratings in "towers of silence," where the ever-near, ever-waiting vultures swoop down and in a few minutes nothing but the skeleton remains. To them, I suppose, the vultures that can be seen hovering constantly overhead are like birds of heaven, rendering the same necessary service our crematoriums render in a far different way.

In Bombay even to a greater extent than in most cities the extreme differences between the very rich and the very poor, the virtuous and the adulterous, the socially acceptable and those discriminated against are glaringly apparent. In contrast to the palatial homes we saw that first evening are the unspeakably crowded tenements in another section of the city; in contrast to the lovely and chaste homes of the law abiding Parsees is Bombay's long "Street of Cages" which is probably the most notorious red-light district in the world. In contrast to the free mingling of all types of racial groups are the British clubs which still exclude dark-skinned people, and the hotels where the policy is to refuse service to South Africans.

That night after retiring I read a most thrilling autobiography of "How a Sufi Found His Lord" by a Bishop Subhan who as a Muslim youth received training in mysticism, then read the gospels, and finally shocked his family and school by becoming a Christian; first an Anglican; then for four years a Roman Catholic; and finally, because Rome did not acknowledge other Christians as "saved" and admissable to heaven, and because in those four years he was not allowed to read the Bible at will, he left that church and became a Methodist. In 1944 at the Methodist Central Conference he was elected Bishop of the Bombay area.

At breakfast the next morning I said to my host, "I am very eager to meet Bishop Subhan whose autobiography I found on the table by my bed last night. Will he be at the meeting tonight?" He smiled and replied, "I am very sure that he will be." Then the Browns laughingly explained that the name of our host was Bishop Subhan!

"That thrills me!" I exclaimed. "Life provides more suspense than fiction does. I have a lot to ask you."

In answer to my questions the bishop told us how his adventure into Muslim mysticism had made of him a spiritual explorer, questing from stage to stage, trying to meet in the unseen world Adam, Noah, Abraham, Moses, Jesus, and Mohammed and finally hoping to reach and enjoy union with Allah. But Allah he conceived to be a god of cruel justice who punished severely. When he opened the gospels to learn of Jesus, ranked as a prophet in the Muslim hierarchy, he found not only a prophet, but a loving Savior who was willing to die for the sins of mankind. This Savior changed his life. His Muslim friends tried to persuade him that Christians had falsified the gospels—"Jesus had done nothing unusual; it was Judas that was crucified and Jesus had escaped!" What inestimable difference Jesus' Passion has made! Had his opposers been able to prove that he had not died, the power he holds over the world today could not have been.

The Brahmo-Samaj sect of Muslims, Bishop Subhan explained, makes much use of Jesus' teachings in presenting an eclectic viewpoint. They tried for a time to gather young John Subhan into their fold but he was determined to go all the way with Jesus as

Lord and Savior. His religious affiliations reminded me of Rufus Moseley who had hopped in and hopped out of so many religious fellowships: Baptist, Christian Science, Pentacostal; and each withdrawal was marked by the blessings of a love feast! This Bishop Subhan has passed through periods of persecution, but he still loves and is loved by the Roman Catholics, and through his continuing love and friendships with Muslims has been converting scores of them to Christ.

Now for a look at Hinduism. It is made up of a conglomeration of beliefs and rites—the multitude of beliefs and rites of all the peoples who have become a part of India through thousands of years. Therefore, it is unlike other religions which have definite dogmas and creeds to which adherents must subscribe. Hinduism looks with tolerance upon all religions, regardless of dogma and creed. It has full confidence that if believers will observe the one thing Hinduism does insist upon—a working steadily upward with a hope of improving their situation in life—they will eventually arrive at the "Ultimate." It accepts with respect any religious philosophy or practice which brings the whole personality into contact with the "Central Reality"—the deity or deities it reverences—whichever the case may be. It makes room within itself for the philosophy of the Gandhi-like individual at the top of the "scale," whose ability to meditate profoundly upon the Absolute is coupled with compassion for the masses and unabated effort to lifting the standards of living through justice and honest dealings. It also makes room within itself for the philosophy of the ignorant, half-civilized ones at the bottom of the scale whose worship of a multitude of deities and godlings is filled with superstition, nameless fear, and efforts of appeasement. It places the worshippers of the Absolute as highest in respect; second, the worshippers of a personal God; third, the worshippers of incarnations of Rama, Krishna, and Buddha; fourth, the worshippers of ancestors, saints, and sages; and lowest of all are the worshippers of petty forces and spirits which might be found anywhere in anything.

Most of the vital religions of the world have an incarnation of God in visible form that can be revered and loved. Islam has its Mohammed, Buddhism its Buddha, Zoroastrianism its Zarathustra, and Christianity has its Christ. It is so much easier for Christians to understand God because the "Word became Flesh and dwelt among us" so we might behold His Glory, Grace, and Truth. Hinduism alone has tried to survive under a God who is an abstraction—The Absolute. But when the worship of Buddha in India began to crowd Hinduism off the stage, the Bhagavad-Gita was revived with the "saintly" Krishna as its hero, and, as a result, Hinduism has regained dominance in India today. Buddhism, pushed out of its native land, has found its refuge in Ceylon, Burma, Indo-China, Japan —in fact has spread all over the rest of Asia.

Religion has to be "beheld" before the human mind can grasp it, and the human heart cherish it and the human soul adore it. God needed to become Flesh.

The craving of the people in the past for a king or a queen had its roots in this same desire to have the abstract ideal made concrete in visible form.

I was thinking how we have our flag, but it is not a sentient creature and doesn't do for us what Queen Elizabeth does for England, Ceylon, Australia, and the entire British Commonwealth, when I suddenly caught a hidden secret in the Indian worship of the cow. The cow of India becomes a living symbol of a creature uniquely adapted for adoration. Queen Elizabeth appears in Australia and New Zealand only once in ten years but the cow is always with the people of India. They meet her on every street. She is obviously a different "creation" from us, so does not arouse envy or jealousy, because we are not like her. There is nothing in her personality we criticize or abhor because an inferiority complex is aroused. And she, thank the Lord, sees nothing in our personality she is tempted to criticize or detest. She possesses all the "Fruits of the Spirit" described by Paul. How richly endowed she is with peace (the serenity of centuries is in her face), long suffering (watch her patiently pull the heavy cart), goodness, gentleness, meekness, temperance and trust. She doesn't stop you with a frown and ask whether you are "saved," or tell you you are foolish if you believe in prayer; she doesn't remind you that the words "capital" and "cattle" come from the same stem, and if you don't worship the Profit System you must certainly be a Communist; she doesn't put you under a third degree about your income tax; and you can overwork her and underfeed her and she forgives and forgives and forgives.

A tranquil statue of seated Buddha may lift some souls but he is just a statue, always in the same place, like a picture in a frame. But the cow is a moving picture in three dimensional technicolor, and she exhibits the dynamics of peace and patience and meekness and gentleness in every action and reaction of life right before one's eyes. Yes, I know a lot of human, "self-righteous" critics that would be more uncomfortable to live with than this "holy" cow!

The next day Bishop Subhan took us to Friendship Center where poor and hungry little children spend the day while their mothers work for a paltry rupee a day, approximately twenty-one cents in our money. I never saw a more glorious group of fifty happy children. They were seated on the floor all ready for lunch, but they joyously postponed it to come out to the lovely enclosed yard and sing for us and reenact a pageant they had presented at Christmas time. Roland took color pictures that are precious. There were Jewish, Mohammedan, Hindu, and Christian children in the group —all blossoming under the tender supervision of the native Methodist worker, Miss Childs.

Finally, the day closed with a wonderful meeting in the Bishop's church at six thirty attended by upward of three hundred fine Indian Christians from all the churches of the city. We presented our customary triple-header: first Roland, then Marcia's picture message, and then my talk.

Through a confusion in dates we found Bombay and Poona had both advertised us for the eighteenth of February: in Bombay the seventeenth and eighteenth, in Poona the eighteenth and nineteenth. When the mistake was discovered, our sponsors in both cities were greatly perturbed. We quickly relieved all tension by assuring them we would divide our team on the eighteenth and provide a speaker for each city.

Next morning Roland and I met with the Christian ministers and leaders of the Bombay area and in our two-hour conference laid foundations for prayer groups and, because of their enthusiasm, perhaps an annual Camp Farthest Out gathering for additional training in the teachings of Jesus in the years to come. Roland remained for another hour with them while the Bishop took Marcia and me to the railroad station for the trip to Poona.

At the station we saw, as we had often seen, the littlest, oldest porter present carefully hoist our two heaviest bags to the top of his head and carry them up the stairs, across the viaduct to the other side of the tracks, and down again. Also while waiting for our train, we watched with interest the arrival of a very tall, white-bearded

Moslem "saint," accompanied by a score of his disciples who were enroute to a "convention" at some Moslem shrine. They piled up their luggage and settled themselves on top of it while awaiting their train.

It was an experience to ride for three hours on a second class Indian railroad, boxcar shaped with few windows and with benches facing each other along the opposite walls, exactly like fourth class in Germany. We ate our lunch of chicken sandwiches which the Bishop himself had prepared for us.

When we arrived in Poona Mr. Aimee, tall and very dark-skinned, the Y.M.C.A. Secretary, was easily recognized in the immense crowd. He drove us to the home of the Crawfords, outstanding missionaries, where we were to stay. After depositing our luggage and washing up he took us to the Methodist Church where Marcia gave a chalk talk and I addressed a group at the six-thirty meeting. At the same hour Roland was speaking in Bombay. It is wonderful the way we were equipped to meet dilemmas that necessitated our being in two places at once.

The next day Roland arrived. His address in Bombay on Jesus' laws of prayer had so thrilled everyone that the Bishop had begged him to return in 1956 and hold meetings in all the Methodist churches of Bombay.

The minister in Poona wanted Roland and me to visit many sick folk, an impossible task, so we asked him to invite the ailing ones to the parsonage at 3:00 p.m. In an hour's address, well interpreted by Mr. Aimee, Roland strengthened their faith in the Great Physician and made clear Jesus' requirements for healing. Then we both prayed for all those present, such sweet little children, such beautiful mothers, and such dear old people. Later the Crawfords entertained us at a tea for religious leaders and workers. I found myself seated between two of the sweetest, most Christ-like of men, who, when I queried them about their religious beliefs, revealed that one was a devout Jew and the other a devout Parsee. Each was living his own religion faithfully, but in this "broad-minded" atmosphere of India both were passionately eager to get all we could give them of Christ.

After another meeting later in the evening at which all three of us had spoken, Mr. Crozier, Director of the Methodist Spiritual Life Camp, drove us in his bus to Nasrapur where the first Camp Farthest Out in India was to be held.

CHAPTER XIV

NASRAPUR—THE FIRST CAMP FARTHEST OUT IN ASIA

WE WERE THRILLED WITH THE CLEAR MOUNTAIN AIR, BEAUTIFUL setting, and the splendid accommodations at Nasrapur, and as the campers began to gather from all over this section of India our joys mounted higher and higher. Mr. Crozier is one of the most loving and lovable of men, and his wife one of the most efficient, devoted, and industrious women I ever saw. She was busy every moment, keeping everything in running order, and seeing that every guest was comfortable.

That evening as I eased myself into my bed, very carefully draped with mosquito netting, I heard a hyena howling and laughing outside. Mr. Crozier slipped a flashlight to me under the netting and cautioned me never to step out of my bed in the night without first making sure there was no cobra or scorpion underfoot. I wondered! However, the windows were wired against snakes and I encountered no scorpions. The only mosquito I saw was inside my mosquito netting and needless to say, I put a blessing on him and sent him to insect heaven. Accommodations here were really lovely, the food was good, the atmosphere was as delightful as California at its best, and the places for the meetings were perfect. About forty people were there for the full time; two-thirds were Indians, the rest missionaries from churches or mission centers throughout this area; in other words they were leaders who would spread their influence to many. The joy, peace, and exhilaration of being in a Camp Farthest Out again was like heaven. There is simply no comparison between the cumulative blessings of a camp such as this and the scattered sessions in a limited series of meetings in a city—excellent as the city meetings may be.

The people were amazed, thrilled almost in a state of ecstasy. Our tall, dark Y.M.C.A. Secretary of Poona, Mr. Aimee, exclaimed,

"This camp must be perpetuated. It is the greatest thing in a spiritual way that has ever hit India. Many churches are spiritually dead, many Y.M.C.A.'s are just marking time; this type of camp can put new life into the dead bones of India's Christianity. I am going to start prayer groups all over Poona, when I go back, using the folks from this camp as a nucleus. If you need a chairman or planner for future years I will be willing to act. [He with Mr. Crozier and Louise Fisher would make a great planning team.] Connect us up with your American movement," he continued. "We will do anything to make this movement grow. Send one of your band every year." Then Louise Fisher, who had been a missionary in that area for years, a saint if there ever was one, told us how by using Indian musical instruments for devotion through motion, since pianos are scarce in India, and how by training a native art teacher and finding other competent native leadership, similar camps could be held every year, led by Indians themselves. With message-bringers like Bishop Subhan, Mrs. Welthy Fisher, and others we were destined to meet, such camps could be very wonderful.

A beautiful Parsee woman rushed up to me after one of my talks and begged permission to print some of my ideas in the Parsee magazine. She said she had been taking notes on our prayers and wanted to print them too. She was learning to love our Jesus, she said, along with her Zoroaster and wanted her people to know Him, too.

The creative writing class proved a splendid outlet for stimulating ideas from these earnest folks; the devotion through motion on the roof garden, even without a piano, was entered into with enthusiasm; and the painting class was simply outstanding. Indians are all potential artists, and they love color; but best of all, every picture illustrated a message. A camp of this size is powerful and thrilling when everyone takes part in every activity as they did here.

The next evening Dr. Hivali, founder of Ahmednagar College, along with three men on his faculty arrived at six o'clock to take me on a hundred mile drive over very rugged jarring roads to the college. Riding with us was Marylin Munson, a former secretary to Roland in his Chicago church and now a missionary here in India. She left us at Poona. As we rode along, Mr. Motley, business manager of the college and distributor of famine relief, explained that their college was in the center of the famine district where failure of rainfall had brought starvation to many. He said the best food to meet the emergency was powdered milk sent by the United Brethren and "Meals for Millions" sent by the Foundation Farthest Out under the direction of George Hales. They also found "Viet" vitamins sent by Stanley Jones of great help for the convalescent in hospitals and for the undernourished. Tons of American wheat had arrived shortly before we came, the old Liberty Ships laden with this wheat making a tremendous sight in the harbor of Bombay, as also did the long freight trains of the wheat as they moved into the Poona area.

Marylin Munson gave us a graphic picture of the famine situation when she told of one boy who had worked two days digging grass, then on the third day walked twelve miles to a place where he could sell the grass for five cents and then walked back home. This five cents had to buy food for three people to last them three days.

It was late when we reached our destination and early the next morning President Barnabas of the college (Hivali's son-in-law) conducted me through the grounds of the fastest growing college in the world, only seven years old. At 9:00 a.m. I addressed seven hundred college men and women in their auditorium. Since there were many religious faiths present I was not permitted to speak specifically of Christianity (according to Indian law proselyting is banned). So I reminded them as I had done before my first audience in New Delhi how we all originated from common stock in the Himalayas, and all belonged to one great Brotherhood under God. . . . With my concluding words I received a great ovation of applause after which a beautiful college girl climbed the platform and put an immense garland around my neck, far larger than the Hawaiian leis, and another girl gave me an immense bouquet.

Then the crowd escorted me to the site for the new residence hall for men where I was to lay the cornerstone. After giving the prayer, I was handed a trowel with which to lay the plaque in the cornerstone. A dozen students flashed pictures of me adorned with the flowers and garlands. Then we marched to the foundation for the residence hall for girls and again I wielded the trowel. I love college boys and girls, and to realize that my name engraved there— and my love—will undergird these residence halls for all time even as my prayers had undergirded it seven years before, almost brought tears to my eyes. Dr. Hivali explained to the students how I had prayed with him in America when this college was first contemplated, and how its success was based upon prayer.

Then I went into the chapel where only Christian students came, and there I could go "all the way out" in speaking to them about Jesus. When I finished, a dozen students expressed such an ardent desire to come to our camp at Nasrapur that we arranged right on the spot for twenty to come for the last three days of the camp. Dr. Hivali offered to pay transportation and I offered to pay the board and room. Their coming furnished the capping climax of the camp, for these enthusiastic youths will spread the "contagion" of Jesus among the young people wherever they go.

The following day, after I returned to camp, Dr. Matthews, President of Chatiapati Shivaji College, arrived, bringing with him a white-bearded, white-haired, saintly Hindu known as Karmaveer Bhaurav Patil, who not only founded the college but also founded fifty high schools and hundreds of elementary schools all over this area. He is known as India's "champion of mass education." I asked this old saint to use part of the creative writing hour to tell the story of his life and his dream to establish over one hundred high schools by the "historic year of 1957." He hoped and expected to take me to his college on Friday, but Roni Singh from Lucknow and Louise Fisher, my two solicitous guardian angels, thought that a second hard long ride over the bumpy roads would be too strenuous for a man of my age. So Roland went in my place.

This journey of Roland Brown to Satara was very fruitful and some of his remarkable experiences are worth recording. When he spoke in the college chapel it was crowded to the doors. The principal businessmen of Satara had invited him to address their Service Club and, when they found his schedule already over-full, they came in a body to hear his address at the college.

He was shown over the entire project—one of a series of amazing colleges and schools where the students can help earn their way. Under guidance of President Matthews he took pictures of the boys in their outdoor kitchen doing their own cooking, of other boys leveling land on the hillside in preparation for raising splendid crops of fruits and vegetables. He was taken around their sugar plantation, and watched the processing of the sugar cane.

All of the older boys are required to work one or two hours a day, thus making the schools self-supporting. This whole project of Mr. Patil consisting of four hundred and fifty schools is one of the finest missionary enterprises in the world—and yet, it is not a Christian mission! Any of our Christian missions could learn much from a study of this remarkable educational work which is being done under the leadership of this Hindu follower of Mahatma Gandhi.

The day Roland arrived, this aged saint fell and sprained his ankle so badly he could not attend the opening meeting. Roland was taken to his home afterwards where he found Mr. Patil lying on a blanket on the floor. The room was without windows and without any furniture. The only property which this dear man seemed to possess was his shiny automobile which someone had given him, and which made it possible for him to get around to supervise his far-reaching work. He was delighted that Roland Brown had come to his home to see him. Roland sat down on the floor beside him and placed his hands on his badly swollen ankle and asked the Divine Physician to make it well. Immediately the old gentleman arose, assembled members of his family together in a place where the light was better so Roland could photograph them all. He informed them that the pain was gone.

Roland doubted if many people would be present at the afternoon meeting because there had been only a few hours to spread the word about it. But when he arrived he found the church crowded with hundreds of people already waiting. For an hour he talked with them about the wonderful Love of Jesus, and how he came to meet every need in our lives. When the service was finished, no one wanted to leave. Instead the people came forward and knelt down that he might pray for them. Back and forth across the front of the church he passed, placing his hands upon the heads of these dear people and praying that God might meet every need in their lives. Many of them were Christians, but probably the greater number were not. At leasty twenty were Hindus wearing their typical turbans. Roland reported that the scene he could never forget was that of dozens of young mothers kneeling and holding their babies in their upstretched hands so that he might touch and bless the infants. For these babies were all sick, and evidently word had gotten around that the Christ, reaching through Roland, might heal them if they could have him touch them.

"How my heart went out to all these dear souls," exclaimed

Roland, "and how I hungered that they might all know Jesus and love him as I did. This is the great challenge confronting the Christian Church everywhere. The world knows that Christ came to save us from our sin, sickness, poverty, and tribulations—and if He really lives in us He should be able to do today what once He did. What I witnessed and experienced at Satara is a tribute to the Christian Church, as well as a revelation of the hunger and expectancy of the human race."

One day Mrs. Roi, an Indian woman whose brown face expressed a great deal of character, was seated beside me at the table when I suddenly turned to her and exclaimed, "I can tell by your face that you have had a life of rich experience which somewhere, sometime, must have left a deep impact upon others. Tell me your story. I mustn't leave until I hear it."

Very modestly she told it. As a social worker she had gone into a village to start a school, but she found that the children could not come because they were earning a rupee a month for watching the cattle. So she introduced bee and poultry culture and paid the same children several rupees a month for an hour's work a day tending the bees and the chickens, persuading the villagers to turn the cattle jobs over to old men, and let the children come to school.

She helped the sick and, to the amazement of the villagers, she even nursed a mean man who had done his best to oppose her. The villagers asked why she helped an enemy. She replied she could not do so of herself, but that her God had directed her to do so. They insisted that no God would require an individual to help an enemy and accused her of lying. So she opened her Bible and showed them the chapter and verse. When she read them the passage, "But I say unto you, love your enemies, bless them that curse you, do good to them that hate you, and pray for them which despitefully use you, and persecute you" (Matthew 5:44), it so amazed them and so awakened their curiosity that they wanted to study her Bible. The result was that half the village became Christian. Then twenty nearby villages, hearing of her work, asked her to start schools for them, and so the work spread.

Since the gods the people worshipped were in the form of idols they could see and touch, they next asked her to *show* them her God. She said she had no graven image to show them, for her God was spirit and resided within each human being. They asked her to prove her contention, so she invited them to come to her house to hear her read the Bible. Thus many more were converted. This quiet woman, sitting beside me, from that moment became to me a living sermon. "If you are really filled with Christ, you become contagious." This was the theory, the conviction, the technique upon which the camp had been operating all week, the best examples of which were to be found among the campers themselves. With all these wonderful people around us, Jesus became more and more contagious to those who were meeting Him for the first time.

Freedom of worship is guaranteed in India, but since the new government forbids Christians evangelizing with the intent to make converts, the folks attending camps informed us that the CFO method of conversion through example and contagion might be the key to Christianizing India. At the close of my last prayer group the Parsee woman said, "Could we sit here in silence awhile and feel the presence of Jesus?" I was thrilled at this spontaneous testimony to the way Jesus was invading the hearts of the peoples of different faith. Earlier that same day a proud Brahman youth in my writing class had written a tribute to the teachings of his loved Hindu religion; but on the last night of the camp when the time came for him to depart, he clasped my hand for a long time and said he wanted to keep in touch with me always, and vowed that he was going to become a student of my books on prayer and on Jesus. Then he confessed that the camp had influenced him to become "very eager to become a fisher of men."

The last three days at Nasrapur were glorious. The fifteen men students and six women students from Ahmednagar College were simply aglow with gratitude for being there and the last evening asked to meet alone with me so they could tell me face to face what an inspiration the experience had been. Art! Rhythm! Everything they loved! A tense little American missionary told me on that last day how for the first time in her life her whole mind, heart, soul, and body were released to God, a sentiment many other missionaries echoed.

Board and room at this camp was seventy-five cents a day! It cost me only forty dollars for the twenty-one students for three days, and when the beautiful Parsee woman, Mrs. Neigis A. Chinoy, left the camp, she and her mother gave me a check for fifty dollars. As we give to God, He gives to us. These Parsee friends were at the train in Poona waiting to garland us as they said goodbye. We gave them Jesus and they gave us flowers. But, best of all, they gave us receptive hearts!

CHAPTER XV

PRAYER MOVEMENTS IN MADRAS AND COCHIN

RETURNING TO BOMBAY IN ORDER TO GET OUR PLANE WE FLEW TO Madras where O. V. Alexander of the Y.M.C.A. took us to the Y.W.C.A. where rooms were reserved. Early in the afternoon we were taken to Miss Appasamy's school for girls where Marcia drew pictures illustrating familiar hymns for the four hundred young pupils and later for the three hundred high school girls, and Roland and I addressed the groups. My talk was fair but Roland hit the bull's eye, rang the bell, and won every heart! From the vantage point of my seat on the platform I could watch their ready response to his every word and smile. During the whole of this remarkably God-directed journey there was never any strain concerning "what we should say." Always when one of us gave just an "average good" talk, then the Lord provided a perfectly brilliant talk through the other one. In such circumstances it was actually fun anticipating how our Lord was going to express Himself, as both of us felt that our messages were not ours but His.

After tea at the school we were taken to the Y.M.C.A. patio where, under the changing sunset sky, a dignified Indian judge introduced us to some four hundred eager listeners. Again Marcia painted and the three of us tried to open the eyes of our audience to Jesus and the Kingdom. We were afterwards thronged by folks for personal prayers, and didn't get to the Appasamy home for supper until half past nine. It was a native Indian meal of rice and curry with several other native dishes added; only two of the dishes were so highly seasoned as to be "too hot" for our western "palates." It was a fascinating experience: a section of banana leaf for a plate, no silverware, so we ate Indian fashion, with our hands.

Half the people at the Nasrapur CFO, using unleavened bread to dip up the curry, had eaten with their hands. The Indians do this so gracefully, using their fingers so deftly it seemed like a trained art, and a rite. The rest of us had western food and used silverware. We watched how they washed their hands thoroughly before and after the meal as in Jesus' day. I found myself sympathizing with the complaints of the Pharisees when they chided Jesus' disciples for eating with "unwashen hands." Jesus had used that occasion to make known, two thousand years ahead of modern doctors, the significance of "psychosomatics!" "Not what goes into the mouth defiles a man, but the wrong emotions inside him defile the man."

We really enjoyed the meal this delightful Appasamy family had prepared for us. Thirty folks came to the party that followed. It merged into a prayer meeting, and as they spread out their problems before us we prayed that Jesus would solve them all.

Mr. David, an agriculturalist, revealed another of India's major problems in a nutshell. The farmers with whom he works get one rupee apiece for eight hours of hard work. Their wives get half that amount, so between them they get thirty cents a day, enough for one meal a day but not enough to give strength for so much hard work. The coolies who are black as Numidians (wearing only a loin cloth) pull heavy loads at a rupee or a rupee and a half a day. They sleep beside the streets at night, no roof for their heads, hardly food enough. In this area, if the monsoon rains are inadequate, there is a real famine. Miss Appasamy suggested that perhaps because the skin of their entire bodies is exposed to sunlight the coolies absorb vitamins through their pores to make up in part for their lack of food. Mr. David said the rains had failed to come for three years following the American experiments with atom bombs. I have heard the same reason advanced for the long drouth period in Texas. If there is any possibility these experiments are to blame for the drouths, and if we continue them, will the Father continue to listen to us? The long drouth caused the girls' college buildings to crack so that several must be replaced, and the school must raise $20,000 to replace them. "Yes, Lord, India needs adequate rains, more food, more 'roofs,' more money in pay envelopes, more of almost everything."

I told them of our experience at Camps in praying for rain, and they all agreed this might be the solution. "Some of us who have had long experience with prayer," I said, "have come to the conclusion that the elements of nature respond to prayer more quickly than human beings; animals next, children next, and adults slowest of all." To illustrate this I told them the following story:

In 1942 when we were holding a Camp in Alabama, where a long drouth was destroying the crops, a Dr. Adams, who had spent a year with the Hopi Indians, insisted that if God listened to the praying of our American Indians, He should listen to devout Christians when they asked "in faith believing." So we lifted our faith and joined in a simple prayer-chant under his direction:

> *"Send down rain; send down rain; send loving Father rain;*
> *Send down rain on thirsty lands; send loving Father rain."*

"First, chant it softly," said Dr. Adams, "the second time, louder, the third time very loud, then again softly, then hum it, and finally let it sing itself in your subconscious. Now only two cautions: don't tell anybody and don't look for clouds."

That very night the rain came and saved the crops of Alabama. Seven times we have used this method of prayer with phenomenal results, but such results come only after a group has been together long enough to meet the conditions for effective prayer. Some of the results were almost unbelievable.

Next I told them how for five years Florida has been touched by only one hurricane. Dr. Adams, now ninety years of age, with a group of about seven people who share his faith, gather for prayer whenever a hurricane is reported approaching Florida, and every hurricane but one has changed its course. When it comes to animals we all knew of occasions where love and prayer had brought wild creatures under control. That led us to wonder how much longer must we wait before love and prayer will turn aside hurricanes of hate and hurricanes of war, and bring wild men and wild nations under control?

Serious situations are bound to develop where people are forced to live on twenty-one cents a day. First, communications are endangered; indeed all American air mail is placed in jeopardy, since there is a great temptation here among mail clerks to tear off the twenty-five cent stamps, equal to a full day's pay, and destroy the letter. Second, the low wage has filled India with beggars who make begging an art. The most effective beggars are the sad looking, disheveled women with tiny babies in their arms. White tourists one after another drop rupees into their cups. So all a clever male beggar need do is to marry several wives, then the more babies he has the more money he takes in. Third, low economic standards open the country to Communism. Teachers in elementary schools, getting six dollars a month, are naturally tempted to teach Communism to the children and their families. Poor pay creates criminals, beggars, and Communists, and countless other problems.

Nehru had just returned from giving one hundred addresses in the Coimbatore territory where we were to hold our next CFO, but in spite of his fight against Communism the Communist vote there almost equalled the vote for his Congress party. If Communism ever gets a majority vote in India there will be only one party. Nehru and all opposition will be liquidated and the followers of Karl Marx will take over. If India goes Communist, all Asia goes Communist. We in this country are convinced that our democratic way of life is the best way. It is best because its roots are mercy, justice, faith, love—the teachings of Jesus. Only the unadulterated teachings of Jesus will make this earth "as it is in Heaven." And only the real application of the Sermon on the Mount will make it possible for Democracy to survive. Democracy is basically a doctrine of respect for the individual, for each of God's children.

While Roland went to the Y.M.C.A. to pray with people in trouble, the Appasamy brothers and sisters took me to meet the most amazing starter of prayer groups in India, Mr. N. Daniel of the Laymen's Evangelical Fellowship at 112 Kolambakam Road, Madras 6, India. At the age of thirty-eight, with wife and four small children, Mr. Daniel resigned as principal of a school and stepped out utterly on faith to serve Jesus. With no income except that received through prayer he began a ministry of preaching the gospel, healing the sick, and casting out demons. He is now fifty-seven years old.

His entire family followed him: his wife; a woman of great character, and four sterling children, now grown. They have converted hundreds from Hinduism and hundreds more from Mohammedanism. They have even gone fearlessly into the underworld and today some of their best helpers are reformed criminals. They have established scores of prayer groups and once a year the more than five thousand of these men and women, whose lives have been remade through their efforts, meet for a week's Ashram of love and prayer and praise of Jesus. The prayer groups which Mr. Daniel has established are not content with meeting once a week; they meet once a day. Some of the scores of laborers among their number work three weeks a month, and give the fourth week to preaching the gospel without pay.

"And get only a rupee a day when they *do* work?" I asked.

"Oh, less than that!" Mr. Daniel exclaimed.

The Appasamys and other great souls I met in Madras attend a prayer group that meets once a week in his home. I felt a marvelous closeness to this man.

At lunch I found Roland enthusiastic over the men's prayer groups he had found functioning in the Y.M.C.A., one of them, believe it or not, made up largely of policemen. So, here at last in Madras, in the heat of India, we found the heart of a vital prayer group movement that will penetrate and vitalize the entire land.

The night of March second I was booked to be on a program in the great Memorial Hall at the "Annual Public Meeting and Triple Jubilee Meeting in Commemoration of the one hundred fiftieth Anniversary of the Bible Society of India, England, and the World." The meeting was to open at six-thirty and was to end before eight; there were to be two other speakers. A detailed annual report on the number of Bibles sold was to be given and two anthems were to be sung. In such a heavy program, with a very limited amount of time available, what kind of a vital message could I bring to an audience of over a thousand, all strangers to me?

I felt heavy and helpless that afternoon, just as I often feel when facing strange situations for the first time. And just as always happens, the good Lord takes this "empty shell," called Glenn Clark, and amazes both him and his audience with what comes through. Not that it is so wonderful, but it is so much better than what could be expected from such a source! What came through me in the fifteen minutes allotted proved to be an address that I know only the Father could be responsible for. I didn't need to remain for the rest of the program, so I slipped out with the Browns in time for another very important meeting we were to address at the Y.M.C.A. Here in very friendly surroundings Roland, Marcia, and I gave them in abundance of all the Lord had been pouring into us. It was a "full, rich load."

The next morning we were announced for a miniature Camp Farthest Out in one of the largest churches. The crowd that came filled the auditorium and all stayed for the entire morning. Early that evening, with a city official as chairman, Roland and I, without Marcia's help, addressed four hundred people for an hour and a half. Bishop Appasamy had arrived from Coimbatore and sat on the platform and opened and closed the meeting with prayer. To our delight we found that some of the police officials of Madras had been coming to all of our meetings, and the men's prayer group to which some of them belonged met each night all the time we were in Madras, from ten until six the next morning, praying for the success of our meetings. Contacting such men and undergirded by them was one of the most heartening experiences we had in all India.

I must here pour out my gratitude to the good Lord for giving me these wonderful partners in the Browns. Hearing Roland day after day addressing these people in foreign lands makes it easy to see why in his previous journeys he had such remarkable success in England, Wales, Finland, Holland, Denmark and Germany. As a boy I used to study the methods of orators and had a secret desire to become an orator myself one day. Instead, God enabled me to get my (or rather His) messages across in a conversational way without benefit of oratory. But I appreciate oratory when used unselfishly for the Kingdom's sake. I loved to watch the audiences as Roland Brown poured love upon them and drew love forth as an expert pipe organist woos music out of his organ. His voice is adequate for any hall, and it is well-controlled, expressing true subtlety of meaning. His gestures are meaningful, and he adjusts his message to Christians or non-Christians with remarkable sweetness and tact.

Now let me confess why I interject this eulogy. It is because the complex audiences and situations we met on this trip would overwhelm one man, at least it would Glenn Clark, but with Roland at hand I am under no strain. If the hall is too large for my voice to reach the farthest corners, or if my message is too complex for some, I have no concern. All I need do is turn to this travelling companion and let his enormous voice and contagious smile take all into the presence of Jesus. If he speaks first, when my turn comes I find that the soil is plowed and harrowed and ready for the seed which I came to plant. I can see now why Jesus sent out his apostles two by two.

After our last meeting the Y.M.C.A. secretary, Mr. Alexander, paid a twenty minute tribute to our team which, to be very honest, bored me no end. But to my amazement the packed audience sat patiently through every word of it and then rushed up to express individually their love and gratitude and to ask for our continued prayers.

From Madras we flew to Coimbatore where another Y.M.C.A. secretary, Mr. Williams, met us between planes and outlined his plans for our three days of meetings in Coimbatore when we should return there a few days later. Then we flew on to Cochin where K. K. Chandy and a civil engineer who has constructed many of the new public buildings in this area met us and had lunch with us in a hotel fronting the Arabian Sea. The engineer opened a map and outlined the Christian history of this southwestern portion of India as follows:

St. Thomas, one of Jesus' Twelve, is said to have arrived in India in the first century and to have converted many. This Thomas "church," established by dear old doubting Thomas, is thriving today and is the oldest Christian church group in history. It is now known as the Syrian church. Seven hundred years after the days of Thomas Nestorian Christians came from Antioch and the spread of Christianity gained momentum. In 1500 St. Xavier, a Roman Catholic, arrived with Portuguese traders and, finding that these so-called "Syrian" Christians did not have the Roman Catholic trademark, he applied the Inquisition, killing many of them and burning most of their records and religious books. For more than half a century the Roman Catholics dominated the area until the Hindu Maharaja, bless his heart, established freedom of worship. Now the Thomas Christians equal the Catholics in number and once a year they meet fifty thousand strong for a great convention, something like the Feast of Tabernacles was for the Jews. This convention—the largest Christian audience in the world—was often addressed in the past by Sherwood Eddy, and now is addressed by Stanley Jones. Stanley Jones is a man sent of God for such mass movements. He is America's great Christian troubadour in this strategic land.

We rented a taxi and with Mr. Chandy and our eight pieces of luggage rode sixty miles to the Ashram. This ride was through the lush, tropical India we were eager to see: coconut palms, banana trees, thatched huts, and ubiquitous, near-naked children. Three times we had to cross rivers on ferries made of flat rafts supported on dugout canoes and poled by muscular Indians. If on this ride south we had come face to face with a rogue elephant our adventurous longings would have been completely gratified. The engineer told how, while driving along a lonely road one night, his automobile had been attacked by a rogue elephant and he barely escaped from the car and hid in the darkness while he watched the crazed creature completely demolish the car. Wild elephants in droves roam this area but are seldom dangerous unless they are alone and "mad" like the old rogue was that night.

At last we reached the Ashram. This Ashram is a permanent gathering place for groups of individuals of like mind and spirit, very similar in spirit to the Camps Farthest Out. It is taken care of by three or four saintly people who live on a simple subsistence level, dependent entirely upon the largess of God. This Ashram, under the leadership of K. K. Chandy, also directs a "Boys' Town" in an adjoining area, where orphan or delinquent boys are adopted "in love" and are trained in the three R's, trades, good citizenship, and Christian love. The accommodations at the Ashram were very simple but they gave us their best. Marcia had the only bed with mosquito netting. Everyone sat on mats on the floor or ground during our addresses and we three (with the metropolitan bishop) were the only ones who sat at a table for meals. We asked for spoons to help us eat our fried eggs, an expensive item of food but specially purchased for us since their chili-seasoned curry was unpalatable for our "anaemic" taste. We enjoyed "filling-up" on their delicious native bananas and papaya. All of the others ate with their fingers, as in Jesus' day. We have never found a group of men and women (more men than women) more dedicated to Jesus or better prepared to receive our messages. By starting with the morning talks at seven and awaiting breakfast until 8:15 a.m. we had an enthusiastic Camp Farthest Out of around seventy-five individuals. Many worked during the day so only thirty-five or forty were present to take part in the creative activities in the middle of the day. But large audiences, often of two hundred, gathered during the evenings. We were truly happy over this whole occasion.

At this Ashram we found several disciples of Vinoba Bhave, who has inherited the mantle of Gandhi. Vinoba is perhaps the most outstanding out-and-out disciple of Gandhi—the perfect "Elisha" for the Mahatmas. But just as Elisha and Elijah were diametric opposites, so were Vinoba and Gandhi the antithesis of each other. He is the man who is carrying out the amazing land program which is bringing new hope in India.

Gandhi was no scholar; his acquaintance with Indian classics was slight; while Vinoba is a brilliant scholar, well versed in Sanskrit and soaked in the wisdom of the past. Vinoba is an accurate student of history and of civilization, not only of India but of other countries. A master of languages, he knows Persian, Arabic, English, and the living languages of Indis, Bengali, Tamil, Telugu, Malayan, and Kanarese. In 1930 he translated that famous Indian allegory, the Gita, into Tamil, and it has sold thousands of copies. He gave brilliant lectures on the Gita which have been translated into a dozen languages. The Gita is his Bible. In times of stress he turns to it and finds immediate peace.

His convictions concerning love have led him to study Hinduism, Buddhism, Sikhism, Islam, and Christianity. His knowledge of the Bible, especially of the Gospels, is astounding. He can quote chapter and verse, and can interpret Jesus' life and teaching with greater understanding than most Christian theologians. His dedication to the love-way makes him look for the merits of all religions rather than for their defects.

He is amazingly brilliant in mathematics and has remained a mathematician all of his life. He makes careful calculations about everything he does, allowing no wastage in his life, either of money or of time. When folks offer to give land he has the legal papers meticulously drawn up with nothing left out.

At the center of both Gandhi's and Vinoba's lives is the law of love, and the expression of that love in non-violence. Gandhi applied this law with phenomenal success in the political sphere and India achieved her freedom from foreign rule non-violently. Now Vinoba is applying it in the economic sphere, showing that it can yield phenomenal results also to free the impoverished from their poverty.

Vinoba's land program began in 1948 when he was confronted by a group of untouchables who threatened to become Communists if that were the only way they could seize land from the wealthy. So Vinoba gathered the whole village together and asked those who had land to divide it with these landless, and to the amazement of all, they did. He then proceeded from village to village until he had distributed twelve thousand acres, which increased to forty-seven thousand as soon as he, in turn, got disciples working in the same way. He sets, as his nationwide goal, the collection of fifty million acres by the end of 1956. When we were in India, he had six hundred volunteers working for him. They go to the small land-holders first, and after they begin to share their small holdings the rich are shamed into giving. Current comment has it that everyone prays when Vinoba enters the district; the poor man prays he will come to his village, the rich man prays he will go around his village. If this movement spreads fast enough, there will be no Communism in India. He is a small man, weighing only eighty-seven pounds, lives on two glasses of Yogurt a day and is carrying out his program on foot, walking fifteen miles a day.

This method gives the wealthy landowner a maximum opportunity to sense his responsibility in society, and exerts upon him a minimum of violent pressure to do so. I couldn't help but think how the crisis the world is in today ought to stir American Christians to start a spiritual crusade that will give the wealthy possessors of Christian-America a maximum opportunity to sense their responsibility to the world before the sleeping dark billions begin exerting violent pressure forcing us to do so.

To our joy this second Indian CFO, like the first, had drawn together a very superior God-chosen group. As usual they were slow the first day in creative writing, also in singing, but brilliant, as we anticipated, in painting, and simply enthralled with devotion in motion. The final day, being Sunday, Roland and Marcia and I went out into the neighboring communities and addressed three big church congregations of the St. Thomas vintage.

The church where I spoke is the most influential church in this area, and the pastor, Reverend John, so skilled in interpreting that Stanley Jones uses him. The Thomas-Syrian type ritual lasted an entire hour and a half, all in the native tongue, but it was so dramatic and varied, and the chanting and singing were so excellent that I escaped any boredom which might have resulted from not understanding a single word. When time came for me to speak I was relaxed and happy and I gave my half-hour address, in spite of the fact it had to be translated sentence by sentence.

At the same hour I was speaking in this Syrian church Roland and Marcia were speaking in two similar churches. The impact of our messages aroused such interest in the neighborhood that I was honored by a very large audience when I spoke in the afternoon and Roland had an immense audience in the early evening. This last audience was so diversified—children and adults, English speaking and non-English speaking—that I was glad Roland had the assignment, as he is an artist in speaking through interpreters. The Reverend John who interpreted for him did a marvelous piece of work. Roland had them laughing at one moment and serious the next, and this talk, climaxing our three morning sermons, and being the final talk of our four-day camp, left a tremendous spiritual blessing with the people. In the united prayer laboratory the hour preceding, which I had conducted, we felt a great union of spirit and a great sense of oneness with Christ. We climaxed the period by a united prayer for India and the entire world.

The next morning we had an opportunity to visit Boys' Town. We talked with the sixty boys who were permanent residents of the "town" plus the one hundred local boys who joined them every day for the training periods. Each boy learns a trade and these boys, mostly from the street, orphans and delinquents, are lovingly trained in character and self control so that they may become self-supporting. Roland addressed them and then we listened to their glorious singing. We saw boys at the loom spinning out new cloth from cotton thread. One of the boys, formerly their "problem case," made Roland an entire Indian costume (dohte) which Roland wore, Indian fashion, in some of the meetings that followed in other cities and countries.

It took us four hours for the return ride in an old Chevrolet to Cochin to catch the plane for Coimbatore. The car broke down when two-thirds of the distance had been covered, so we transferred to a still older and more rickety one, and finally reached the airport just before the plane was to leave.

CHAPTER XVI

COIMBATORE AND SOUTHERN INDIA

AT COIMBATORE Y.M.C.A. SECRETARY WILLIAMS, WHO LOOKS CON-
siderably like Booker T. Washington, met us and took us to the
London Mission where we found comfortable rooms. Almost immediately we were taken to Bishop Appasamy's home for tea, where
we were received graciously by him and his wife, his two daughters,
granddaughter, and son-in-law (a Y.M.C.A. secretary)—a delightful
family group. The Bishop had read—and had loved—*A Man's
Reach,* and in booklets which he had given wide distribution he
had mentioned me often as one who is spearheading a new spiritual
awakening in America. A deputation of young men from New Zealand had just arrived in the city for a ten-day mission for the Youth
for Christ, and they readily complied with the Bishop's suggestion
to postpone starting their campaign until our three days of meetings
were over. We were delighted to find them in our audiences, and we
expressed our deep appreciation for their lovely spirit. We found
wonderful cooperation among all Christian groups in India, conservative and liberal alike.

The Bishop apologetically indicated that we should expect
smaller audiences than in the larger cities of Calcutta and Madras,
but he was amazed that evening to find the Y.M.C.A. auditorium
packed to the doors—some even standing. In the mornings we held
meetings from seven-thirty to nine before people went to work; and
in the evenings we held prayer laboratories from five-thirty to six-
thirty after they returned from work. Then from six-thirty to eight
we gave our two addresses, separated by a chalk talk or period of
devotion-through-motion led by Marcia. Supper was at half after
eight at the Mission.

Every day the crowds grew larger, and the prayer laboratory periods grew more effective and vital. During the middle of the day
we had time to write letters, rest, read, and meditate. One morning

we drove twelve miles to the country home of the much revered Bishop and Mrs. Walsh who have been missionaries in the area for fifty-eight years. The tall, angular, ninety-year old bishop from Ireland had a heart-warming twinkle in his eyes and still retained his quick Irish wit. I was overjoyed to discover that he loved to hear good stories and to my even greater joy I found that he had a number of good ones himself which he was eager to share. I enjoy telling stories and had always prided myself on having the best collection of funny stories since Lincoln, so it was rather frustrating to discover only serious and puzzled expressions on the faces of an audience as an interpreter finished one of our "American" pleasantries built around a play on words—American words.

Here is an example of one of my best stories which translation into a foreign language would completely ruin:

When the brilliant orator, Dr. Roy Smith, was arriving too late for a men's dinner engagement, I found myself in the embarrassing position of "pinch-hitting" for him before a group of men who knew little or nothing of me. I helped to save the situation by means of this story:

"A young minister, who was invited at the eleventh hour to take the place of a famous bishop who had suddenly been taken ill, began the service with these words: 'When a window is broken a bundle of old rags is sometimes stuffed in the aperture to keep out the cold. All I can claim to be in this hour of emergency is a bunch of old rags.' When the service was over a dear old lady came forward and said, 'You weren't a bunch of old rags; you were a real pane.' "

When the laughter subsided the entire audience was with me. Many times on this journey I was in situations where a good story would have eased the way, but, alas, when passed through the sieve of translation all the humor "vitamins" would have been sifted out.

The middle of March is supposed to be the hottest part of the year in Coimbatore, and as we were there at that time and found the climate more delightful than summer days in my boyhood state of Iowa, we agreed that Coimbatore would be an ideal summer resort—which I surmise it is. Our stay there was a welcome respite. We were grateful that we had all weathered the cold of England and Holland and the dust of Calcutta and were now in perfect physical condition. The missionaries of India were frankly concerned whether at my age I could stand the climate and the food, and carry what the Indians themselves said was a man-killing speaking schedule. All through our six weeks in India and Ceylon, regardless of heat, food, or sanitary conditions, each of us was scheduled to speak two or three times every day. We not only met every appointment but squeezed in some "interesting extras." One, for instance, was the real privilege of watching the girls of the London Mission School present a top-caliber review of their Indian rhythmic dances presented in our honor.

Following one of the evening talks a distinguished educator, Principal Hanes, entertained us at a buffet supper in his home where we met all the faculty of his school which had been founded one hundred years ago.

Bishop A. J. Appasamy had prepared the way for us in Southern India by the booklet referred to earlier which had been given wide circulation throughout that area. Over one-third of the contents were quotations from my book. After we left India the Bishop distributed a second booklet among his Diocese in which he expressed appreciation for what our mission had accomplished: "The addresses of Dr. Glenn Clark and Pastor Brown on the dynamics of prayer," he wrote, "made a special appeal to a large group of people in the city of Coimbatore. The Y.M.C.A. Hall was well filled for each meeting. Both these men were so obviously led by the Holy Spirit that all of us who listened to them were much impressed at the very outset by the joy that permeated them in all that they said and did. They were living witnesses to the fact that Christianity is a religion of joy. They brought home to us the abundant love of God for us and what it means to love God and to love one's neighbor. The visit of these two great men has so vitally opened up new vistas of spiritual experience to men and women in this area that they have resolved to live their religion not only at the altar or the pulpit but in the drawing room, the office, and the kitchen. Books written by Dr. Glenn Clark are being avidly sought for and read. Prayer groups are being started at different places in the city. We look forward to their promised visit again to our country in 1955 and hope that then they will be able to spend with us longer time and lead us into pastures new."

During our last evening meeting God veritably opened the windows of heaven and the following morning the blessings that continued to pour forth were like the climactic hours of a Camp Farthest Out. One fine young man cried most of the night at the thought of our leaving.

We reached Madras to find intense summer heat, but as we arrived at five-thirty in the afternoon and were to leave at eleven the following morning we escaped the worst of it. I enjoyed a cooling tub bath, and then we three walked a third of a mile to the Y.M.C.A. (perspiring all the way) and in an outdoor patio had a powerful meeting. J. Edwin Orr, a great evangelist, close friend and associate of Billy Graham, was leading a meeting in the Memorial Hall at six, and immediately after his address he hurried to our Y.M.C.A. in time to hear all of Roland's talk. He and Roland had been classmates in seminary days. Afterwards we had a good visit with this sincere man of God. He told us the fighting Fundamentalists were more bitter foes of Billy Graham's work than the extreme Modernists; they wanted to capture him for *their* group exclusively and were horrified that Billy refuses to go to a city until *all* the churches, liberal and conservative alike, combine in inviting him. Edwin Orr is one of the clearest minds in Evangelism today and because of his understanding and dedication can be a bridge to help bring religious leaders together in unity and goodwill—together around Jesus.

The next morning Miss Appasamy's chauffeur took me to her school where I breakfasted while the Browns breakfasted at the Y.W.C.A.

There are twenty-five teachers on the staff of this school—about eight Hindus and the rest Christians. Miss Appasamy wanted me to initiate them into an Inter-religious prayer group. We all sat in a circle, and after they opened the meeting with a Christian hymn I pointed out the commendable characteristic in Hinduism—respect for all religions—and the glorious power in Christianity—Jesus' redemptive love—and how both Hindus and Christians can have a common meeting place in prayer. I especially dwelt upon the power of prayer revealed in the Great Textbook—the Gospels—and ended with a prayer. Then at their request, while they knelt, I walked around the circle touching their heads as I asked Jesus, my Master, to bring down blessings from heaven upon them all.

At breakfast I sat between Miss Appasamy and her wonderful mother. The latter, after having built this school, turned the leadership over to her lovely daughter. The mother's trip to Delhi (where I first met her) was to induce the government to help finance the reconditioning of the buildings, cracked and rendered obsolete by the long drouth. The government promised 200,000 rupees ($42,000) if she would raise 100,000 rupees or $21,000. How I wish I could raise $1,000 of this needed sum! After breakfast several high school girls demonstrated some of the native dances Tagore recommended for aiding spiritual release. One was the most beautiful expression of "devotion through motion" that I have ever seen. As these Christian Camps open up and spread in India in the years ahead I foresee their incorporating some of these native rhythms, perhaps accompanied by some of the musical instruments, native to this land.

When Roland and Marcia arrived to pick me up their tiny car was so over-crowded with luggage and passengers that Mrs. Appasamy offered the school car to take me and my luggage—accompanied by her—to the airport. We departed India at half past eleven and reached Jaffna, Ceylon at one-thirty that afternoon.

CHAPTER XVII

CEYLON BECOMES MY ISLE
OF PATMOS

AS WE FLEW OVER THE INDIAN OCEAN TOWARD CEYLON I REMEMBERED that Ceylon is an island—one of the world's many important islands. Singapore is almost an island, Hong Kong is an island, Manila is situated on an island, Formosa is an island, Japan is an island, and Hawaii is an island. And so the Lord had arranged the last stage of our journey to be on the seven Islands Farthest Out. Islands have a great fascination for me. While reading the Book of Revelations I have often sat in imagination beside John, the beloved disciple, on the Isle of Patmos with eyes uplifted toward the skies as we awaited God's revelations from Heaven. Some of my greatest revelations have come to me on islands. Little did I realize that the very island I was flying to at that very moment was destined to be for me a veritable Island of Patmos.

Ceylon is a separate nation from India and so we followed the usual ritual of customs inspection. While clearing customs at the Jaffna airport we were greeted by a man in long brown robes, barefooted, but with a face that simply radiated what Matthew Arnold would describe as "sweetness and light." A friend had brought this radiant Mr. Selvaretnum in a car, and we were taken at once in that same car to the American School for Girls where comfortable rooms had been reserved for us. We would be sleeping at the school and would have two of our daily meals there, giving the balance of the daylight hours to the program at Selvaretnum's Ashram, a mile away, where we would find three hundred or more people waiting for what proved to be one of the best Camps Farthest Out ever held.

This girls' school, where we resided in such comfort, is under the direction of the American Board (Congregational) and is the oldest girls' boarding school in Asia. It was founded in 1824 and has had only three presidents or principals, the first one having been

136

head for about fifty years. Miss Bookwalter, a devoted friend whom we had met at the camps in America, had just retired after being its third president for thirty-three years.

Miss Lucy Clark of the staff looked after all our wants including delicious lunches and suppers. Our breakfasts each morning at the Ashram were prepared especially for us at the school and then transported in the same car with us to the camp. They provided a table, chairs, and silverware for us while the Ceylon folks sat nearby on the floor and, as in India, ate with their fingers. We Westerners could well envy the time they save in having little dishwashing, table setting, and chair dusting, although their meals do take much time to prepare because of limited facilities. I might be able to adjust to lack of silverware but I am sure that my seventy-two-year-old joints could never adjust themselves to floor-sitting. But many Ceylonese customs I loved. Wearing sandals and doffing them when entering the chapel appealed to me. Most of the people, however, went barefooted; Selvaretnum, just as K. K. Chandy had done, always went barefooted.

Every morning and every evening, on our way to and from the Ashram, we were driven through narrow crowded intersections at breakneck speed, dodging bullock carts, bicycles, tongas, handcarts, pedestrians, cows, and jogging barebacked men pulling rickshaws— our horn honking every five seconds. It was enough to take one's breath away. I sent my accumulation of soiled clothes to a "Doby laundry"—the only kind of laundry available—where clothes are washed in the river or an open pool and slapped against the stones. When they were returned two days later, half the buttons on my underwear had been slapped away. I did not adjust to local living quite as well as Roland, who most of the time enjoyed going barefoot and wearing that long nightgown sort of garment presented to him at Chandy's Ashram. K. K. Chandy had given me a pair of Indian sandals as a gift as we were departing Kottayam, which now served me well for, since we all removed our shoes as we entered the open air chapel, I found them easy to step into and out of. The closest I came to being "indigenous" was in regard to the fringes of my head; I had not had a haircut for two months, the only barber shops in India appearing to be "just a stool and a towel" along the edge of the street.

We were beginning to think we led charmed lives because mid-

March is supposed to be the hottest time of the year on Ceylon—it is even closer to the equator than Coimbature—but showers every night we were there, something unheard of at that time of year, kept the temperature ideal.

At the first meeting when I gave the opening address, knowing that Ceylon belonged to the Commonwealth of Great Britain, I said, "While awaiting the visit from your Queen, who I understand is coming April tenth, let me introduce you to a very competent 'stand-in,' one who will help you during this interval to pay obeisance in beauty and grace, not to your beloved British Commonwealth, but to the beloved Commonwealth of us all—the Commonwealth of the Kingdom of Heaven. So, pending the arrival of Queen Elizabeth, let me introduce you to Queen Marcia and her Consort Prince Roland." The entire group, seated on the floor of the chapel, greeted them with jocular acclaim, after which I found myself talking to a very attentive and responsive audience. And so we were off to a grand Camp Farthest Out, one of the best we have ever held.

The next morning, as I stepped out onto the porch, one hundred beautiful brown-skinned, black-eyed high-school girls greeted me by singing "Happy birthday to you," and the youngest placed a garland of spiced flowers around my neck. As I looked into those sweet faces I had to pinch myself to make sure that I was awake and that I was not on the Island of Patmos listening to an angel choir. Indeed, this might well have been a dream—a sort of leftover dream following an even greater dream I had experienced during the night.

For a real revelation had come to me that "birthday" night. In the days of the broadsword and the battle-ax people believed that personal duels would always be the fair way to settle grievances. But when the deadly revolver came into the picture and duels became mutual suicide, duelling became a thing of the past. Ordinary human common sense, dictated by a desire for survival, determined that action. In the same way that duelling went out of fashion why could not war go out of fashion? For untold centuries people have been believing wars would never cease. But now, with instruments that could destroy a civilization making war between two nations mutual suicide, why should not the plain common sense of the leaders of nations be sufficient to do away with an outmoded method of expressing hate. Certainly, I said to myself, there must be enough practical gumption among the leaders in the Kremlin and the Pentagon to bring common sense techniques to pass. And if common sense can be a powerful factor in bringing peace on earth, greater than common sense is that "uncommon" sense that comes to men when they pray.

This I called a Revelation—my Revelation on this Island of Patmos. And here is the way this Revelation expanded: In my vision I saw the leaders of the nations looking facts straight in the face and admitting that another war will be nothing but folly and suicide for all nations that participate in it. I could see the leaders making an honest acknowledgment that their armament race is draining the most precious resources of their lands, resources which if expended for peace could bring prosperity to all. Then I could vision their common sense (if they could not find any higher prompter) leading them into an agreement to declare a moratorium on war for twenty-five years, to abolish all armies and all munition plants and enter into a new type of competition between Capitalism and Communism—a twenty-five-year race—to see which could prove itself the better system for uplifting and benefitting humanity. I could vision the wonderful world we shall have when the fifty million men in Russia, China, the United States, France, and Britain that are now either under arms or in munition plants are released in order to build roads, replace slums with modern housing projects, and set to work creating, not instruments of destruction, but instruments of construction! I could foresee the emergence of a new sense of moral responsibility and higher standards of ethics, even in Communist lands, as both Communism and Capitalism realized that in order to win the loyalty of other peoples to their "way of life" each would have to reform themselves before hoping to reform others. To win this "race" against the evils in the other, each of these major ideologies would have to win a more immediate race against the evils within themselves. What a heaven it would be!

This birthday of mine started at 12:01 a.m. on March thirteenth in Ceylon, and thirty-six hours later my family in St. Paul, Minnesota, were just finishing celebrating it there, for Ceylon is twelve hours ahead of the United States in time. So as the earth turned slowly on its axis my birthday was lengthened. Joshua was not the only one who witnessed the sun standing still to give him extra hours necessary to win a momentous battle. I also witnessed my birthday expanding beyond the twenty-four hour length to give me time to concentrate on this vision of Love and Prayer and inspired Common Sense winning an even more momentous battle.

As I was still musing on this idea the next day, March fourteenth, I picked up the Ceylon newspaper containing a dispatch dated March thirteenth and the following statement met my eye: "Mr. Anastas Mikoyan, Soviet Deputy Minister and Minister of Trade, in an election speech at Erivan, Armenia, suggested the replacing of the World's Arms Race by a competition between Socialist and Capitalist systems to raise living standards."

So God was revealing exactly the same idea to me in the East as Mikoyan was expressing in the West—at exactly the same time. Surely it was more than mere coincidence.

Several months later on the eve of the Geneva Convention Malenkov gave a "major policy speech" before the Soviet Parliament in which he said, "The Soviet Government holds that the Capitalist and Socialist systems can quite well co-exist peacefully, competing economically with one another. The Soviet Union favors the general considerable reduction of armaments and armed forces. The Soviet Government has submitted and is defending proposals, the implementation of which could create guarantees for lasting peace." Churchill, in a subsequent journey to Washington, made that the chief object of his trip.

But, we ask, can we trust Russia to comply with such a plan? Only on two conditions. One is that she open wide the doors for United Nations inspectors to see that she keeps any agreements that are made regarding reduction or abolishment of armed forces and munitions manufacture. And the second condition is that we set our praying forces in motion to safeguard the whole procedure.

This world journey had certainly been cumulative. At every city in India our audiences seemed to grow larger. In the city of Jaffna only eight miles from the Ashram there are fifty thousand people. It is the second largest city in Ceylon. Columbo, the largest, has five hundred thousand people. Sunday, Roland addressed an immense assembly in St. Petersburg Church in Jaffna and Monday evening I addressed the same congregation. The church was packed to the doors each night—over seven hundred people—and we were given forty-five minutes to speak to them on the way to attain spiritual heights through prayer. Tuesday Roland addressed them again and on Wednesday Stanley Jones spoke. These meetings were arranged by the pastor, Rev. David T. Niles, who is the successor to John R. Mott as International President of the World Student Volunteer Movement. Dr. Niles had given one of the main addresses at the World Council of Churches meeting at Amsterdam, and since our meetings in Jaffna has given one of the chief addresses at the world Council meetings in Evanston. He attended most of the Camp Farthest Out meetings in Ceylon and his dedicated, talented wife played the music for Marcia's Devotion through Motion.

This camp grew each day until there were over two hundred and fifty at the day meetings and four to five hundred every night. The people participated in all the activities. There were so many teachers and ministers present from the entire Island that we could honestly feel that this assembly represented the educational and spiritual leadership of all Ceylon.

The last full day of the camp was a fitting climax to the cumulative blessings. At eleven in the morning, during a free period, Stanley Jones arrived and was immediately thronged by all of us. We were so happy to greet him and he seemed so glad to see us— old friends from America. He asked us about our experiences thus far and about the next stages of our journey. He said we would find Singapore very responsive, and when we mentioned that we were also going to Formosa he exclaimed, "You will find a wonderful missionary there. She really accomplishes things. Her work among the lepers is outstanding. I can't recall her last name, but her first name is Lillian."

I said, "Her last name is Dickson."

And then Roland told how she had been an outstanding student of mine thirty years ago and how I was especially proud of the wonderful record she has been making on the mission field ever since. She had earned her own way through Macalester College in three years, had made an outstanding record in scholarship, and still greater record in the spiritual field. Through her utter dedication she became a channel for bringing a great blessing to others. She, who had no fortune of her own, helped start a flow of good fortune to Macalester College which has never ceased. In the story of my life, *A Man's Reach,* I devote five pages to this experience.*

* *A Man's Reach* pp. 236–240.

We insisted that Stanley Jones use the half hour before lunch to give a talk. He quickly consented. "An extemporaneous talk," said Selveratnum with his sweet smile and then added, "extemporaneous means unprepared." Stanley laughed, "I was expecting this so I am carefully prepared." And he certainly was prepared. He gave the best talk on the Pentecost Experience in the Upper Room that I have ever heard.

We had an Indian luncheon that day—served in Ceylonese style. We *all* sat on the floor and ate rice curry, but we three novices from the West were allowed spoons. Stanley ate with his right hand like the other natives, but I could not see whether he let them flavor his curry with the hot chile sauce that burned the three of us like liquid fire.

In the evening Roland left to speak in the city of Jaffna while I addressed what had grown to be an immense audience at the camp. It was my final talk there. The next morning Roland gave the final address and I led the prayer laboratory and the camp closed.

Mr. G. L. Cooray, prominent lawyer of Columbo, had driven with one of his sons to the camp, and he let his son drive the car back alone so that he could accompany us on the plane to Columbo. We accepted his invitation to be his guests in his capacious Columbo home.

There are eight million people on the island of Ceylon and five hundred thousand of them reside in Columbo—an immense and beautiful city on the Indian Ocean. The university of Ceylon located there is one of the finest in the Orient and the literacy rate for the entire population of Ceylon is 70 per cent, highest in all Asia, except for Japan and the Philippines. Mr. Cooray is the founder and editor of the *New Lanka,* a "quality magazine" much like our *Atlantic Monthly,* filled with profound articles, excellently written by scholarly contributors from all over the world. We feasted on this magazine while staying in his home. Looking back upon the experience, we realize we were simply "bathed" in culture and enlightenment throughout our entire stay on this island of Ceylon.

Roland and I found we were running competition with Madam Pandit, chairman of the United Nations, who was addressing the women of Columbo at the same hour our meeting was in progress at the Y.M.C.A. but, even so, our hall was full and the audience most receptive. And later that evening when Mr. Cooray took us to an entertainment of native dances and scenes depicting the early history of Buddhist Ceylon, who should arrive but Madam Pandit and her two tall handsome daughters, and amid the hearty acclaim of the throngs were escorted to excellent reserved seats right behind ours.

The next morning the Browns and I took a four-hour train ride through some of the most magnificent mountainous country to be found anywhere in the world—rugged peaks, broad vistas, terraced rice paddies—to Kandy where I was the guest of Principal Walters, head of a large boys' academy, and the Browns were guests of Theodore Grambery, the Dutch pastor of the Presbyterian church called the Scot Kirk. That afternoon I addressed seven hundred boys in the Boys' Academy, while Roland was addressing a special group of women. The streets of the city were adorned with bunting and bamboo poles in honor of (whom do you think?) Madam Pandit, who seemed determined to follow us all over Ceylon. She was to address an audience in the Town Hall while Roland and I addressed another audience in the Scot Kirk. Again there were enough people to go around for our church was full and of course the Town Hall was full. Fifty people remained after the service with special prayer requests, so we concluded with a Prayer Laboratory to take care of their needs. Then I was taken to Principal Walters' home for a late dinner with a number of invited guests, while Roland and Marcia had dinner in the Manse of Rev. Grambery.

Mr. Selvaretnum had told us that a car would arrive early the next morning to take Marcia and me back to Columbo, but we had no word as to who would be escorting us or when they would come. After breakfast we three musketeers addressed three college chapels, two men's colleges and one women's college, Marcia being worked as hard as we men. Then the promised car arrived. A doctor and his wife, who had been at the Ceylon Camp Farthest Out, had left Columbo at four that morning to come and take the two of us back to the big city. Another man had already arrived to take Roland to the beautiful mountain city of Badulla, two hundred miles further into the mountainous interior. I was originally scheduled for that trip, but as it would be a long, arduous journey over steep mountain roads, it was decided at the last moment to assign that job to a younger man and allow me to return to the comforts of Mr. Cooray's home and, incidentally, to address the big audience that was expecting to hear Roland Brown on spiritual healing.

The return trip by car took us through a very picturesque part of Ceylon: rich flooded fields with oxen ploughing knee-deep in water as they prepared for planting the rice while men in the next field reaped the mature grain, and bullocks in still another field trod out the harvested rice. Glorious coconut palms and exotic tropical greenery were a part of every scene. To cap the climax we had our first and possibly last views of Ceylon elephants—passing three of them at different stages of our journey. To our surprise our fellow travellers told us that the elephants are dying out—they are going as their ancient companions of huge bulk went—the mammoths, mastodons, dinosaurs, cave bears, and sabre toothed tigers. Will the mastodons of military dictatorship go next? We were told that the dinosaur was "bowed off the stage" because it has twenty tons of armor plate, and only two ounces of brain. Take heed, ye militant nations of today! Take heed!

That night Marcia Brown gave a chalk talk before a packed church and I gave an address on Spiritual Healing, a subject people are deeply interested in there in Columbo. Saturday morning I got my much needed haircut for a rupee (twenty-one cents) and since I had left my safety razor in Kandy I stepped into a drugstore to purchase another one. The proprietor and all the clerks, recognizing me as a foreigner, gathered about me and asked me about my journey. And when I told them we were building a Belt of Prayer around the world they became so tremendously interested that I could hardly pull myself away.

In the afternoon, it being Saturday, I requested to see a cricket match, a game I had never seen before. It was the most leisurely, drawn out, monotonous affair I have ever witnessed. They even took time out for tea! After Roland arrived with a thrilling account of his journey to Badulla, we went to a packed church where, from four to six o'clock, we conducted a Healing Laboratory. Then we drove through a terrific downpour (I called it a monsoon) to the home of some precious people, who had been at the Selvaretnum Ashram, for our evening meal. That noon we had been guests for luncheon, along with the happy-souled Selvaretnum, at the home of Reverend and Mrs. Nelson who had been born and reared in Ireland; so for the second time in two months I had the luxury of trading funny stories. How we did laugh! What the world would have missed had there been no Ireland!

But Ireland is not the only place where hearts have a lilt and a lift. Selvaretnum found his in the Kingdom of Heaven, and the peace and joy of heaven simply radiate from his face. He wears a sort of Franciscan robe girdled with a cord. He has taken three vows: of celibacy, humility, and poverty. And every minister we met told us what tremendous spiritual influence he has on the island—a sort of modern St. Francis. His love for us and ours for him is a high point of our world journey.

In India and Ceylon we were often the guests of bishops, ministers, Y.M.C.A. and Y.W.C.A. secretaries, college presidents, and other people of outstanding influence, including an ex-Maharajah. On one of the plane trips my seat-mate was the Chief Justice of India and at every station stop on that flight crowds loaded him with bouquets and garlands. We were very "close" seat-mates, for he was so exceedingly portly that the stewardess could not fasten his seat belt, and I am not exactly slender myself. I was happy to converse with him. What pleased Roland and Marcia and me most was not the physical proximity to prominent, delightful people, but the spiritual closeness we experienced everywhere with people of outstanding spiritual caliber. It thrilled us to find spiritual oneness with spiritual giants from among the ranks of the humble and also among the ranks of the prominent and influential. We were greatly moved by the wonderful cooperation we had with all the Christian Churches and ministers and missionaries in every nation. Everywhere we went people wanted us to come back. And we are grateful to God that they felt that way. We were not bringing them something new and strange. We were merely witnessing to something they had known but in the pressure and strain of life they may have "forgotten and lost awhile." All we were trying to bring to them was Jesus and His teachings concerning Living in the Kingdom of Heaven here and now.

Our last full day in Ceylon was a Sunday. That day we spoke in six churches and in spite of the daily rainfall, which kept the temperature beautifully comfortable, the churches were all packed. When we left for the airport early Monday morning accompanied by four or five carloads of well-wishers we felt that our stay at this Isle of Patmos was one of the richest experiences of our lives.

As I settled back in the comfortable seat on the plane I pulled out of my pocket a letter which a young lady of American birth, now residing in Columbo, had handed me just before I left. I opened it and was startled at the message it contained:

"Not satisfied with the conventional religion preached at me from the Christian pulpits of America I came ten years ago to India and Ceylon to sit at the feet of the 'Great Masters' of the East. Here I studied the mysteries of the ancient philosophies and delved into the lore of the modern swamis, but it was not until I attended the Camp Farthest Out at Jaffna and followed all your and Pastor Brown's addresses in Columbo that I discovered that in these camps were all the precious things I had come all these thousand miles to find. I had turned my back on Jesus. This week I have found Him again. The pearl above price that I had sought so long, the completeness and the wholeness of the spiritual life, had been available all the time in my own land, yes at my very door, had I only known where to find it. I shall be thanking the Lord the rest of my life for bringing you here."

CHAPTER XVIII

SINGAPORE—CROSSROADS OF THE WORLD

IT WAS ALMOST 7:00 P.M. WHEN OUR PLANE FLEW INTO SINGAPORE. We had flown miles off our course against stiff head winds to avoid more tempestuous winds that blocked our course.

We were met at the airport by Eugene Hill, head of the Southern Baptist work in this area, accompanied by Polly Cool, who had flown from her Methodist-sponsored mission field in Borneo to be with us, and Elizabeth Hale, a Baptist missionary who had driven more than five hundred miles from her station up near the border of Thailand. Polly had attended several Camps Farthest Out in Kansas, and Elizabeth had attended one in Virginia. We all dined at the home of the Hills and then the three of us were taken to a private hotel entitled "Happy Home" where we shared their friendly comforts during our stay.

Singapore, British Crown Colony at the southern tip of the Malay Peninsula, is aptly called the "Crossroads of the World," where East meets West. Principal port of call on the Europe–Far East route, Singapore harbor is a busy kaleidoscope of ships of all shapes, sizes, and purposes as well as of all nations. The bustling streets are thronged with natives of a dozen different races, and the Hindu Temples, Mohammedan Mosques, and Chinese Temples and an assortment of Protestant churches symbolize the great diversity in the population.

We did not get a chance to go into the Federation of Malaya, but I had a long conversation with an enthusiastic young missionary, Gunnar Teilmann, who, with his wife and three beautiful little daughters, came to a Camp Farthest Out.

Malaya, he explained, is a tropical peninsula about the size of Florida, with a population of nearly six million people. Of these, one-third are Malays, one-third Chinese, and the rest are Indians,

147

Punjabis, Pakistanis, Eurasians, British, Americans, Canadians, Australians, New Zealanders, and a smattering of Thasis, Filipinos, Burmese, and others.

The Chinese control the large part of the wealth that is not European. The wealth is considerable when one realizes that almost half of the world's supply of both tin and rubber come from this small land. These rich Chinese are naturally opposed to Communism, but if Formosa should fall they would be like flowers without roots and might become easy prey for Red propaganda.

The nine independent states, each ruled by a Muslim Sultan, were constantly fighting each other until in desperation they turned to Singapore, a British Crown Colony, which had shown what peace and law could do for prosperity, and they requested the British to take over the management of their states, reserving for themselves full jurisdiction over only the matters of custom and religion.

When World War II broke out, the Communist Party (at that time a recognized, legal, political party) proposed to the British that they would be willing to organize an "Anti-Japanese Army" to carry on a guerrilla warfare against the occupation forces if the British would train and supply them. When the Japanese were advancing toward Singapore, the British agreed. After the war, the remnants of that same force became the Malayan Peoples Army, known as Terrorists, Bandits, or Communists, which has since 1949 carried on terroristic warfare against the people of Malaya with the hope that "Father Mao will come" and that they will be the Communist leaders of the country. As soon as this terrorism had been brought under control, the High Commissioner of Malaya, General Sir Gerald Templer, called in a group of church leaders and said to them, "The Military can win the shooting war against the Communist guerrillas, but there is a more difficult battle to win—the one for the hearts and minds of the people in the New Villages. We are asking the churches to go in and give the people there something spiritual upon which to base their lives. If you will do it, we will give you every cooperation. If you will not, we shall turn elsewhere for help."

This led to the most remarkable cooperative movement among religious sects in the history of the world. There were four hundred villages in Malaya, and the Churches had sufficient personnel to enter only two hundred. So each denomination took as many villages as they could handle, leaving the rest to the others. For the first time in hundreds of years, St. Francis and Martin Luther and John Wesley could look down from heaven upon Catholics and Protestants working in hearty cooperation to carry Jesus' saving message to the peoples of an entire nation. The Churches' Coordinating Committee, sponsored by the Malayan Christian Council, allotted the villages to Methodists, Lutherans, Anglicans, Baptists, Presbyterians, Brethern, and Catholics, granting favors to none and all work in loyal zeal for the glory of the Lord.

We could not take time to visit the Raffles Museum or the Aw Boon Haw Villa with its collection of jades or the Botanical Gardens where rubber was first introduced from Brazil. But we were urgently persuaded to visit the Buddhist Hell. A millionaire Buddhist spent a fortune creating this grotesque park containing figures sculptured in hideous postures of torment. They made Dore's pictures of Dante's Inferno seem as mild as afternoon tea parties. Children who go there have bad dreams for months afterwards. But who wouldn't!

Then we were taken to a Chinese church where we shared an elaborate ten-course Chinese luncheon with thirty choice spiritual leaders especially invited for the occasion. The Browns were good sports and ate with chop sticks but I used spoon and fork. The food was excellent and it was a real experience to be initiated into the Chinese customs of eating. However, in the midst of all the friendly gaiety I was sobered by the thought of the vast amount of time good Christians all around the world spend in eating more food than they need. It may not be good manners on my part but I always begrudge these two-hour rituals in homage to "Lord Stomach," when we spend so little time in prayer and praise in honor of Lord Jesus! Consequently I was in no mood to raise the spiritual tone when it came time for me to speak, so I introduced my ever-ready partner, Pastor Brown, who capped the Chinese hospitality with manna from heaven, even restoring my spiritual equalibrium.

That evening I redeemed myself by holding an audience's close attention for thirty-five minutes and then Roland followed in good Baptist style which these new-made friends loved.

The next morning a little group met with us on the second story balcony of the "Happy Home" and discussed ways and means of holding Camps Farthest Out in this Singapore area of Malaya. Mrs. Chao, Chinese wife of the leader of the Inter-Church-Alliance, was most insistent that Camps were needed and to our amazement she assured us that her husband could find an excellent site for a camp and would be able to guarantee a regular all-day attendance of seventy-five with evening meetings of over three hundred. She repeatedly said that Singapore was the most strategic spot in Southeast Asia and it could draw leaders from Borneo, Thailand, Sumatra, the rest of Malaya, and Indonesia. "The villages," she said, "are ripe for Christianity and the missionaries and leaders need just the kind of inspiration and training such a camp could bring them." With the enthusiastic cooperation of the Southern Baptists, the Inter-Church-Alliance and the China Inland Mission, with all of whom we have had delightful fellowship during our short stay there, a successful camp could be assured, and there is every probability it would multiply into many more camps as the years go by. A recent letter from Mrs. Chao urges us, "Come quickly! We need to learn how to pray. Come before the storm breaks!"

The Superintendents of the China Inland Mission for all Southeast Asia were holding their annual convention in Singapore during the time we were there, and a half dozen of them played "hooky" and attended our meetings. Four of their number roomed at the "Happy Home" and after breakfast the next morning Mr. Harris, one of their most vital leaders, sought us out. He said they had all been driven out of China but had found the villages of Malaya ready to welcome them with eager arms. The Mandarin language, which the Inland-Missionaries learned in China, enables them to reach the Chinese in Malaya as effectively as in China. Every missionary available is needed in this new territory. He said the China Inland Mission would welcome one of our camps and would cooperate with us in every way. He concluded with the words: "The fields are white for the harvest but the laborers are few."

When I refer to what the Camps Farthest Out could do, I refer to it merely as a symbol of what all Christian movements can do. The Ashrams, the Disciplined Order, the International Christian Leadership Movement, the Moral Re-armament, the Wider Quaker Fellowship, the Youth for Christ, the China Inland Missions—together with all the efforts of all Christian churches and their missionary endeavors—are the real hope for saving this world. It is not the Pentagon Building or the Munitions Trust—or even the United

Nations. It is thrilling to think of what all these Christian groups and movements can do if each one will hold fast in loving commitment to the highest light God has given it, and then, in His Name, will all work together in harmony toward the same goal. We can be one in impact, if not in compact. We *can* become one in Jesus and then the impact of His love will be adequate to save the world. Yes, to put it in its simplest terms, Jesus and His love are the real hope of the world.

The Camps Farthest Out, of which there are now fifty in America and all around the world, is an interdenominational movement dedicated to making Jesus' teachings realities in the life of individuals and of nations. They indoctrinate people not in this creed or that creed, (the people coming from their various churches have their own creeds) but they indoctrinate people in the actual reality and truth in the teachings of Jesus, in the power of prayer as He taught it, and in the vital part the church must play as the instrument God has chosen to redeem the world.

The world-shaking movements in history did not have their beginning in great masses of lukewarm people. They usually began with a mere handful of men and women thoroughly indoctrinated with complete faith in the central truth for which their movement stood.

The sweeping rise of fascism and naziism in Italy and Germany followed the thorough indoctrination of a small group of individuals. Gandhi liberated one-fifth of the human race from the greatest empire of modern times by indoctrinating a little band of devoted men and women with faith in the power of non-violence. A basic activity of the Communists, wherever they seek to take root, is indoctrination, even among non-Communist prisoners-of-war. All movements undergirded by convictions resulting from thorough indoctrination grow with tremendous power.

The philosophy of indoctrination is simple: if you have something worth selling, sell it—with your life and with your words and with your actions. If what you have is not worth selling, forget it. When the church stops indoctrinating people, then other organizations and "isms" start. Why did the church stop indoctrinating? Because the church became ashamed of its doctrines. Think it over!

This has happened whenever the church forgets the basic teachings of Jesus as central and imperative and becomes absorbed in things marginal or tangential. Bishop Sudham of Bombay told us how his ancestors were among the Mongol invaders who, through some combination of circumstances, had contacted the living message of Jesus somewhere along their march and were completely open to becoming Christians until they found that the most pressing problem of the Roman prelates at that time was the question whether their vestments should or should not have tassels.

Students of mine returning from the First World War have told me that they came home expecting to participate in the greatest spiritual awakening in the history of the world, and all they found was the Modernists and Fundamentalists fighting over the first and second chapters of Genesis.

When Christians lost faith in their Faith up sprang Nazism. Right or wrong, the Nazi faith inspired commitment—a serious, passionate commitment to a cause they felt worth selling and therefore it was easy to sell. Communism, too, revolves around faith and commitment. Right or wrong, it is a living ideology. To believe it is to want to sell it. When Germany ceased believing passionately in Jesus Christ they started believing in the right of the German race to rule the world; when Russians lost faith in God they started believing in the right of the working class to rule everyone for the good of humanity.

The most thrilling thing that man can come to appreciate is the absolute truth that we have a Loving Father, more powerful than all the rulers of the world; and the most exciting fact that follows is that prayers in accordance with Jesus' teachings directed with love and faith to that Father are more powerful than all the atom bombs ever produced. Because the rank and file of Christians do not believe this, it becomes utter boredom in their ears. No wonder Christians cannot sell Jesus and his teachings on love, faith, and prayer—they are not thoroughly indoctrinated with them.

What Christians need is thorough indoctrination. Listening to a lecture here and a sermon there cannot do the job. Casual reading of the Bible cannot do it. Attending church services once a week cannot do it—even if the ministers really believe what they preach, although many of them do not. To indoctrinate a people with a Christ-like love and faith, a nucleus of the most vitally dedicated of them must be drawn apart and trained by Christ until they are as zealous as any of the followers of Lenin, Hitler, and Gandhi. I know this can be done. My knowledge is based on the fact that the groups that I have mentioned and many other groups have been doing this indoctrination for so many years that when the crisis comes I know that the power of their prayers will outweigh the power of the hydrogen bomb.

And when the crisis comes it will not be precipitated by Russia but by China. The time has come when we should make a careful appraisal of this great sleeping giant that has just commenced to open its eyes and look around. The American public is too inclined to think of China as a sprawling mass of ignorant peasants unable to move as a united whole. That is the way the country has appeared for the last three hundred years. We forget that China has existed as a nation three times longer than any nation except Egypt and India, and as one looks at that long span of history he will discover the outstanding feature of her growth has been a mysterious rhythm of alternating expansion and contraction as inevitable and as powerful as the ebb and flow of the tides.

One moment China is a perfect picture of ruin, feebleness, and desolation—the helpless football of the nations. The next moment she experiences one of her tidal comebacks, surprising the world with her amazing, unexpected, overwhelming strength. For three thousand years this rhythmic pattern has been reproducing itself. Twelve times in the last thousand years China has alternated between periods of sprawling weakness and united strength. The firm hand of the Communists was all that was necessary in this generation to set in motion a unifying, electrifying comeback that we are reluctant to recognize. Within two years she has emerged as a world power capable of winning two wars against two of the greatest fighting nations of the last century. The period of the ebb tide is over—China is now ready for the flow. When the flow really gets started I doubt if any mere human force in this generation will be able to stop it.

A quick summary of this mysterious rhythm of recurring ebb and flow is as follows: First, China produces a surplus population. Then the crowding at home causes individual Chinese to seek opportunities abroad as bankers, merchants, small traders, or farmers. They gradually take over the financial control of the new country and gradually they grow into large strategic advance guards. The population continues to increase until the nation is bursting at the seams, and when that time comes, the government sends troops to follow the colonists. When the troops come, the Chinese who once were guests become the masters. Thus the territory of China has been steadily expanding for more than three thousand years.

At Singapore one could see clearly that all the conditions now exist for another great expansive movement of New China. At the end of the seventeenth century the Chinese census indicated a population of about a hundred thousand. Today the population is claimed to be four hundred and fifty million, but a Communist spot-census shows a population of six hundred million. Again China is bursting at the seams and is ripe for another step in the recurring pattern of digestive imperialism. The Chinese advance guards are already waiting in almost every country in South Asia. In Malaya, of which Singapore is the key, the Chinese are actually as numerous as the Malays and in addition are ten times as rich. As I stood in Singapore I felt like a mountain climber standing under a vast ledge of snow where the crack of a gun or possibly a mere whisper might start the avalanche.

CHAPTER XIX

THE JESUS WAY ALONE SUCCEEDS

ALL I COULD THINK OF AS I FLEW FROM SINGAPORE TO BANGKOK WAS the imminent danger hanging over all South Asia and how all human means seemed powerless to prevent catastrophe. Never in all history did the world need the statesmanship of Jesus as it needs it now. Had the love way of Jesus been adopted two thousand years ago, there would be no Palestine problem today, and had His love way been followed by nations in this generation there would be no Communist problem today. The shame of our age is the amazing way in which so-called Christian Governments have overlooked and ignored the statesmanship of Jesus.

Arnold Toynbee defines Communism as an "Eastern criticism of the West's failure to live up to her own Christian principles in the economic and social life of a professedly Christian society," and he shows how the Russians have borrowed this "spiritual weapon" and turned it against its makers. "Thus the spiritual initiative has passed from the Western to the Russian side, and we Westerners find ourselves thrown upon the defensive for the first time since the Second Turkish siege of Vienna in 1682." Toynbee feels that Russia offers a more attractive spiritual fare to the Far East than we do. "The truth is," he reports, "that in offering the Chinese and Japanese a secularized version of our Western Civilization we have been offering them a stone instead of bread."

Communism gets its power from taking Jesus' doctrine, which He announced at Nazareth in His pre-inaugural address in the words, "The Spirit of the Lord is upon me, because he hath anointed me to preach the gospel to the poor; he hath sent me to heal the broken-hearted, to preach deliverance to the captives, and recovering of sight to the blind, to set at liberty them that are bruised."

This is almost word for word the program the Communists offer. They preach *their* gospel to the poor and, as the overwhelming majority of the people of Asia are terribly poor, they have an immense audience to preach it to. And as half the babies born in Asia die before their first year there are millions that are broken-hearted. Still more millions are captive to ignorance and blind to the vast stores of world knowledge, and finally (and this is the Communists' strongest weapon) they promise to set at liberty those that have been bruised by centuries of colonialism and the terrific exploitation which this domination by the white race has brought. By exchanging the name of Jesus for the name Marx this doctrine, kidnapped from the Man in Galilee, is spreading like wildfire over the entire earth. But because it is only half of what Jesus proclaimed, merely the arms and legs as it were, with the very heart and lungs left out, when it is confronted with the whole of the Christian message, it is like an earth-bound bird with a broken wing in the presence of a heavenly bird which mounts into the heights with wings as of eagles.

There is very little danger of Communism's penetrating England or Sweden. In these nations Protestant Christianity has been preached and respected for so many years that it has naturally found expression in democratic legislation and in adjustments between capital and labor upon a more equitable Christian basis. Through a limited amount of socialized industry and medicine and the development of Christian cooperatives, these nations have been safely innoculated against the Red plague of Communism. In contrast to these nations, France and Italy and Greece, which followed the ancient law of taxing the poor and exempting the rich, hang on the precipice of Communism.

But the most striking contrast along this line can be found between Indo-China and Burma, two nations that border the land I was approaching, Thailand, one on its east and one on its west. These two nations, with approximately the same population, have an equally strong hatred of imperialism. Both are bordered, just as Thailand is, by Red China on the north, and both had Communists leading their anti-imperialistic movements. Of the two, the Burmese Communists were the more powerful at the outbreak of the civil war, having most of Burma supporting them. No country was more badly ravaged by the war than Burma. Two and a half million acres of rich rice land had become useless jungle. Five thousand villages were reduced to rubble. The oil wells and flotilla were wrecked. The lead mines, installations and electrical equipment had all been destroyed by actual warfare and by the retreating British. Tens of thousands of homes were demolished and millions of persons were forced to flee. The national capital had been lost, most of the industry destroyed, and postwar production was only 57 per cent of prewar production. Here was perfect soil for Communism, and the Communists were ready. They mobilized three quarters of a million peasants and proceeded to move in. Even the non-Communists looked to Moscow as their main friend and next-door neighbor.

Indo-China was not in nearly as great danger from Communism as Burma, but the events that followed proved conclusively the thesis that I have presented: that the Jesus way, by which I mean the just and merciful way, applied to national relations, has never once failed, and that the power-politics-way has failed whenever tried. In Indo-China, France refused to grant independence, whereas in Burma, Great Britain granted it. In both nations the Communists tried to force their autocratic methods, slavishly imitating the Soviet and Peking dicta. In Indo-China the French obligingly fed grist to their mill by continuing their imperialistic tactics, while in Burma the Socialists adopted the Jesus program as quoted in Luke 4:18 and began preaching good news to the poor and release to the captives and setting at liberty those who were oppressed before the Communists could claim priority to the program. In other words, the Burmese leaders met the fraudulent propaganda of the Communists with resounding progressive deeds that sent the followers of the Kremlin running for cover. They not only exposed the Stalinist ruthlessness but countered with solid social achievement of their own.

Contrast this procedure with what was going on in French Indo-China. Here most of the land was owned by landlords who extorted rents from their tenants often amounting to 50 to 70 per cent of the year's crop; and the peasantry was in the grip of moneylenders, many of whom charged 40 per cent interest for the period between planting and harvesting one crop. This domination of the moneyed over the moneyless was one of the principal causes for the bitterness against the French colonial occupation which enabled the Communists, under Ho Chi Minh, to secure mass support for the long-drawn-out armed struggle.

In August, 1952, Prime Minister Van Tam of Indo-China told Chester Boles, our ambassador to India, "When the Communists capture a village, their first move is to announce that all land now belongs to those who till it, and all debts are cancelled. As a result," he continued, "the peasants are wildly enthusiastic. Then with the ebb and flow of battle the French Union forces again take over the area and close behind them come the landlords and the money-lenders. 'Where are our back rents?' they say. 'Where is the money that you owe us?'

"How can we beat the Communists in such a war?" he asked.

Seven months later, when Chester Boles again saw the Prime Minister, Van Tam said, "Do you remember our last conversation about land reforms? Since then we have made great progress. Now when the French recapture a village they let the peasants keep the land which the Communists gave them. So today throughout Vietnam people are saying, 'The sensible man prays that his village will be conquered by the Communists and then recaptured by the Vietnamese or French. For only then can he become a small landholder without becoming a Communist.' "

In Burma the Communists did not fare so well. Here they started to introduce land reform in the brutal pattern employed in China. They took over all land, rich and poor alike, and divided it on what they termed equal shares. The richest land owners were usually killed. Some people were allotted land that was worthless and others land that was well irrigated. No provision was made for education in farming techniques. No one was given credit for seed and animals. Cooperatives and cooperation were not heard of, and everything ended in a fiasco.

Then the Socialists came in with what I call the Jesus method. Their land reform was based on realities. Rentals on land were reduced. A Tenancy Disposal Board was elected by the peasants to see that occupancy rights were protected, that loans were given for seeds and cattle and that no one was shifted to a tract which did not yield him a living. The worst burden on the peasantry was the debt owed to the moneylenders, and these debts the government wiped from the books. Thirty million dollars in loans were made to needy peasants, and they also were later canceled. No peasant had to be killed in implementing this program. Word came to us while we were still on our journey that the Burma government had finally decided that the nation was sufficiently pacified to go ahead with a full-scale development program. They started building cement and fertilizer factories, initiating large scale irrigation schemes and electrification, while ten million acres were distributed to landless peasants. What they call "mutual aid teams," of five families each of those who had received this free land, were organized to work their land together, sharing a tractor and other necessary machinery.

With this practical demonstration of what I call the Jesus method of doing things, there is little wonder the Burmese switched allegiance from the apparent radicalism of the Stalinist reform to the true radicalism of the Socialist method with its sane concern for human welfare. The results were soon apparent. Communism lost its hold upon the people. Instead of the Communists being greeted in each village as liberators as they were greeted in Indo-China, they were greeted as highway robbers coming to steal the people's rice and cattle and giving nothing but bureaucracy, poverty, and death in return. The Communist military effort was reduced to pathetic impotence.

In contrast, a quarter of a million French troops spending one and a half billion dollars a year (half of a billion of it American money) were able to hold only eight per cent of the Indo-Chinese territory.

Burma, with an army of less than fifty thousand, spent only a small proportion of what the great powers were spending to save Indo-China, and the Communists were being swept out with no aid from the United States or Europe in the way of arms and armies. But I am glad to say that the money for Burma's development program did come largely from the United States—indeed one of the best jobs of pump-priming ever done. But the money contributed for the constructive work in Burma by the Jesus-blessed method was a mere fraction of the millions we poured into Indo-China in attempting to save her by the devil-blessed method of war and destruction.

Any sane person could see clearly the futility of the United States endeavoring to induce the United Nations to come to the aid of Indo-China when nine-tenths of the Indo-Chinese did not want that aid. Their hearts were with the Communist invaders who, they felt, had come to set them free from the imperialism of the white nations. While France had made a number of concessions to Indo-China, their point of failure was in their stupid refusal to make basic concessions in the field of economic opportunity and political freedom. That gave the Communists the entering wedge they needed. Yes, Toynbee is right, the Communists have borrowed the spiritual weapon of the Christians and turned it against its makers.

"Burma is the only country," writes a foreign correspondent, "where democratic socialism has defeated Communism both militarily and ideologically. It has demonstrated a lesson the professional anti-communist must learn sometime—that in a final analysis only a democratic revolution aimed at providing political freedom and economic opportunity can triumph over the appeals of Communism among the under-privileged millions."

Since arriving home I read these words of Supreme Court Justice William O. Douglas in the *Look Magazine* of October 15, 1954:

"Morocco is another Indo-China in the making. Unless French policy is reversed and drastic reforms introduced Morocco will explode with a violence only Africa knows. The desire for independence is, indeed, the most powerful political force in the world. It operates today in Morocco to produce murders, riots, strikes, and an all-out conspiracy of the masses against the French.

"The French own all the industrial plants, the choice lands, the mining claims. The Moors are the serfs, the farmhands and for their labors get no more than fifty cents a day, live in squalor and misery with hardly enough to keep them alive. Child labor appears in a vicious form.

"The French have not only practiced discrimination; they have built an economy based on discrimination. Under French rule, Morocco is a Police State. It is a crime for three or more Moors to hold a meeting. A press that criticizes the French is suppressed. Suppression by the French in Indo-China of all Nationalists, left the field to the Communist, Ho Chi Minh. The same thing is likely to happen in Morocco if the Nationalists are long suppressed.

"Whatever may be the political tides in France, one thing has become increasingly clear. All colonialism must come to an end. Independence is the most powerful slogan of the century. America has the first historic claim to that slogan. We should reclaim it. The day we do we will have acquired a moral authority among the people of the world that no force can ever destroy."

CHAPTER XX

BANGKOK AND HONG KONG: DANGER SPOTS

ARRIVING AT BANGKOK IN THE EARLY EVENING WE TOOK THE BUS some eighteen miles to the airport office in the city, reaching there at seven-thirty, where we were joyously met by Gladys Hopewell, the lovely young Baptist missionary whose name had been given us in Rome by Juliette Mather. Miss Hopewell directed us to the Mission Home of the Hanson's where we were served a fine supper.

We were booked to fly on to Hong Kong at seven the next morning but were telephoned that the plane was late—would not arrive until noon. That would put us in Hong Kong after nightfall. Because Hong Kong is girdled by mountains and the airport is nested among them, no planes are permitted to land after dark; therefore we would have to remain in Bangkok all day and leave shortly after midnight reaching Hong Kong at eight the following morning.

For those who have read *Anna and the King of Siam*, Bangkok and Thailand (the present name for Siam) will hold a special fascination. It is fantastically strange in its life and customs and fantastically picturesque in landscape and architecture. Countless canals (called "Klongs") thread the city making Bangkok an oriental version of Venice, and much of the daily life and business of the people is conducted on or along these canals. But most of this beauty of Bangkok was marred for me for it was impossible to ignore the debris and scum on the water or the squalor along the streets. It seemed that not only was there pollution in the canals, but in the manner in which the people live, and that Bangkok, more than almost any other city I had ever been in, needed physical hygiene, mental hygiene and, above all, the spiritual hygiene of Jesus.

In the last chapter I contrasted Indo-China and Burma as examples of how to and how not to resist Communism. If you look at a map of Asia you will see that one of these lies on one side of

Thailand and the other on the other side, three nations, like three little birdlings, nesting right under the wings of Red China. There they stand like three dominoes where, if one falls all three will go down. Indo-China is toppling toward Communism. The other two are safe, as yet, but let us hold our breath and pray that corruption is kept out. Wherever pollution and corruption control a nation the doors open wide for Communism to enter.

Having all day Thursday for sightseeing we visited the very famous and elaborate Marble Temple of Buddha constructed entirely of marble shipped from Greece and, after removing our shoes and entering the main chamber, we were awed to silence as we caught sight of the shrine: gold, jewels, flowers, and blazing lights surrounding the seated figure of the giant, gold-leaf covered Buddha. The edifice, with its ornate trimmings and lavish, glittering shrine, must have cost millions. Turning away from the shrine we found statues of Buddha everywhere. They lined the immense hall —each figure larger than life, alternately a seated and a standing figure.

Then we went to another temple and saw the famous "Reclining Buddha"; he is as long as half the length of a football field, completely filling a structure large enough to hold twenty thousand people if he weren't taking up all the space.

Bangkok is certainly a city of contrasts. Where else does one live astride the centuries as literally as in this city with its wide paved streets and age-old canals; its splendid thoroughfare leading to a modern parliament building housing a modern law-making body, but at the back of the lot behind the parliament building stand the King's elephants awaiting the King's return from Europe (which he much prefers as a place to live, to his native land); its modern rice and sugar mills in contrast to the single roomed, wooden houses built on piles erected on rafts and moored in the river; its street car system in contrast to the out-door bathing and clothes washing along the canals bordering the highway. In the harbor are ships of all nations, as modern as tomorrow; but parked up the river are the stunning "row boats" which played a colorful part in the recent coronation, one of them one hundred thirty feet long, dragon shaped, manned by some seventy pairs of oars, with a throne at the stern for the King and Queen.

Three-fourths of Thailand's foreign trade passes through Bangkok harbor, a harbor extending for nine miles, crowded with godowns, warehouses, and trading posts of all the famous companies of the Orient and most of the well known western companies. Immense amounts of teak, rubber, and hides are being loaded on huge freighters for export. Then one must not forget the river, with over one hundred rice-milling plants along its banks, leading up into one of the world's best rice-producing areas. If the free-world lost this rice-exporting center, things would go bad for the rice-importing countries such as Japan.

I was told that one of the most typical sights is the early morning exodus of priests. There are thousands, perhaps a hundred thousand, of these Hinayana priests. Hinayana is the southern and simpler form of Buddhism. Incidently, I chuckled over having the Presbyterians in there converting the Buddhists, for Hinayana believes in a neat kind of predestination stemming from about the time of Christ that holds that only a relatively small portion of the people can be "saved," while Mahayana, the other type of Buddhism, makes salvation free to all. Just as the sun touches the horizon the priests pour out to beg their morning food and alms. Even the scholars come forth, as is their duty. The people respond generously, too. No priest says "thank you" for the privilege is the donor's, who thus lays up merit for himself.

These priests are a vast untapped source of power. I was told that if Christianity could send its best representatives, including some scholarly missionaries who could reach these priests and raise their level of education, and impart to them a drive for service, and make them aware of God's love as well as of his justice, what a tremendous thing might happen in Thailand! They said that when missionaries do not "black-out" the teaching of Buddha, but let them serve as an old testament to the Gospel's New Testament, it has been found that Christianity can move into Buddhist countries with relative ease.

In many ways it seems to me that Thailand would be the easiest Asian land, possibly excepting Korea, to Christianize. And a Christian nation so placed geographically would be strategic. Thailand commands respect in Asia for it is the only country never to have been conquered or colonialized.

Mr. Calvin Chao, the remarkable Chinese Missionary of Singapore, whose wife had cabled him to meet us, called on us at the

Mission Home and our conversation was so fruitful that we saw a blessing in the fact that our airplane was delayed. He certainly is a key man to arrange plans for effective spiritual work in this eastern archipelago. The head of the Bible Society of Thailand also called.

Seated at the table with us at every meal were a man and wife representing the Pentecostal group of Finland, and another couple representing the China Inland Mission. The Finnish couple had a very sick child, a two-year-old with a high fever, and they asked our prayers. The healing was so immediate that the grateful parents said we had come to them like Paul and Silas.

The Hansons have entertained missionaries from all over Asia, such as Walter Judd and Lillian Dickson, dear friends of ours; and all the China Inland Mission folks have known our friends Dick and Marion Springer who now have a regular pastorate in the state of Washington.

Thus, wherever we go we discover God is inter-weaving our many spiritual friendships into a tapestry of love and good will. The people there at Bangkok mapped out a splendid three day program for Roland when he returns another year. There is no question but that he will spend half his time hereafter abroad. The field is indeed white unto the harvest, awaiting the reapers.

It was midnight when we boarded our plane for Hong Kong.

When we arrived at Hong Kong, we didn't know what to expect. Not a single word had reached us in response to the letter we had sent to the name handed us by Miss Mather. Imagine our surprise and joy to find at the airport a half dozen lovely people with eager faces asking if we were Clark and Brown. It was another lovely Southern Baptist group, and we were very willing that they take complete charge of us. They registered us in a beautiful modern hotel with running water and ultra-modern conveniences, accommodations rarely encountered on a trip such as ours. Then they took us at once to the Baptist Seminary where we addressed an auditorium full of wonderful Chinese students, with the very light of their souls shining in their faces. When Chinese are fine, they are among the finest people of the earth, intellectually and spiritually. The students and faculty all proudly joined in escorting us through their classrooms and dormitories and in showing us the magnificent

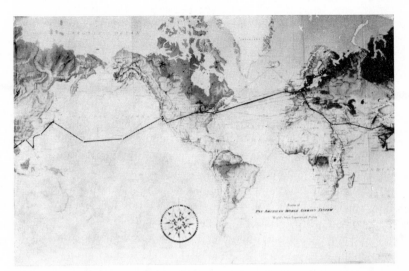

MAP OF OUR WORLD-ENCIRCLING JOURNEY: Ireland, Britain, Holland, Germany, Italy, Greece, Egypt, Jordan, Lebanon, Syria, Iraq, Pakistan, India, Ceylon, Maylaya, Thailand, Hongkong, Philippines, Formosa, Okinawa, Japan, Wake, Hawaii, United States.

COUNCIL RING OF FIRST EUROPEAN CAMP FARTHEST OUT, Swanwick, England. Seated: Marcia Brown, William Wood, Glenn Clark, Frank Rhead, Roland Brown.
Standing: Maurice Buckler, Norman Renshaw, Stanley Cox, John Maillard, Will Milne, Ernest Jeavons.

Glenn, Marcia, and Roland inside Parthenon on Acropolis. Mt. Lycabettus in background.

MARS HILL, ATHENS, showing Glenn, Marcia, and Roland reading Paul's famous speech to the Athenians, Acts 17. The Acropolis in background.

INSIDE THE KING'S CHAMBER, THE GREAT PYRAMID OF GIZA. Glenn Clark standing in sarcophagus.

EVANGELICAL MINISTERS' ASSOCIATION OF CAIRO. Ibrahim Said standing directly behind Glenn Clark.

THE SPHINX, Egypt, with Marcia, Roland, and Glenn on camels. The Great Pyramid of Giza at right. The excavation near pyramid at extreme right is where King Cheops' "Soul Ship" was discovered shortly after we were there.

MOUNT OLIVET, JERUSALEM. The Garden of Gethsemane
in foreground at left of Roman Catholic structure covering rock
where Jesus knelt in agony. Down the road at left Jesus rode on his
triumphal entrance into Jerusalem.

THE GARDEN OF GETHSEMANE, Jerusalem. In the footsteps of Jesus.

ARAB REFUGEE COLONY in Valley of Baracca, Bethlehem. There are 61 Refugee Colonies in Jordan where the 870,000 Arabs live since fleeing from Israel in 1948.

THE TAJ MAHAL, Agra, India.

CAMP FARTHEST OUT, NASRAPUR NEAR POONA, INDIA.
Roni Maharaja Singh, Dr. A. V. Matthew, Karmaveer Bhaurav P.
Patil, Glenn Clark, Roland Brown, G. C. LeRoy.

ART CLASS, CAMP FARTHEST OUT, KOTOYAM, INDIA.
K. K. Chandy third from right.

DEVOTION IN MOTION, CAMP FARTHEST OUT, KO-
TOYAM, INDIA.

panoramic view of the entire harbor from their hill, and then produced a dozen cameras to take pictures of their "famous visitors." That noon, at a lovely potluck luncheon prepared by the wives of the faculty, I had the joy of telling the wives and faculty members of our vision of all the Christians of the world being linked together in prayer. I never had a more attentive and cooperative audience eager to be a real link in our Belt of Prayer.

In Hong Kong there is a strong nucleus of the finest upper-class educated Christian Chinese that can be found anywhere. The churches are packed with these Chinese who are working hard to spread the gospel, a nucleus which will be very, very important when China is again open to Christianity. There are amazing prayer groups among them.

Hong Kong is a magnificent city of magnificent buildings surrounded by magnificent mountains, but faced with a tremendous problem. Because of the influx of immigrants (mostly Christian) from Communist China, the population of the city has risen from one million to two and a half million in two years. The food has to be carefully distributed and even the water rationed—and as far as sleeping quarters are concerned, thousands of the newcomers must sleep on the streets. This city is like a window looking into Communist China and I learned much about China while here. There is a strong feeling in Hong Kong that China, which has always absorbed and converted all its conquerors to the Chinese pattern, will eventually transform Communism in like manner. *War and the threat of war between them and the free world* tends to unite the common people on the other side of the Red Curtain behind Communism and thus this process of liberation from the inside is delayed. All over Europe and Asia we were told that McCarthy's vicious attacks on all who oppose him is discouraging men throughout the world from raising their voices in behalf of reforms which could stop Communism from spreading—lest if they raised their voices in behalf of much needed liberal changes they would be attacked by McCarthy as traitors to the established order.

Roland and Marcia took a long ride to where they could look behind the Curtain into Communist China. In the meantime I walked to a nearby church where I addressed a splendid group of young people. Elmer Galt, an American who has represented the

Church World Service in Hong Kong for many years and knows the refugee problem here better than any other man, walked me back to the hotel.

"For the last year and a half now," he said, "I have been administering relief sent from America for this city. We are facing a terrific problem. How can a tiny colony like this take care of a population of two and a quarter million when only half of that number was formerly considered a maximum for its economy?

"This complex problem," he continued, "is being grappled with by government, by business circles, and by voluntary agencies with results that are truly remarkable. These refugees are here and they are staying here. There is no place for them to go. Migration doors in every direction are all but closed. The only door through which they could pass in appreciable numbers would take them back into China. Nothing short of military compulsion could send any considerable percentage of them there. And to what? To a worse sense of being surplus outcast! to worse poverty! to hostility and suspicion! and many would meet certain persecution. We can't force such a fate on them. A half million are still in real need and one hundred and fifty thousand of that number are in such distress that it is next to desperation."

"That's serious," I said. "What are you doing to relieve the situation?"

"Well," he replied, "we are doing our best and there are dozens of other welfare agencies, each doing its bit in cooperation with the authorities to relieve the distress. There is good cooperation among all of us. We have established a 'Welfare Workshop' for training apprentices in weaving rattan products; and a cottage industry where women missionaries supervise the training of women in embroideries. We've distributed sixty thousand pounds of Kansas wheat flour to fifteen thousand people; and two hundred and sixty bales of used clothing which came from the United States in splendid, clean condition; and we have constructed temporary mat sheds to house fifteen hundred refugees. The United States has dumped its surplus milk in the form of a milk-powder over here. Thank the Lord they didn't dump it into the sea but 'overseas'; and the United States Government reports enough powdered milk on hand to keep sending it for two years longer. Thousands of children in free schools for the underprivileged, thousands more in the street-urchin clubs and in orphanages, numberless tuberculosis patients and nursing mothers—some twenty-five thousand people in all are being blessed by this gift."

When I returned to the hotel that night, my mind was filled with foreboding for the future of Hong Kong, this great trade center and cultural pivot in the heart of Asia.

My concern for Hong Kong's economic future lies in the fact that its trade figures for February, 1954, was a third less than a year previous. The Communist occupation of China, which is primarily responsible for Hong Kong's business decline, has made matters worse by pushing the refugee squatter population up to two and a half million which is a million more than the economy can absorb. With Hong Kong's accumulated wealth fast shrinking and no major business improvement in sight, the fear is that relief agencies will be unable to hold back starvation indefinitely, and acute hunger tends toward lawlessness, food riots, and chaos.

Should conditions worsen, should the work of Elmer Galt and others like him not be able to continue, then Hong Kong's extremity becomes Red China's opportunity. Some observers feel this is precisely what the Communists plan for Hong Kong—an economic disintegration into which they can move as the "rescuing angels."

CHAPTER XXI

THE FRIENDLY PHILIPPINES

SATURDAY AFTERNOON, MARCH TWENTY-SEVENTH, WE ARRIVED AT the Manila airport on our magic carpet after an easy flight from Hong Kong. Looking down on Manila Bay as we came in we could see a countless number of rusted and dismantled hulks of vessels blasted by our bombers in the final days of the war. Most were submerged with only an occasional mast showing above the water, but the shadowy forms beneath the surface were clearly visible from the air. One entire ship lay on its side on a sand bar as if it had been coughed up by the sea and another, following some mighty explosion, was strewn in huge sections all along the breakwater.

Several days later I remarked to Mr. and Mrs. Morgan, who took us in a power boat around the Bay, that it might be smart for the Manila Chamber of Commerce to leave the wrecks just as they lay; they could easily serve to draw thousands of tourists to see permanent reminders of the greatest world war in the history of mankind. For we had discovered that the prosperity of Greece and Rome came chiefly from the trade of tourists drawn there to see the ruins of a glory that was past. I did not know as I came flying in that I was entering one of the two worst bombed cities of the entire war—only Warsaw being worse hit. And the irony of the holocaust in this friendly city was that most of the destruction came not from bombs dropped by enemy Japanese flyers but from shells from American battleships in the final effort to drive the Japanese out. War does not pay. We, the winners, in the process of winning destroyed the very foundations of a prosperity we were trying to preserve.

To our joy we found that those, among the throng of greeters lined behind the wire barricade awaiting the arrival of our plane, who were waving most eagerly were a little band who were waiting to meet us. I recognized among them Presiding Bishop Sobrepena who had been a student of mine thirty years ago, the most brilliant Minnesota college orator of that time, and today the most brilliant pulpit orator in the Philippines and potentially one of the most influential men in the Archipelago next to the president of the Philippines himself. With him were his lovely wife and his beautiful daughter who had also been a student at Macalester College. In the group were two other lovely people we were destined to see a great deal of: Mr. Stephen Smith, executive secretary of the Foreign Missions work of the United Church and his brilliant wife, Viola Smith, who, besides conducting a religious radio broadcast every Sunday evening, is director of a great choir of several hundred voices. We had the precious privilege of hearing the choir rehearse the Hallelujah Chorus before leaving the Island.

Roland and I addressed five packed churches Sunday morning and evening. In the afternoon Marcia talked to the women's meeting while Roland and I addressed a specially summoned meeting of ministers and church leaders.

Monday and Tuesday on the Campus of White College at Los Banyos, eighty miles from Manila, we three conducted a miniature Camp Farthest Out attended by a group of some of Manila's finest church leaders and workers.

On Wednesday and Thursday at the summer resort city of Baguio one hundred and twenty-five miles northwest of Manila we conducted another miniature Camp attended by over one hundred people, chiefly leaders from the entire Island of Luzon, including a number of teachers from Silliman College and Manila Union University. Baguio is four thousand feet above sea level and is called "the land of eternal spring." This idyllic mountain summer resort enjoys a climate probably unsurpassed anywhere in the world. On our drive along the mountain highways we were thrilled with the magnificent Alpine scenery and the ever fascinating panorama of one of the man-made wonders of the world—rice terraces rhythmically mounting the steep hillsides. Rev. Smith carefully arranged our journey both up and returning so that we would not go through the intermediary "Huk" territory in the dark. The day before, a party had been ambushed by these mountain Red-sympathizers and seven travellers had been killed. At certain points, as nightfall approached, we passed soldiers standing guard with uncovered cannons ready at a moment's notice to go into action. At one place we had to stop to let a mile-long caravan of army trucks loaded with soldiers and cannons go by.

This insurrection by the Huks had its rise from so many causes that it would be unfair to ascribe it to any particular malpractice or any particular people. Many of the brave village boys who joined the guerrilla-underground and carried on ceaseless resistance to the Japanese invasion, instead of being rewarded for their patriotism, were terribly mistreated when the war was over. When they saw that vast sums sent by the United States to lift the standard of living were largely used to feather the nests of office holders and influential folks of wealth they continued their revolt against exploitation and now directed it, not against foreign oppressors, but against the injustice and oppression of their own leaders. On the other hand, many of the brave village boys were given financial assistance and were paid in good cold dollars for all they lost in the war. But many of the guerrillas had always been brigands, and the war and the exploitation that followed were congenial to their way of life. Many who had been farmers before the war preferred the quick profits of a brigand's life to the stolid, profitless ways of peace.

The average Filipino tends to be a little more adolescent in temperament than the Anglo-Saxon and the Chinese. I believe the waves of juvenile delinquency which have swept over our nation following our two great wars find a parallel in this Huk uprising in the Philippines following a war which wreaked far more havoc on the homes of their people than anything that has happened to our nation since our Civil War days.

President Magsaysay, just elected, has brought an end to all that graft. He offered each of the Huks a cow and five acres of land, and came down with an iron hand upon all who did not meet his terms. Although he was a Catholic he guaranteed complete religious freedom for all. I consider him the Abraham Lincoln for this land at this time.

In one of our meetings Bishop Sobrepena said that in 1898 there was not a Protestant on the Islands while the last census of 1940 estimates some 600,000 and today there are probably 1,000,000 Protestants. The Philippines is the only Christian nation in Asia. The splendid growth of Protestantism is due to the remarkable work of American missions, beginning shortly after Admiral Dewey sank the Spanish fleet in Manila Bay. I was a high-school student at that time, but I shall never forget the poem Eugene P. Ware, a

Civil War comrade of my father, wrote celebrating that historic occasion: "Dewey was the morning upon that April day, etc., etc."

The accident of Admiral Dewey's happening to be in the far Pacific with the United States war ships when war broke out between Spain and the United States led to a series of events that made the United States a World Power over night, with colonies for the first time in the Far East—an accident which, by the way, has helped to involve us in two world wars. For us it might have been better if the "accident" had never happened, but for the Philippines, American tutelage became a blessing. While all the other white colonial powers exploited their colonies without returning comparable service, the United States sent hundreds of school teachers, many of whom died of tropical diseases, and established the best school system in all Asia. Years ago a Filipino whom I complimented on his good English, after extensive travelling in our country claimed a little proudly that they used better English in the Philippines than we do in the United States because they used literary English and we used "slang." This may be an overstatement, but at any rate the fact that English is the second language in these islands is one of the assurances that they will not go Communist. For let me assert again that the Communists have never taken an English speaking country, proving that language is the great binder of ideologies. Now every land in Asia has made English its second language with the exception of China and Formosa, and the latter, I believe, has recently put English into the Public schools.

Another bond of gratitude the Philippines feel toward us is that we kept our promise and gave them independence. Indeed it is a stirring thing in any capital on July fourth to see the United States Embassy and the Philippine Embassy celebrating the same national birthday, and to feel the warm appreciation of the two countries.

And finally we taught them the meaning of democracy in ways that make other neighboring nations look upon them with envy. Indeed, if the United States had adequately advertised over the Voice of America all the good we had done for the Philippines instead of depending upon arms alone, we might have won all of Asia.

At the time we arrived in the Philippines the new President, Ramon Magsaysay, was intent upon implementing his new program of sweeping out the graft and initiating his Christian offensive against Communism. With one hand Magsaysay held out this "Christian social action program," five acres and a cow for every rebel who surrendered, and a promise of rural roads and artesian wells to lift the standard of living in general. With the other hand he threatened to apply the "big stick" of ruthless warfare against those who did not fall into line. These were the stern peace terms he was then offering the Huks:

1. Surrender, by stages, of all Huk forces and their arms.
2. Maintenance of government sovereignty over all parts of the country.
3. Trials for rebels charged with crimes, with permission to plead for clemency if convicted.
4. Resettlement of pardoned guerrillas on government land.

Little did we know that the very week we were holding meetings of prayer in the Philippines, these policies were beginning to bear fruit.

And while we were constantly passing the long lines of army jeeps loaded down with soldiers, vivid reminders of the Big Stick policy in Magsaysay's left hand, little did we dream that already his right hand, with its pro-Christian solution of social justice and mercy, was reaching deep into the hearts of the rebels preparatory to bringing the struggle to an end.

A daring *Manila Times* reporter, named Benigno Aquino, had made contact with the rebel leader, Louis Taruc, the elusive Huk terrorist. The reporter found Taruc soft-spoken, clear-eyed, and warm in manner, and bitterly against colonialism and tyranny; a Nationalist first and a Communist second. He said, "The people have spoken and overwhelmingly elected President Magsaysay. It is for us to accept the verdict. I am ready to negotiate a peace settlement." He demanded a "cease-fire" with all military operations frozen while he consulted his Huk advisers. President Magsaysay refused to agree to a "cease-fire," which would simply take pressure off the guerrillas, so negotiations bogged down. Magsaysay's retort was to order the army to launch a powerful new operation to "get Taruc," an operation of which we were the unconscious witnesses. Ten thousand men, armed with cannon, and with dogs and cavalry to track down the Huks, plunged into the wilderness. We were in the midst of our own operation of building the last strands in our

Belt of Prayer around the world while this powerful operation of President Magsaysay of building a Belt of Democracy around the Philippines was at its height.

Shortly after we left the Philippines, Louis Taruc accepted the terms offered by Magsaysay with only one stipulation, that the word "surrender" not be used in official documents. To this Magsaysay agreed, though only on the understanding that Taruc would accept all the other peace terms unconditionally.

Shortly afterward the radio was broadcasting the good tidings that Taruc was calling off the "civil war." Communism had been blocked. Democracy had won.

CHAPTER XXII

FORMOSA—UNDER THE SPOTLIGHT

FORMOSA IS ABOUT THE SIZE OF HOLLAND AND HAS ABOUT THE same population. The name is Portuguese and means "beautiful," a reference to the high mountain range stretching almost the whole length of the island. The Chinese call it Tai Wan, which means "terraced fields"—referring to the fertile valleys where the population is concentrated. No one starves in Formosa, and one of the things that impressed us most was to find that there are no beggars in Formosa.

We knew no one in Formosa except the Rev. and Mrs. James Dickson, missionaries under the Canadian Presbyterian Board, and they were on furlough for a year. However, just before we left Hong Kong word came that Lillian Dickson had returned. James had been detained in America.

When the plane door opened at Taipeh at ten o'clock the night of April second, whom did we see awaiting us right at the foot of the "ladder" but Lillian, her smiling face all but lighting the air field. She had driven a little jeep to carry our eight pieces of luggage, about all the tiny car could hold, and had the foresight to have a taxi waiting to carry us three pieces of human baggage "in state" to the "Friends of China" hotel.

"Nothing but rest tonight," she said. "But tomorrow, Saturday, I have invited all the Christian young people we have contacts with to my place at three o'clock for an afternoon of games, a picnic supper at five-thirty, songtime at six-fifteen, and talks by you two from seven to eight. I invited all the ministers to come, too. Then Sunday, Dr. Clark is to speak to my lepers at their church out at the Government Leprosarium in the morning and Mr. Brown in the evening. Mr. Brown will be preaching at a church here in town in the morning, and Dr. Clark goes to a different one in the evening. Monday you are to meet with all the ministers of the city at the

Y.M.C.A. and in the afternoon I have invited the missionaries to a tea at our Compound where you will address them. Tuesday you address the Presbyterian Seminary, and Wednesday and Thursday we shall fly to the mountains where you can meet and address my mountain people who have built one hundred and seventy-five churches with their own hands. Friday you're off to Tokyo."

So there it was, everything taken care of perfectly by Lillian and the Lord! At the hotel we found Rev. Tan awaiting us and Lillian introduced him as "the minister who heads up the three hundred and sixty churches on the Island." He is a Formosan of slender body but almost as expansive with love and joy as Lillian. Saturday morning the Pan American airlines informed us that their Friday plane for Tokyo had been taken off and we would have to leave Thursday, cutting our Formosa visit by one day. When we broke the news to Lillian she said, "That won't hurt our plans any. We can arrange to fly to the mountains Tuesday morning and fly back Wednesday afternoon, and we shall postpone the Tuesday meeting at the Theological Seminary to nine o'clock Thursday morning. You can still have time to catch your one-o'clock plane to Tokyo. God is arranging everything."

And so our schedule for Formosa, which until the previous day had been a piece of blank paper, now became a whole writing-pad filled in by the fountain pen of God!

Saturday afternoon more than a hundred of the finest young men and women in the Orient gathered on the wide lawns of the Canadian Presbyterian Compound where the Dicksons make their home and participated merrily in a half dozen different games all going on at the same time, while we staid elders were invited to drink tea in the parlor. I left the tea party after a good visit with Dr. Taylor and Mrs. MacMillan, missionaries in this field for the past forty years, and went out to watch these happy young people. It was a love hour for me. All I could do was to love them. After the lawn supper and some fine singing by the young people I addressed them, Dr. Taylor serving as interpreter, and Roland followed.

Sunday morning, while Roland addressed the church in town, Lillian took me ten miles out to the Church of the Lepers. As I sat on the platform and looked deep into the faces of the two hundred unfortunate stricken ones before me, my heart went out to them. So this was to be another love hour. The entire center section of the church was filled by young soldiers of Chiang's army who had contracted the disease somewhere and it had been diagnosed since their arrival in Formosa. Only a few in the entire audience showed advanced leprous lesions or noticeable disfigurement, as most of the very ill were confined to their beds, but they were listening to me over the loud speakers. Two vested choirs sang, one a male choir in the soldier section, wearing white vestments; another a choir of mixed voices wearing blue. Half a dozen of the young women had faces almost as beautiful as my own lovely daughters and again I say, my heart went out to them. I wanted to shake hands or even hug them all, but such direct contact is forbidden even though this Hanson Disease, as leprosy is properly called since the discovery of the bacillus by Hanson, is far less contagious than tuberculosis. The week before our visit, the untainted babies of leprous mothers had been brought out so the mothers could see them, and the anguish of mothers who could not touch or kiss their babies, or even live with them, must have been great. After the service a large group followed us to the gate and sang a song of farewell; three happy little boys, who were infected, joining most enthusiastically of all.

There was much good in all the religions in the Orient as we saw them. Confucianism has a splendid system of ethics, and Buddhism with its stress on asceticism and the search for wisdom could be made, under the loving guidance of Christian missionaries, their "Old Testament" background for Christianity. But it is Christianity, with its loving Father and Redeeming Christ and positive faith in Immortality that is the Religion of Hope. It so surpasses all other faiths that there is really no comparison.

The transformation among these hundreds of lepers under the ministry of Lillian and her helpers is almost unbelievable. A leper colony can come as near being a hell on earth as any assembly of human kind. Suicides occur daily. But when Lillian the "Little Mother" arrives with her accordian which delights their ears, and her "Good Tidings" that inspire their hearts, this place of doom becomes a place of hope. They have something to look forward to, if not in this world, in the next. I shall always carry with me those happy faces, and I can never think of them without thanking God for sending Jesus into the world.

As our jeep started and we turned our faces away, Lillian's happy smile was replaced for a moment with a look of sorrow.

"I never know when I leave them," she said, "whether I will ever see them again, because if the Communists come the first thing they will do will be to liquidate the lepers as economic liabilities."

Then she took me to a building a mile distant where the uncontaminated babies are taken care of, babies whose leprous parents can see them only once in three months but never touch them. These tots merely smiled at us, but when time came to leave and I waved goodbye, they were all galvanized into action and responded vigorously waving and calling, "Goodbye." When we were getting into the car they lined up at the door, three deep, calling and waving; an unforgettable sight.

The lepers had been made very happy by Lillian's announcement, when she returned from America the week previous, that the *Christian Herald* had promised three new buildings, one for occupational therapy where they can learn to make things for sale, and two "Houses of Hope," where patients in the process of cure by the new treatment for leprosy can live until they gain confidence enough to return to the normal world of work again. The first year a healed leper is released he has an extremely difficult time as he lives in constant fear of being shunned by former friends. One of the new buildings will house men, the other women during this period of adjustment. Doctors will continue to examine them and at the end of a year if they remain symptom-free they can take the next step of becoming self-reliant in the world again.

I had confined my talk to the lepers that morning chiefly to the need for the prayers of all so-called "shut-ins" for our Belt of Prayer. The part that interested them most was this little parable of the "Fanner Bees:"

> It was a glorious night of midsummer—a moon at full and a host of stars. The old bee-garden was bathed in soft crystalline light—and ever so light a breeze lisped in the treetops. At the door of one of the hives we came to a halt. There arose from the hive a sibilant note . . . persistent . . . not unlike the sound of sea-waves . . . advancing . . . retreating.

> "They are Fanner-bees," whispered the old bee-keeper. "It's their job to keep the hive sweet and fresh. They're standing

with their heads lowered, turned toward the center of the hive. Their wings are moving so rapidly that if you saw them you would think you were looking at a gray mist. They are drawing the bad air through one side of the entrance whilst the pure air is sucked in on the other side."

Standing there close to nature, listening to the bee fanners, I felt close to one of nature's wonders, the mystery of the hive life. Presently the old bee-keeper stooped to the hive, holding a lighted candle in his hand. Instantly the light was extinguished by the strong air current, those infinitesimal bee wings, moving in unison, making a draft so strong that the candle light was instantly quenched. Think of it!

As we stood there in the star-lit garden, the old preacher said, "The Fanners—drawing out the bad air, letting in the fresh. Isn't that how people who call themselves Christians ought to act." If we had enough fanners, if they were as keen on their jobs as those bees were on theirs wouldn't the great hive of the world grow sweet and fresh?

I asked that at least seventy (either as individuals or as a "Fanner Bee Club") use their leisure time to pray for their loved ones, their nation and the world. Lillian says she will find the seventy.

The young minister who interpreted for me is named "Everlasting Life." His brother, "Resurrection," is studying at Princeton Seminary, and his younger brother, "Born Again," is studying in Formosa.

The mother of these uniquely named young men, who understands no English, played the organ at the church where I spoke in the evening. She played the hymns beautifully—all familiar tunes but, of course, they were sung with Formosan words. The church was packed and the excellent interpreter made it very easy for me to give my address on Prayer, the Greatest Power in the World. These Formosans, like their Chinese cousins on the mainland, all wear poker faces in church and think it impolite to show any feeling. But I could sense down inside me that I was really reaching them.

Monday morning Lillian took us to lead the devotions for a group of about one hundred and fifty Nationalist Chinese women, wives of soldiers who had come with Chiang's army from the mainland.

Madam Chiang has interested them in spending Mondays sewing for the families of the soldiers. Sewing together this way helps to keep up the morale of the women and it certainly lifts the morale of the soldiers to know that somebody cares. They are mostly Confucianists, Buddhists or atheists—only a few Christians, but Madam Chiang has this devotional period because she wants them to hear a Christian message. Lillian played her accordian while they sang a Christian song and then I told them how prayer can bring peace. Lillian translated my talk into Formosan and a young man, her chauffeur, translated her translation into Mandarin which is the dialect of those who came from the mainland. Little did I know that the one thing these displaced persons do *not* want is peace. They want the Communists driven out of China by force. Smart Lillian edited my speech (leaving out the peace emphasis) and the chauffeur who did not understand English repeated her version in Mandarin, so all went well. Perhaps all my speeches should be put through a double filter in that fashion. After I finished Roland spoke on Love. Each woman had been seated behind a sewing machine, and how the machines did buzz the moment we were finished!

When we left the building my eyes were still filled with the picture of those serious faced, devoted women, and as we stepped out on the street I saw a battalion of Chiang's army march by, made up of the oldest soldiers in point of age in the world, averaging twenty-eight years old. I turned to Lillian and said, "In America we talk of the danger of a Communist drive against Formosa. Here I find everything is geared for an invasion in the opposite direction. Is that true?"

"It certainly is," she replied. "If the American government held out the slightest promise of backing him up, Chiang would plunge into the invasion at once. The two million people who came out from China with Chiang's government, five hundred thousand of whom are soldiers, are looking forward eagerly to the day when Communism will be driven out of China and Chiang will be restored to power."

It seems that the five hundred thousand soldiers who came from the mainland are being trained to become non-commissioned officers in the new divisions which Chiang hopes to raise when he returns to China. He is convinced that most of the armies sent out against him will join him. His army is excellently equipped, mainly with American help; there is a small but strong air force, and there is a small but impressive navy. To date Communist China has few naval forces. However, Russia can furnish Red China with enough jet planes to destroy Formosa in a few hours.

I do not share Chiang's optimism.

From the meeting with the Chinese women, Roland and I were taken to a gathering of ministers where we both spoke, after which we joined them for a Formosan lunch. There I had an opportunity to get well acquainted with Hugh MacMillan, that splendid Canadian co-worker of the Dicksons, and learn more about the conditions in Formosa and the urgent need for the work of the missionary.

In the afternoon we three met many more missionaries at a tea given for them in our honor by Lillian. After supper at the weekly prayer meeting of Christian missionaries—all of whom could understand English—we had a wonderful fellowship and our messages seemed deeply appreciated. In my talk, among other things I told how Lillian had helped bring the gymnasium to Macalester.* Our hosts in the home where the meeting was held had graduated from St. Olaf, and several other missionaries were from Hamlin, both of them Minnesota colleges, arch rivals of Macalester College in football and track. When I had been a coach at Macalester how often I had led my teams against theirs!

I had a particularly good visit with Miss Jenkens whose parents were missionaries in China and cousins of Agnes Sanford, mother of my lovely daughter-in-law. A tall chap who was graduated from Hamlin about the time my daughter, Marion, was graduating from Macalester asked me to autograph *A Man's Reach*. He has two copies of *I Will Lift Up Mine Eyes* which, he said, he and his family live by. He quoted his mother as saying, "Some say Glenn Clark is a liberal, but if he is I am liberal, too." These missionaries are all conservative but their fundamentalism is like ours and centers around the fundamentals of Jesus. It is not the fundamentalism which gets preoccupied with fighting about rituals and creeds.

The next day we drove up into the mountains to a mountain church. We had hoped to go still further inland but while we could get reservations to fly in, we could not get reservations to fly out.

---

* See *A Man's Reach*, pp. 237–240. Harper & Brothers, New York.

Lillian said the block in reservations might be providential as the only landing field is grass-covered and if it rained, and it rains frequently, might not be safe. God, she said, was taking care of us.

The story of these mountain people, who have until recently been head-hunters, is one of the most romantic chapters in missionary history. Formosa has long been a mission field occupied by English and Canadian Presbyterian Missions, but their early labors were confined to the Chinese who formed the vast majority of the population. No Christian work had been undertaken among the primitive tribes who dwelt in the central mountain fastnesses because the Japanese, who ruled the Island from 1895 to 1945, repeatedly refused to permit the evangelization of these aborigines. The official policy was to leave their primitive, animistic faith undisturbed, yet the Japanese police who supervised them did not hesitate to impose Shinto practices upon them.

Now witness the power of prayer! When all modes of action are stymied, prayer, like water dammed up, can move like a giant waterfall.

In 1895, after the first Sino-Japanese war, China was compelled to cede Formosa to Japan, but the Formosans refused to recognize the treaty and declared Formosa to be an independent republic. Whereupon the Japanese navy promptly made a landing in the north and the local government rapidly collapsed before their force of arms. Only the liberty-loving Highlanders swore never to submit, and the aboriginal snipers took heavy toll of the Japanese troops in the dense thickets and deep gorges.

The Japanese were eager to exploit the forests of camphor and other valuable timber within the aboriginal territory and were prepared to conclude an honorable agreement with such worthy foes as these mountain tribes. But who among the mountaineers was wise enough to match the cleverness of the Japanese—who could be their interpreter and negotiator? Their choice fell upon one of the mountaineer people, a woman named Chi-oang, thirty-six years old at that time (1895), who could understand Japanese and speak Chinese fluently as well as her native Taiyal tongue. Through her good offices, peace was concluded between the Japanese and the Taiyals to their mutual satisfaction. The Japanese authorities never ceased to be grateful for her services and allowed her more freedom of movement in going in and out of the aborigi-

nal territory than others, who were required to get a police permit.
Wherever she went she was known as the woman who made peace
—"Chi-oang the Reconciler." Little did the missionaries know,
when they started to pray for the mountain people, that God's
answer would be to call Chi-oang to the higher task of reconciling
men to God.

When my former Macalester College long-distance runner, Rev.
James Dickson, met Chi-oang in 1929, twenty-five years after she
had achieved peace with Japan, he found a frail fifty-eight year old
woman with the distinct tattoo mark of the Taiyal tribe upon her
face. She was the first aboriginal person he had met who could
speak the Formosan dialect and he urged her to go to the Tamsui
Bible School. She thought she was too old but James induced her
to attend the school for two years.

Now comes the miracle—the wonderful answer to prayer. When
the missionaries returned to Formosa after the second world war
they were amazed to find that seven thousand of the aborigines,
whose forefathers had been head-hunters, had become Christian.
During the war an underground Christian movement, one of the
most remarkable movements in modern missions, broke out among
the mountain tribes, through the unquenchable faith of Chi-oang
and a young helper.

When Chi-oang stepped into heaven the Dicksons caught the
torch and now one hundred and seventy-five churches have sprung
up all through the mountain tribes, built by the people themselves,
filled with the zeal of first century Christianity. Although they are
probably the poorest people in the Island, the churches are self-
supporting. The secret lies in the fact that they all tithe. Some
churches send a tenth of their tithe to James Dickson to help other
churches. Yes, Jesus is wonderful. God is good!

Here on Formosa the revelation that came to me was how close
heaven is to earth. The lovely people in the Leper Colony especially
live very close to heaven; in fact, these victims of fate, exiled from
family and friends, have almost nowhere else to look but to heaven.
On the streets of Teipei, thronged with exiled "nationalists" separated from the mainland of China only by a narrow strait which
bombers loaded with death could span in six minutes, I looked
at people whose lives could be wiped out in a twinkling of an eye.
Never did I realize how fragile human bodies are and how tempo-

rary life on earth can be, as I did here. And never did I realize more strongly how only the solutions that are born in heaven can ever solve the problems that are born on earth. Something like this must have been in the mind of the consecrated church organist when she named her three sons, Everlasting Life, Resurrection, and Born Again. These three sons are all wonderful preachers now.

Everlasting Life, the chief helper of Lillian Dickson, together with Lillian's beautiful daughter, Marilyn, were the ones who took us up to the mountains where the head-hunters lived, the courageous mountain folk who have been changed by the magic of Jesus into soul-hunters. Mounting higher and higher, crossing shaky bridges, looking down through deep gorges into glistening rice paddies and flowing streams, surrounded on all sides by cone-shaped mountains decorated here and there with lace-like waterfalls, we came at last to villages of bright-eyed people and still more bright-eyed children. In my travels, I have found that all mountaineers, whether in the Alps of Switzerland or the highlands of Scotland, have bright eyes. We paused finally before a church built by the hands of the mountain folk, and hardly had Roland got his camera set on a tripod ready for shooting, when down the mountain, up out of the gorges, and from every nook and cranny of what at first sight had appeared to be nothing but barren wilderness and bare hills came flocks of children running at breakneck speed, followed by mothers with babies slung on their backs. When all were lined up for the picture, they began to sing Christian hymns, and when we finally said goodbye they ran after us singing a dear familiar melody but in unfamiliar words, "God Be With You Till We Meet Again."

Divinity students at the Seminary where James Dickson is president are assigned churches to serve, the salary for which service helps defray their seminary expenses. Everlasting Life was the most brilliant student in his class and was offered the church that paid the most but, as no student wanted to go to the mountain churches that paid the least, Everlasting Life turned down the better offers, and spent his four student years serving four mountain churches, climbing rough mountain paths every weekend from morning to night.

The car carried us until the road ended, then we walked and climbed, and even travelled part way on "push cars" on narrow-gage tracks propelled by coolies who live in the low-lands. At every home where we paused, if a face that radiated light appeared, we were told "That is a Christian." No one qualifies to be a Christian among these mountain folk until he drops smoking, gambling, and drinking. Another requirement almost startled me. In days of old no man could hope to win a maid until he had proved his strength and valor by bringing home a head. Today, no one is admitted into full church membership as a fully fledged Christian until he has saved a soul. What a world-shaking transformation!

I practically never saw a baby of this island that was not in a sling on a mother's back, or on the back of an older sister or brother. Some of these carriers however were no older than eight or nine. And I never saw more contented babies. Often they are sleeping, their little heads bobbing backwards, lulled to sleep by the rhythmic walking of the carrier. Newton Dillaway, expert on child psychology, claims that there are no psychopathic or neurotic people among the races where little ones spend their babyhood attached to their mother's backs in this fashion.

Other psychiatrists would question that statement. But I do know from experience that babies nursed under the "Holt system" where feeding hours were definitely adhered to, and babies' hunger-cries between times went unheeded, could have produced a race of neurotics had not the grandmothers intervened and insisted that the little ones be picked up, cuddled, and fed whenever the pangs of hunger called. We three on this world journey have certainly been "babied" by God, who has carried us carefully tucked away in His knap-sack, not letting our feet once strike against a stone. Several times, for instance, air companies have changed our schedules, but every time God had it work out for the best. Never were there better treated babies than we three "little ones" being trundled along from place to place, from country to country, lulled to sleep or stirred awake by the rhythmic step of our Loving Father, who has never allowed us to become detached from him for one single minute.

Here is an example of the way in which God opened doors for us. On the second day that we were in Formosa, an attractive looking woman with a Madonna-like face and soft cultured accent came to Roland Brown. "I am Miss Franks, a Baptist missionary," she said, "and I just received a letter from Japan saying you were to be here. We want you to address the Baptist Theological Seminary tomorrow if you can." Through the Dicksons we had contact with the Presbyterian Seminary but we had no contact with the Baptist Seminary. So Roland gladly accepted and when he finished his address of forty minutes the students crowded around him and some of them begged him to give them more of the same thing that evening.

Miss Franks invited the three of us to dinner at her mountain home that evening, saying she would then take us to the gathering the young men had asked for. The wife of the president of the Baptist Seminary, Mrs. Culpepper, was one of the guests, and we had one of the most wonderful meals we had had on our journey. Miss Franks has a vegetable garden (with lettuce which can be eaten safely) and an excellent Chinese cook. The Compound where she lives will house over one hundred people, and before we finished eating she and Mrs. Culpepper began planning a CFO there for some future year. With the Baptists, headed by Miss Franks and the Culpeppers, and the Presbyterians headed by the Dicksons, this island has opened all its doors, and other groups will help to reap the harvest ahead.

When we arrived to meet with the "few" young men who had asked Roland for this extra meeting, we found almost the entire student body filling the room. After stirring songs led by a remarkable young song leader, Roland and I addressed them through a capable young interpreter whose words flowed like a mountain stream, and whose facial expressions and gestures were perfect replicas of ours. The audience would have stayed all night to listen if we had been willing. They would not let us go until Marcia told and illustrated the story of the Good Samaritan with them participating! How they loved it!

They were dynamic young men with spiritual power and genius shining from their eyes.

"Some of these young men you have influenced tonight," said Miss Franks, after we left, "may change Formosa in years to come."

When these young ministers have churches of their own they can certainly recruit hundreds of twice-born Christians who could help save not only Formosa, but the world.

When the Browns and I returned all aglow to the Friends of China Hotel, Roland telephoned Lillian and reported on our wonderful evening. She had good news in return. The next morning we were to address the Presbyterian Theological Seminary of which James Dickson is president. She reported that the half-hour Chapel was to be changed to an hour Chapel to hear us both, but I was to speak first beginning at nine in the morning because now the Baptist Seminary was arranging a special service for me there from nine-fifty to ten-thirty.

Thursday morning I kept the appointment at the Presbyterian Theological Seminary, giving a half-hour address through a translator, and Roland followed with a twenty minute talk; then President Culpepper of the Baptist Seminary took me to his Seminary to give a half-hour address before his choice young men and women, many of whom I had addressed the night before.

Never were more First Century-type Christians to be found anywhere than these future ministers of Formosa. God has certainly prepared the soil for us to plant our finest seed. Jesus is wonderful! God is good!

The Presbyterian Church of Canada has carried most of the Protestant work in Formosa, but since China went Communist, Formosa has received one hundred and fifty missionaries representing twenty denominations and missionary organizations who have come out from Old China. They work in harmony, with the exception of a few groups who think they are the recipients of the only true light from heaven, who here, as everywhere else, are the "problem children" in this family of Christ. The tremendous increase in the number of young people going into Christian work is one of the most hopeful aspects in Formosa today.

CHAPTER XXIII

THE RACE BETWEEN CHINA AND INDIA

IF THERE IS A THIRD WORLD WAR IT WILL NOT BEGIN WITH OUR previous enemies, Japan, Germany, or Italy. Neither will it begin with Russia. The place where it will start will be Red China, and while its ultimate aim will be Singapore, the initial push will probably come from China's passionate desire to reclaim that part of her land which she believes Chiang has stolen from her—Formosa.

But the war with which we are actually face to face right now is not a shooting war—it is a war of ideologies. And the arena where the first round is even now being fought is Asia, and the chief contestants are India and China. There is no question but that Communist China and Democratic India are right now in a life and death race against Time to demonstrate which will attain the eagerly sought goal of economic security first. And according to what I have learned from missionaries and responsible persons who have penetrated behind the bamboo curtains, China seems to have made a flying start.

United States News and World Report, a conservative magazine, recently issued the following report: "In China *there are almost no flies.* Peiping's swat-the-fly campaign has been a sensational success. *Public health* is improving by leaps and bounds. *Crime* is disappearing. *Beggars* are not to be seen. *Prostitutes* have been converted into zealous Communists. *The opium trade* has gone. *Drunkenness* is rare. In short: Everybody is working hard, happy, delighted with the Communist Government, which wants only peace. Or so some of the Atlee party said."

India, following Gandhi's example, is striving to build, as one Indian has phrased it, a "responsible society as an alternative to the materialism of the Communism of U. S. S. R. and the Capitalism of the U. S. A." To develop a responsible society is a slow process but

187

its gains are permanent when once achieved. In contrast to this slow method, China, with its dictatorship, its ruthlessness, and its un-Christian doctrine that the end justifies the means has been moving very, very fast. The contrast in methods is illustrated by the fact that India required a half century of non-violence before she was able to cast off the yoke of British Imperialism without the firing of a gun, while Red China, in a quick uprising against Chiang Kai-shek and through the slaughter of many thousands of landholders and moneylenders, achieved her ends within a few months.

The problem confronting India today is, can she bring about her land reforms fast enough and raise her standard of living more rapidly than China raises hers. At this date Vinoba's "land gift" crusade is the most effective means of achieving that end. It is undoubtedly one of the greatest movements of "applied Christianity" in the history of the world. Says Vinoba: "My aim is to bring a threefold revolution. First, I want a change in people's hearts; secondly, I want to create a change in their lives; and thirdly, I want to change the social structure. This method of change is in tune with the cultural traditions of India. It contains in it the seed of economic and social revolution. And lastly, *it can help in the establishment of peace in the world.*" That he is succeeding is attested by Nehru's statement that now 85 per cent of the land is peasant-owned whereas a few years ago only 15 per cent was so owned.

It is folly to think the Communists can be driven out of China by force of arms. Asia is in dire need of many reforms and the Communists are proclaiming that they alone can do the job. The only way to beat them is to beat them to it. To do this will be no small task.

A Chinese, who owned thousands of acres in China, said to me, "The Communists are in China to stay, and Chiang Kai-shek's hope of driving them out is futile. They are soundly anchored there for the following reasons:

"First, they have seized the land from the rich landowners, of which I was one, and distributed it to the landless. That aroused the enmity of 5 per cent of the people who were landowners and won the loyalty of 95 per cent.

"Second, for centuries young women have been compelled to marry men selected by their parents, regardless of love. Now the

Communists are granting young women freedom of choice, and those who have been unhappily married to brutal husbands may have the marriage annulled. This release from an intolerable tradition has won the loyalty of the young women."

To these two reforms mentioned by the Chinese gentleman, I will here add some others reported to me by missionaries and others who have been behind the bamboo curtain.

Third, one of the first things the Communists did was to abolish the opium traffic which had been the greatest curse ever placed on China. One hundred years ago opium was banned in China, but British gun boats entered port cities with the demand to restore the traffic because its ban was hurting the profits of the British opium raisers in Burma. Thus the Communists have righted a great wrong which the greed of Capitalism had fastened upon China.

Fourth, little had ever been done to control the rivers which every other year overflowed their banks and created the famines that caused millions of deaths by starvation. Had the United States sent earth-moving machines to Chiang instead of man-destroying machines (which later fell into the hands of the Communists) and if they had brought the rivers under control, the grateful people would never have turned to Communism. One of the first things the Communists did was to regiment hundreds of thousands of men and women with spades and wheelbarrows, and they dammed up the rivers, imitating our Tennessee Valley Project, saving millions of lives. Indians who witnessed this process returned to India in awe. "I saw eight hundred thousand people working with their bare hands," exclaimed an Indian correspondent in 1952.

Fifth, they put an immediate end to corruption in government and stabilized the currency.

Sixth, they initiated a school system modeled after the Russian school system, and it is spreading quite rapidly.

Seventh, they ended epidemics by vaccinations and inoculations and have swept flies and mosquitoes out of the country.

Eighth, through confiscation of surplus food supplies where the harvest has been good and by controlling the distribution of it they have helped alleviate famine conditions where the harvests have failed.

Ninth, by helping Indo-China win her independence, they have impressed Asia with the idea that they are the saviors of all the nations that have been for years victims of the imperialism of the white races.

I might be tempted to doubt some of these claims if they had not been made by responsible authorities who know the actual state of affairs. One of the missionaries who had come from the interior of China told us, "When Mao came into Peking he challenged the young Chinese to gird themselves for five hard years of sacrifice and labor to build up a great new China. And they responded heroically to the challenge. In the meantime too many of us missionaries were giving tea parties, and too many of our ambassadors were giving cocktail parties. The only way to beat the Communists is not with lukewarm troops obeying the feeble orders of lukewarm generals armed with weapons to destroy, but with an army of men and women completely obedient to the great laws laid down by Jesus and filled with faith in the power of love and prayer to save the world."

In spite of the fact that some of the hastily built dikes finally gave way under pressure of the highest crest the Yangtze ever reached,* bringing a recurrence of the famine conditions, there is no question but that the Chinese Five Year Plan is progressing faster than the Indian Five Year Plan.

And right here lies the danger: the Chinese government feels under no obligation to consider their methods under terms of human life and liberty in winning this contest to raise the standard of living, whereas Democratic India must adjust her progress to the will of her people. China, with her Communist dictatorship, with clock-like efficiency is producing reforms at tremendous speed and is spreading propaganda about Communist achievements all over Asia. The Chinese are a smart people, and those directing the Communist reforms are the smartest of all. As previously mentioned, in all the Asiatic nations we visited we found the Chinese were con-

---

* Twenty-four years ago a Yangtze flood drowned one hundred forty thousand and left ten million homeless, and the famine that followed in its wake brought death by starvation to fifty-two million men, women, and children. This past year the Yangtze River reached a flood crest of ninety-seven feet, the highest in its history, too high for the handmade dikes to contain it. The area flooded is China's heaviest rice-producing country, and as a result, the Communist reforms had a serious setback.

trolling business houses and, with the exception of Egypt and India (and, we were told this was true also of Indonesia), they usually control the banks as well. Wherever we went we found the Chinese outsmarting the native inhabitants at every turn.

The Indians may be as wise or even wiser than the Chinese, but they are not as clever, and the field where they are least clever is the field of propaganda. If the contest between Democracy and Communism is to be decided by propaganda, the Chinese will win hands down.

It is easy for critics sitting in comfortable arm chairs today to go back over past history and point out where and how China could have been saved from Communism. Most criticism is summed up in a slogan of five words: "Too little and too late." The slogan is correct but the application is wrong. The too little and too late should be applied not to the military field but to the ethical field. Had our statesmen and capitalists helped Chiang to bring about the needed reforms before the Communists beat us to it, Democracy would now be so anchored in China that neither force of arms nor of propaganda could drive it out.

Chiang Kai-shek has evidently learned the lesson which he failed to learn in time to save China. In Formosa, where he was faced with the same political and economical issues on which he was beaten in China, he has, in the last two or three years, put through a land reform program which could serve as a model for every free nation in Asia. The Nationalist government in Formosa now permits no one to own more than ten acres of land nor to own any land which he does not till himself. These reforms have brought about an extraordinary increase of output of rice per acre, so much so that there is no starvation and no beggars in Formosa. But unlike the Communist agrarian reform, the landlords in Formosa have been compensated, partly in cash and partly in industrial bonds. Had Chiang brought these reforms to pass while he was in China, Mao's victory would have been impossible. But, alas, we have been too little and too late in China with everything but guns!

In a former chapter I stated my conviction that if these land reforms had taken place in Indo-China in time, Communism could never have come in. Undoubtedly one of the chief influences that prevented such steps being taken sooner was the fear that to advocate such reforms would bring one under the attack, by McCarthy and others, of being a subversive. Efforts to spread the ownership of land might be labeled the first step in "creeping socialism."

Although the credit for the land distribution in Formosa went to Chiang, and for the land reform in Japan went to General Mac-Arthur, the man who actually did the job in both nations was Wolf Ladejinsky. When the reactionary leaders in America forced Secretary Benson to withdraw him from his post as United States Agriculture Attache in Tokyo, ostensibly as a "security risk" because he had been born in Russia, Ryutaro Nemoto, formerly Minister of Agriculture of Japan, said, "It is ironical that the loyalty of a man who is responsible for making a majority of the Japanese people firmly anti-Communist should be suspected because of his Russian background." It is to the credit of President Eisenhower that he immediately induced Secretary Dulles to send him at once to Indo-China to help save that land as he had helped to save Formosa and Japan. Had he been appointed as Agricultural Attache in Indo-China in 1951, Communism would not be in control there today.

The immense place that reactionism and corruption played in opening the doors for Communism to gain control of China is vividly told by Olin Stockwell, a missionary to China who was held in solitary confinement for fourteen months. In his remarkable book, *With God in Red China* he shows how money sent to a corrupt government where those who handled it were interested only in personal gain was like money poured into a well.

"In China," he writes, "corruption, which is the twin sister of inflation, flourished. F. G. Ho, financial adviser to the Central Bank at Chungking, told the Rotary Club there quite frankly one noon that the Chinese inflation and economic collapse were entirely due to the bankers who were more concerned about making their millions than in putting China on her feet.

"The U. S. sent out repeated commissions," continued Olin Stockwell, "and their reports were so discouraging that the State Department did not dare release them. Probably Secretary Dean Acheson saw the picture in its true light and wanted to insist on no more help to China unless she cleaned house. However, some of our congressmen and their friends raised the 'Red scarce.' They argued that no help to China and any attempt to discipline her would mean Chiang's defeat. So they voted down Acheson's proposals and sent more help. The battles were not lost at the front but in Nanking and commercial centers where the money-changers were salting away their millions in American banks. Communism has never won in any country where there was economic stability and honest government. Chiang struck out on three counts—no political democracy, uncontrolled inflation, and corruption in government."

Mrs. Mary Austin Endicott, in her book, *Five Stars Over China,* writes of the terrible corruption discovered by her husband, Rev. James G. Endicott, Chairman of the Canadian Peace Congress, and son of the Moderator of the Union Church of Canada. On Page 231 she writes, "The most terrible evidence was his discovery in 1944 that three million conscripts in Chiang's armies had starved to death because of corrupt officers who had sold the men's rations on the black market." A report like this tests my credulity, but it does imply that something was decidedly wrong.

No wonder Chiang's troops ran away in flocks to join the Communists, taking their arms, freshly sent from America, with them. It was such a defection that turned the tide in favor of Communism. American army officers testified before Congress that "the Nationalist army could have defended the Yellow River line with broomsticks if the soldiers had had the will to fight."

That Chiang Kai-shek may have realized the situation better than some of us think is evidenced by a remark he recently made: "If I had had a few hundred thousand honest Christians to put in leading positions, developments would have taken a different course."

I have reiterated in this book over and over again that wherever the Jesus way has been used Communism has been kept out. The man who came closest to applying this way in China was a Christian named Yen. At the close of the First World War, James Y. C. Yen, a graduate of Yale University, returned to China fired with a determination to help set his people free from the bonds of ignorance, poverty, and disease. He had been educated in America by the Boxer Indemnity Fund which, under the urge of our Christian missionaries, had been returned to China by Teddy Roosevelt. The Chinese used the fund to send each year around two hundred topranking students to American Universities, among whom Yen and Mao were outstanding examples. Yen became Minister of Education in Chiang Kai-shek's Nationalist Government and initiated a program that, if properly supported, would have saved China. His program consisted of sending village development teams of four workers to every village. One was an agricultural expert, one a literacy expert, one a public health expert, and one a specialist in teaching democratic self-government. More than twenty million people were reached by this program before the war brought it to what was hoped was only a temporary stop. In 1945 when the war ended Dr. Yen asked Chiang Kai-shek for the resources to spread this tested village development into all of rural China. Chiang was impressed but insisted that a military victory over the Communist forces was the first order of business.

"When we have crushed Mao Tse-Tung's armies, we will give full support to your plan," he is reported to have said.

"But you cannot defeat Communism on the battlefield," Yen is said to have replied, "until you have first conquered it in the villages and rice fields; it is the poverty and hopelessness of the peasants which is giving Mao his chance."

Chester Bowles, who reported this incident, drew the following conclusion, "No one knows whether the tragic debacle that followed might have been averted if Dr. Yen had had his way, but we do know that Mao's strength in the villages continued to grow and that his peasant soldiers, fired with the hope of land and plenty, defeated the dispirited Nationalists in battle after battle." Then Mr. Bowles reiterated what I have quoted on a former page, "American army officers testified before Congress that the Nationalist army 'could have defended the Yellow River line with broomsticks if the soldiers had had the will to fight.'" Indeed I would like to repeat that testimony on every page of this chapter for it is such a stupendous task to make the American public realize that China was lost not because of lack of military preparedness but because of lack of spiritual preparedness. *The Readers' Digest* for March 1955 relates how Jimmy Yen's program is building bulwarks against Communism in the Philippines today.

The method that Yen tried in China with such success is the method our Point Four Directors were using in India when Chester Bowles was our ambassador. (The recall of Chester Bowles from India in this time of crisis was one of the most unfortunate steps our nation has taken in regard to India.)

Training the villages in literacy, agriculture, public health, and democracy would change all of India in a few years, if carried on wisely enough and widely enough. Russia has sent one hundred thousand trained technicians into China. The United States cannot find twenty-five hundred to send to India.

Listen to this warning: "Russia, under a dictatorship, taught a hundred million people to read and write between 1925 and 1935," reported a man who knew the situation. "China is spreading literacy even faster. They have a passion for learning. To match this, India's democratic government must teach two hundred and fifty million illiterates by 1972." Frank Laubach, whom Chester Bowles described as the "world's leading expert on literacy programs," is the one we should put in charge of this work.

The strategic time for America to help India in this critical race is now, not after the race is lost. The tragic fact is that if democratic India fails to keep up with China in this contest, all Asia will turn to Communism as the most efficient way out of ignorance and misery. "In defense of tiny strategic Greece," writes Chester Bowles, "the United States in four years contributed more than twice as much as India needs to make a success of her Five Year Plan. One would think that the time to aid India is *now* while she is safe herself, and while her chance for success is good."

If India were blessed with coal mines and oil fields and waterfalls to furnish power for industrialization, she could easily carry her heavy population load. Lacking in these sources of power she is already looking forward to another source which will make all other forms well nigh obsolete. I refer to the unlimited, unmeasured new discovery called atomic power. Scientists in India are already prophesying that within twenty years, through new found uses of atomic energy, all India's industrial problems will be solved.

The greatest help we can render India right now is to have the right type of ambassador. Chester Bowles was just that. We could not find a better representative than he was. Ever since his recall I have been praying that the right successor be chosen.

I believe that this prayer which, by the way, is being shared by thousands of others is now being answered. John Sherman Cooper, following his defeat by Alvin W. Barkley of Kentucky for reelection to the Senate, was offered the ambassadorship to India by President Eisenhower. At first he refused to accept it, but two months later, when both Secretary of State John Foster Dulles and President Eisenhower had used their best powers of persuasion, he considered it seriously. However, it was not until he was informed that the members of the Indian government were convinced that he was exactly the man for the place that he realized the President was not trying to find a job for a defeated Republican but was seeking a man who was willing to give all that he had in one of the most important undertakings in the most sensitive spot in the world where the cold war between Communism and Democracy is at its height.

Having made this decision he relinquished his lucrative law practice and dropped all thought of trying to be elected to the Senate again, and threw himself whole-heartedly into preparing himself for this new task with an enthusiasm and devotion that is simply thrilling. He makes no secret of his admiration for the people of India, for its role as the hope of democratic government in the Far East, for its efforts to abide by the rules of freedom, of due process, and of constitutional methods.

However, he knows well the obstacles that lie ahead. He knows how often we lose patience with Prime Minister Nehru of India. He knows how hard it is for Americans to condone India's apparent lack of concern about Communist aggression in Asia. But no matter how often we lose patience with the Indians for their unwillingness to fall in with many of our plans Cooper realizes that we must rely upon them to carry forward in their part of the world the things that are important to us. We must choose, he feels, between democratic India and totalitarian China. After all, he believes, there are no more contradictions among the Indians than there are among our own people.

"If they seem cantankerous," he said, "it is because they are so much like us."

As Cooper views his assignment, it is to understand the difference in attitude taken by our Government and by the leaders of India, to interpret our views to them and their views to us.

"India not only is anti-Communist," Cooper says, "but it is the only truly democratic state in the East. They have a Constitution based on ours. They have a Bill of Rights. They practice due process. They have a free judiciary. They cast the largest free vote ever cast in any country. It is terribly important to us that India, and not China, become the leader of Asia. We must keep that in mind whenever we lose patience with Nehru. We must remember that when Nehru does something we don't like, he is expressing the independence of his country—he is demonstrating the spirit of nationalism in contrast to the Communist imperialism exemplified by Red China.

"No other country has spoken more clearly for true freedom than has India. That was why the post of ambassador there was one job I could not turn down. India is important to us and to the future of the world. It is of tremendous importance that we have good understanding and good relations with India. There are many points of disagreement based on misunderstanding. I hope I can have a part in removing those points.

"I am going to make this the supreme effort of my life."

CHAPTER XXIV

WE FIND A MAN OF GOD IN JAPAN

IN 1952, WHEN ROLAND BROWN AND I WERE MAKING TENTATIVE PLANS to fly from our Hawaiian Camp to Japan, Starr Daily reported a dream in which he saw the plane in which Roland and I were flying, as we neared Japan, crash and dive into the sea. Because Japan was not ready for us at that time we postponed our journey until 1954. As we were flying from Formosa to Tokyo we ran into some dense clouds and high winds that made the plane creak, so we did a little praying and instead of diving into a sea of destruction we dived into a sea of Love. In America nearly everybody is having bad dreams of the world's plunging into a sea of war. If we get enough people to pray with faith enough, I am confident that we shall see the entire world immersed at last in a sea of Love.

As gently as a bird lights upon a bough our plane alighted in Japan. Merrell Vories and his helper, Narmi Kawa, and Reverend Galen E. Russell of the Tokyo Union Church were at the airport to greet us. After a visit at the Russell home, where we made plans for our three weeks stay, Merrell and I left the Browns as the guests of the Russells and went to the Y.M.C.A. to spend the night. I sat up late reading the barrel of mail I found awaiting my arrival.

Friday morning we wanted an early start to the International Christian University of which Merrell is the architect, and as the Y.M.C.A. restaurant did not open in time, the two of us took a taxi to the railroad station where a little later we were to meet the Browns, hoping to find a restaurant there. Finding no restaurant open that early we took recourse to a fruit stand. The little Japanese woman in charge cleared a place in her shabby shop while her husband scouted up a couple of half pint bottles of milk and with bananas, chocolate bars, cookies, and milk we ate our breakfast as their two cute little progeny watched us with big eyes.

"White people to them are like elephants and monkeys in a zoo," said Merrell. "We are better than a circus to them." The dear little mother tried to press back the money Merrell wanted to pay her, and only through persistence did he succeed in making her take it.

Tokyo is the third largest city in the world and to reach the suburbs, where the International Christian University is located, required a long ride on a train. In the station trains were constantly coming and going, ejecting onto the platform thousands of kimono clad people who hurried by us and were swallowed up in the stampeding throng. It was a relief when our train came and we experienced the miracle of finding seats.

As we rode out of the railroad station Merrell told me that practically all of Tokyo had been leveled by bombs during the war and an almost new city has sprung up since, not of wood and paper but of steel and concrete. In every block we saw a new building going up.

It is almost unbelievable the speed with which Tokyo has transformed the shambles left by the war into one of the most modern of cities of concrete and steel. It was not until later we learned the secret by which they had outstripped all other war-torn lands. The secret lay in a clause written into the new Japanese constitution forbidding arms- and munitions-making; therefore *all* their energies could be channeled into reconstruction. The paradox of war is the way it has transposed some of the time-worn slogans: "to the victor goes the spoils" now reads "to the vanquished goes the spoils." Jesus tried to teach us some of these things without our having to go to war, but we could not believe Him. "He that destroyeth by the sword will be destroyed by the sword." "The meek shall inherit the earth." "The last shall be first."

As we approached the university an immense airplane hanger could be seen nearby. "People wanted to tear that down," said Merrell, "but I said it could make the perfect frame for the athletic center. We can put an arena in the center, large enough for all the great indoor or outdoor games, and one wing can be transformed into a gymnasium and the other wing into an immense auditorium."

This university has a special place in my heart. While it was still but a dream, I had the honor of breakfasting in the Prince George Hotel in New York City with its architect, Merrell Vories, and its President, Yuasa, and Carl Balcomb, to pray with them for God's blessing upon it. To meet the president now in his spacious office and sit with him and Merrell in a newly completed building, while Roland took the usual photograph, was like participating in the christening of a precious child.

This university will be limited to six hundred undergraduate and one thousand post graduate students. It will take care of large numbers of students who formerly had to go abroad to complete their work. Every professor will be a Christian, and the influence of this university upon the future of Japan cannot be measured. It will be a lighthouse for the Orient with the Lamp of Eternity shining from it. Everything about it has the element of permanence stamped upon it. For instance, the marble floors, laid according to the pattern of the palace of the Doges in Venice, will last for five hundred years. Protective devices on the steps will make them last as long as the floors. Every detail was planned as only a master architect, who has been on the job for fifty years and who relies on a greater Master Architect, could plan it.

Although only the first of many buildings is completed it is already in operation with a carefully selected faculty on the job. Going through the grounds, whom should we meet but Dr. Bryn-Jones, a close friend of mine, formerly of Carlton College—one of the greatest authorities on foreign affairs in the state of Minnesota. In going through the library the first objects that caught Roland's attention were two copies of my book, *What Would Jesus Do?*

As we took the train back to the center of the city we thought how wonderful it would be if in every land—yes even in our own—there would be an International *Christian* University where every member of the faculty would be a *Christian,* and where every student would be inspired to ask, before undertaking any project, *"What would Jesus do?"*

The next morning we took the train for Omi-Hachiman. In transportation Japan has not yet caught up with the demand. To secure reservations on trains one must plan days in advance. Merrell had purchased our second class railroad tickets for the long trip to Omi-Hachiman two weeks before we arrived. At the station we saw people lined up in rows extending almost a city block waiting to enter the inexpensive third class cars. Two-thirds of the people in Japan who travel third class must stand, only the lucky first comers getting seats. Our reserved seats could tip back, almost sleeping-car fashion, when we wanted to rest. Our turn in the dining car was also arranged in advance and the steak dinner which costs $1.50 was the kind that would cost $3.00 on an American train. The train announcer, whose voice is heard by loud speaker in all the cars, suddenly startled us with "The Emperor's private car is attached to the end of the train that will pass us in seventeen minutes." Outside we could see people in every village we went through, as well as along the countryside, lined up in long rows waiting for His Imperial Majesty to pass. These gatherings of people were the great sight for us, the unforgettable sight, not the royal car, for when His Majesty's train passed, it was at lightning speed.

"Before the war," said Merrell, "they would have had all the curtains drawn on windows through which the Imperial train could be seen, as it was forbidden for anyone to look at the Emperor on the same level—only from below. Since he has announced that he and his ancestors are not divine, the people seem to love him all the more." Then he told us how, when the War Party tried to prevent his announcing that the war was over by keeping him under guard in the palace, he had a servant smuggle a phonograph record out the back way. When the war lords heard his voice speaking to the nation, many of them committed suicide in the palace grounds.

I must tell you a little about this man Merrell Vories. Fifty years ago he accepted a teaching position in a Japanese government academy with permission from the authorities to teach Christianity outside working hours. In this Buddhist ridden section the character of the loving Jesus so appealed to the boys that three hundred and sixty attended his Bible class and were fast becoming Christians. The Buddhist priests, taking alarm, asked the academy officials to discharge him but the contract prevented discharge. So they incited the tough boys to set upon the lads who came to the Bible class and beat them up.

The only protection Merrell and the Bible class boys resorted to was prayer; they met twenty minutes before school time every day to pray. The persecutors seeing the radiant faces of the boys coming from the prayer meeting sent two spies into the gathering to see what they were secretly plotting against their persecutors. To their amazement they found no plans of vengeance were being made; instead these Christian boys were praying for forgiveness and salvation for their oppressors, and for patience and Christlikeness under their own persecutions. That was too much for the spies; they were overcome and melted into tears in that very meeting they had come to report on. This led to so many of the "bullies" joining the Christian group that the Buddhist priests in desperation pleaded to representatives in the Provincial Assembly, and it became a political issue whether or not the American teacher should be permitted to teach his religious convictions. The pressure soon became so great that the Principal was forced to ask for Vories' resignation.

After building up this wonderful Christian work, to leave was unthinkable. But how could he support himself without a job? Again he turned to God and again prayer saved him. His hobby had always been architecture. When he felt the call to foreign missions he had hesitated for a long time, pondering whether he could not render a greater service for the Lord by staying in America as a successful architect and supporting *three* missionaries. Under conviction of the Holy Spirit he had relinquished his beloved architecture to enter the mission field. Now in his hour of need, with no means of self support, he turned to the old hobby he had given up long ago. Prayer brought him guidance to ask some missionaries if he could do their architectural planning for them. His work was so well done that he was soon in demand all over Japan until he had thirty architects working under him with offices in many cities. The result is that instead of supporting three missionaries in Japan, as he would have done if he had remained in America, he became a missionary himself and is today supporting three hundred missionaries, if we count all his Christian co-workers as missionaries, who, by their lives as well as testimonies, are contagious influences for leading people to Christ.

This man who came to Japan fifty years ago without a cent, not supported as most other missionaries are by Church Boards, today is directing an amazing evangelistic work carried on by twenty-three full time religious workers through the Omi Brotherhood, assisted by hundreds of volunteers. The Omi Brotherhood maintains fifteen regular preaching centers, thirty Sunday Schools, four kindergartens, three schools, three night schools, two day nurseries for the children of farmers during planting and harvest seasons, several farmers' institutes, two magazines, correspondence evangelism, a lending library of Christian books, Bible study by mail, and relief work of various types. The Brotherhood built the first tuberculosis hospital in Japan and supports its six doctors and twenty nurses.

The reason I am so interested in the work of Merrell Vories is because he is a living manifestation of what the world so needs—the application of the teaching of Jesus in all the areas of life—the school, the factory, the playground, the home, everywhere. The Architectural Department of the Omi Brotherhood, for instance, is just as much an evangelistic agency as the church. It evangelizes its clients and the workmen who construct the buildings. In fact its influence is felt throughout Japan for the public knows that here is one architectural firm which employs no one who drinks or smokes, which not only demands Sunday rest and a maximum of eight hours per day of work for its own staff, but which seeks to obtain like conditions for the lowest laborer on any job it superintends by putting a Sunday-Rest clause into all its contracts, a firm which neither accepts nor gives "commissions," and which is trying to put into everyday practice the principles of Jesus Christ. This knowledge has a slow but sure influence throughout the building and labor trades, which are not being directly evangelized by any other agency.

When his neighbors scoffed at the idea that the principles of Jesus could be applied to modern business, Vories accepted the challenge and set up branch factories for producing Mentholatum and Air-wick, all the net proceeds to be devoted to Christian work.

Now it so happens that public education in Japan is supported by the government through the Junior High School level, but only the well-to-do can afford to go through Senior High. So the Omi Brotherhood hires only girls from poor families to work in the Mentholatum factory; the girls work only five hours a day but are paid for eight hours. The other three hours they attend classes in rooms set aside in the factory for that purpose. Merrell employs excellent teachers to give the one hundred and twenty girls a full three year Senior High School course in five years. Vories took us through the factory, and I have never seen a happier set of girl workers.

When we reached Merrell's home all of us took off our shoes in the vestibule and moved about in special house slippers. Merrell shared his bed-room with me. A man who might have been a millionaire limited his salary to One Hundred Dollars a month in order to support this work for which he is giving his life. Every month he and his wife entertain and feed and house at least one hundred guests.—"Inasmuch as ye have done it unto one of the least of these . . ."

Beginning Saturday night and continuing through Tuesday evening Roland and I gave fourteen addresses, including one to teachers, one to high-school students, and one to doctors, nurses, and patients in the tuberculosis sanatarium, and the balance belonged to a series of meetings we conducted in the Central Church of the Omi Brotherhood. When time came for us to leave one of their speakers gave a moving testimony of appreciation from the entire Brotherhood. They felt our coming was especially timely as just a month previous they had established twenty-seven prayer groups, each composed of twelve persons, a forward step that is destined to bring great blessings upon the entire community.

The day before we arrived in Japan, Kagawa, addressing two thousand persons in Tokyo, used as one of his strongest appeals for them to adopt the Christian way, the fact that in communities where the Christian influence was strongest the crime rate was always the lowest. He cited Omi Hachiman Prefecture, where the Omi Brotherhood is so strong, as the best of all. "There has not been one murder committed there in the fifty years that Merrell Vories has been there," he said. One year Vories received the medal granted by the largest newspaper in Japan, with five million circulation, as the most valuable man in Japan.*

---

* For full story of Merrell Vories see *The Voice by the Lake* by Glenn Clark, Macalester Park Publishing Co. Price $.50.

CHAPTER XXV

PRODUCING PEARLS AND PRODUCING SAINTS

ONE MORNING THE STATION WAGON OF THE OMI BROTHERHOOD TOOK us on a long ride over rough roads to Shima where we found ourselves overnight guests in a glorious hotel. The next day was planned for us by the Brotherhood and all we did was to follow directions. A private launch took us to the greatest pearl farm in the world. Some years ago a Mr. Miki Moto discovered how to make millions of dollars through a process of irritating oysters scientifically in order to facilitate nature's production of pearls. Mr. Vories had written him of our coming and he was expecting us and even had gifts ready for us. He was ninety-six years old and saw few people but he gladly welcomed us. His sixty-year-old son is an enthusiastic Christian but he said, "Father is one-half Christian, one-half Buddhist, and one-half Shinto." Before we left, Marcia suggested I ask God's blessing on the old patriarch. When his son was told of the prayer he was overjoyed. Since our return to America the newspapers have carried news of his death.

We learned a lesson from this pearl merchant who traded all the ordinary methods of gathering pearls for a method of producing them that is so extraordinarily successful that he could have bought up all the other pearls in the world if he had wished. Indeed his "pearl above price" is the power of creating pearls without limit.

Merrell Vories and Miki Moto were two men entirely opposite in type and in purpose but both were creators of miracles, holding each other in mutual affection and esteem,—two remarkable personalities who have made real to me two of Jesus' greatest parables: the parable of the mustard seed, planted by Vories, and the parable of the pearl without price, discovered by Miki Moto.

I have given much space to the mustard seed that Merrell Vories planted; permit me to interpret the parable of the pearl that Miki Moto discovered.

Pearls are created through the intrusion of some foreign, alien substance into the oyster which, when imbedded in the soft part of the oyster, sets up an irritant that stimulates the oyster to build a covering of its own around the intruding particle which results in the creation of the pearl.

Every saint I have met seems to have gone through some sort of an experience where an intrusion entered, although in many cases the "foreign substance" usually took the form of some sorrow, sickness, or even sin, which forced him to turn to God. Just as pearls are rare, so saints are rare. Just as pearl divers spend weeks bringing up hundreds of oysters from the ocean bottom only to find one pearl among them all, so students of human nature can spend weeks, months, yes years scrutinizing people before they will find one saint. Open the oyster and look into the heart of the pearl and you find the irritant; look into the soul of that saint, and you will find the sorrow, disappointment, or tragedy that created that sainthood.

Just as this Japanese pearl merchant sought far and long to find a way of inserting a material irritant in ways that would create pearls not at random but by the thousands, so I have been seeking long to find the "positive" spiritual irritant to insert into the hearts of men that will create not an isolated saint here or there but an entire army of saints who can pray with power. As I left the presence of this great pearl merchant I was simply obsessed by a tremendous thought: "As no power on earth can bring the world out of its present dilemma as quickly as the united prayer of an army of saints, why cannot we apply the secret formula used so effectively by this great pearl merchant in the material world, in an equally effective way in the spiritual world?" In other words, why not produce an army of saints here and now?

Miki Moto's daring hypothesis was that if pearls are produced by the chance intrusion of some irritating, evil, abnormal foreign substance that sets the pearl-producing process in motion, why cannot as perfect, if not more perfect, pearls be produced by the careful, gentle insertion of a carefully designed and lovingly prepared substance, in fact a miniature model of the very pearl it was destined to produce.

So while we were conducted through all the secret chambers of this "pearl factory" learning all the successive steps for producing pearls, our minds and hearts were alert to discover a similar pattern and technique for producing the army of praying people we had come all around the world to find.

Whenever I seek for spiritual guidance my thought always turns to Jesus, and I couldn't help but think of how gloriously Jesus would use this as a parable for producing saints. To make the parable complete we must start at the beginning. First, mussel shells are imported from America. From them are cut little cubes which are moulded and polished into tiny globules, miniature models of the pearls they are intended to produce. Then these miniature models are carefully inserted into the soft flesh of the living oyster, care being taken not to injure the oyster. The oysters so treated are placed in wire basket containers which are fastened to floating rafts and suspended four to six feet under the surface of the ocean where the pearl producing job can be adequately done. Four times a year the baskets are drawn up and the shells of the oysters are cleaned of all barnacles and dirt. The wire containers protect them from the customary enemies of oysters—the starfish and the octopus.

Tracing a parallel in the spiritual world I began to wonder if there were not a better way of producing saints than by the intrusion of trouble, suffering, persecution, and other negative elements. I can surely recall some Christlike souls who never went through the fires of sin, suffering, and catastrophe, but received their impetus into the spiritual life by the invasion into their lives of some heavenly inspired persons whose lives had become miniature reflections of Jesus himself. Whenever a radiant contagious spiritual leader lets a part of his real contagious experience of prayer and love be injected into the heart of another, something permanent happens. To get the full value of such a dynamic awakening the one so affected should, if possible, withdraw for a season from his old sinful, material environment and let the vital experience ripen in a silent, creative way, just as a grain of wheat must lie in the soil for awhile away from the eyes of men until the power of growth is sturdy enough to fulfill the Divine Plan for which it was created. Paul gave the perfect example of such a program when he tells us in Galatians how, after his experience on the Damascus road, he withdrew for three years in the desert to give that experience time to fructify and bear fruit.

So why wait until a Third World War brings disaster, suffering, and sorrow into people's lives to form the "irritant" to create saints? We spend so many billions producing hydrogen bombs and jet planes; why not use a tithe of that sum to underwrite spiritual training camps where people can be trained to use the most powerful forces in the history of the world—love and prayer?

Why a tithe of that sum? Because God challenges us by saying "I'm not going to require that you risk everything in order to prove what I tell you is true. Just bring 10 per cent and put it into My storehouse to be used My way and 'prove Me now herewith if I will not open the windows of heaven and pour you out such a blessing you will not be able to contain it.' "

But just as the insertion of this perfect pattern of mussel shell into the body of the oyster does not complete the creation of the pearl, so one camp experience, no matter how inspiring, does not complete the job of producing a saint. The wire container in which a dozen or more "impregnated" oysters are placed is symbolical of the prayer group to which everyone so "impregnated" should belong. And the large rafts to which these containers are attached by powerful chains can be likened to the churches that keep them safely moored. As the containers are drawn up three or four times a year to have barnacles and other evil accretions washed off, so the seekers should be drawn up into Retreats, Conventions or Camps for recleaning and refilling with renewed dedication and renewed inspiration several times a year. Then after three or four years of this growing and cleansing process we might actually find ourselves surrounded by an army of saints.

It might startle the world to contemplate seriously the production of saints on a mass production scale. To turn them out on an assembly line as automobiles are turned out would seem absurd on the face of it. But if raw farmer boys in Germany, England, and America can be converted into military machines on a mass production scale; and if untutored Chinese peasants can be turned into ruthless Communists in an even shorter time, it should seem logical that if saints or near saints are the only known antidote for the evils these other groups produce that they, too, should be produced at a far faster rate than they are being produced at the present time.

People may laugh at this dream. But thousands of folks laughed at Miki Moto when he proposed his dream. Edison, for instance, told him that one of his deepest wishes had been to invent a way to produce pearls in quantity but even he, the greatest inventor of all time, had given the project up as impossible. Miki Moto persisted and by following the simple laws of injecting a tiny replica of a real pearl into the heart of each oyster and then merely clearing the way for God and Nature to complete the work, the miracle was accomplished. If we are as faithful to our dream, which is really God's dream, as this old Japanese was to his, will not God bless us, too?

As we were driven to Kyoto we were told that one of the fine things that happened in World War Two was the fact that our Armed Forces were instructed not to drop any bomb on or near Kyoto or Nara because these spots were ancient capitals of Japan and also because they contain as great treasures as any city in the whole world and our government wanted these treasures preserved for world culture. The Japanese gratitude for this sparing of their heritage is beyond telling. To many, it overbalances the destruction of Hiroshima and Osaka for our planes flew right over Kyoto to get to Osaka, twenty-five miles distant.

As our route led right through Kyoto, we attended the famous Cherry Blossom Festival. The performers are several hundred Geisha girls in beautiful costumes.

These Geisha girls are sold to their owners by parents too impoverished to support them, one reason that led Kagawa (born out of wedlock of a Geisha mother) to start the cooperative movement to lift thousands out of poverty. They are trained from little girlhood to be "entertainers,"—to dance, sing, and act and play instruments. In fact, they are the only girls in Japan who in the past were given as thorough an education as the boys. They can converse upon almost any subject—history, politics, art, music, literature. Statesmen sometimes depended upon the insight of brilliant geishas. In contrast to them, aristocratic women, and most of the other women of Japan, were practically never educated. They are not professional prostitutes as is the common belief, although they often slip into prostitution, as they are trained especially to entertain men. If it were not that they are the legal property of their "owners" they would not be different from the ballet girls and the night club entertainers in our own America. But there is this great difference—while the American entertainers are specifically trained to put on a "front" of coquetry and animation in everything they do—the Geisha girls are trained never to show any animation on their faces whatever. However, in both cases, their behavior is a "stage front." The American ballet girls come on stage with blank faces until they get fully under the footlights when they put on a stylized smile; they too, are actors putting on a gay exterior but their vivaciousness does not stem from joy in their hearts. The Geisha girls may be smiling before they come on the stage, but when they get fully under the footlights their faces take on stylized masks. To watch an hour of entertainment by these Geisha girls was like watching animated dolls, indeed when it was all over I felt that I had been watching a puppet show for the entire hour. The banjo players who lined one side of the wall never moved their heads, all facing obliquely away from the stage so that not one action of the play could they see. The drum beaters along the opposite wall looked another way; no movement of the head, no expression on the face! How they could keep such immovability I could not imagine. As is my habit when watching the people in all these lands, I looked into face after face wondering what thoughts were hidden behind those expressionless masks; what deep feelings and yearnings were locked beneath those motionless shoulders.

These two sets of musicians were like the strophe and antistrophe of the ancient Greek chorus, and their singing and chanting were about all that was audible. The acting and dancing was slow and rhythmical, mostly in pantomime. Only occasionally did an actor speak and then only one or two words. Their faces were also as expressionless as masks; and then I recalled that in the Greek dramas the actors actually wore masks; and the word mask came to stand for the theatre.

As my mind was still centered on the process of producing pearls and saints, I suddenly realized that here, too, was a case of mass production. These Geisha girls all looked as expressionless as paper dolls stamped out on a printing press or as Ford cars turned out on a production line. What a contrast their lives must be to the joy-filled lives of the Christian girls working in the Mentholatum factory at the Omi Brotherhood!

When we reached Osaka we were invited to be the speakers at the noon luncheon of a group of business and professional leaders. Next to Kagawa and Merrel Vories the man I especially wanted to meet in Japan was Captain Fuchida who had led the raid on Pearl Harbor, which he himself has written up brilliantly in the February, 1954, *Reader's Digest*.

Imagine my surprise and joy when I found him sitting directly opposite me at the table. Imagine my still greater joy and surprise when the chairman announced that the Captain would give a fifteen minute talk while we were waiting for the dinner to be served. Another joy was to find Alice Grube, one of my loyal students of Macalester, 1930, and a missionary to Japan for over twenty years, seated at my left, quick to translate in my ear the speech of Captain Fuchida as fast as he gave it.

He told how kind and forgiving he found the people of America when he visited our mainland a few years ago, and how deeply impressed he was with the resolve of the Doolittle flyer, Sergeant Jacob De Shazer, to return to Japan and give his life to winning Japanese to Christ after being captured by the Japanese and confined and brutally treated in a prison camp. He spoke feelingly of the daughter of two missionaries to the Philippines, both of whom had been beheaded by the Japanese. What overpowered him was that he found the daughter had not only forgiven the Japanese but was planning to go as a missionary to bring them Christ as she felt they needed Him most.

"I could not understand such enemy-forgiving love," said the Captain. "Where did men find such love? I had never heard of people's returning good for evil. I desired to discover the source of this power that could remove hatred from the hearts of people and change them into friendly, loving individuals. I became more and more ashamed of my own revengeful spirit. When I found that a book called a Bible had changed many lives, I wondered if it might change mine. So I bought a Bible for myself.

"I started to read it. I became absorbed in it. When I came to the Gospel of Luke and faced the crucifixion of Christ I was amazed by his words, 'Father, forgive them for they know not what they do.' Jesus prayed for the very soldiers who were about to thrust a spear into his side!

"Here was the source of this miracle of love that can forgive enemies! Suddenly I could understand the story of the American girl whose parents had been slain. I could understand the transformation in Sergeant De Shazer's life. I am not ashamed to say that my eyes filled with tears. Immediately I accepted Jesus as my personal savior.

"I am positive of my conversion. There was a time when my back was turned to Christ, but now I look to Him in faith. I firmly believe that Christ is the only answer and the only hope of this world.

"Eleven years after Pearl Harbor! Little did I dream that eventful morning that my view of life would be so revolutionized. Today I am a Christian! I say it over and over again. This is the message I send to all mankind with a fervent prayer that there will be 'NO MORE PEARL HARBOR.'"

As I watched Captain Fuchida speak I realized that here was one who had found the Pearl Above Price. Here was one who was well on the way to becoming a "saint in the making," himself. Two people from America, an army sergeant and a woman missionary, had penetrated into the sensitive heart of one whose daring action had brought our nation into the World War. As the oyster, when impregnated with a globe of mussel shell, builds a perfect pearl about it, so this Japanese captain, whose soul had been impregnated by the forgiving spirit of these two Americans with spiritual muscle in their souls, was now experiencing the process of being changed from a son of the world into a Son of God.

I had a dream of Captain Fuchida's travelling with me some day from city to city, he speaking on NO MORE PEARL HARBOR, and I speaking on TRANSFORMING PEARL HARBOR INTO SOUL HARBOR. My heart was filled with a prayer that the Lord would raise up an army of religious leaders with enough "spiritual muscle" in their souls to create saints by the thousands, with hearts centered in the living Christ. Yes, Captain Fuchida is right. "Christ is the only answer and the only hope of the world."

CHAPTER XXVI

BUILDING BROTHERHOOD IN JAPAN

ONE MORNING I WAS INVITED BY ALICE GRUBE TO GIVE THE CHAPEL talk at the Presbyterian Academy for girls. This was a thrilling experience. I met the superintendent and the principal, and then, with the fifty teachers on the platform behind me and the fifteen hundred and fifty Japanese girls from thirteen to nineteen years of age in front of me, filling every seat of the auditorium, I talked for forty minutes. I wished that Roland's color camera had been there to record that sea of responsive faces.

Before we left Osaka we went to see the feudal lord's castle, greatest of its kind, and also went through a large department store built by Merrell Vories, more artistically appointed than Marshal Field's. On one occasion we met with fifty men representing the Democracy in Action Movement that had been established the year before by Melvin Evans of Chicago—a representative group of business and professional leaders of western Japan.

On another occasion we were guests of the Rotary Club. It so happened that the International Industrial Exhibit was on and representatives of manufacturing companies from all over the world were in the city. One-tenth of those present were guests from overseas, so while I was limited to fifteen minutes I was able to "tell the world" about our journey to build a Belt of Prayer around the world. As nine-tenths of the local members of this Rotary Club were Buddhists I was cautioned not to stress Jesus but to deliver a message of good will from America, which I did with all my heart. However, these single addresses do not produce pearls above price —they are like the random diving into the sea *hoping* that one or two pearls will be found among the scores of shells brought to the surface.

An approach to the Miki Moto's method of producing saints, as pearls, was granted us in a two-day Retreat of leading businessmen of western Japan, who took over a hotel in Nara for this purpose. This was another of the "Democracy in Action" groups established by Melvin Evans the previous year. Here we were again cautioned not to proselyte for Christianity, as most of the group were Buddhist, but to show how true religion worked out in practice. This was right along my line so in my opening address I told how Jesus and Buddha did not invent their laws, they merely stated laws that were as old and as permanent as the law of gravity and the law of the tides. I then told my parable of the bees. The bees' loyalty to the Queen, I compared with our loyalty to the King of Kings, expressing the first Great Commandment; the bees' teamwork exemplified Jesus' second Commandment, love for others. Then I closed with the story of the fanner bees which keep the hive sweet and clean.

Roland was perplexed about what he should say because his talks are all Christ-centered, but asking the Lord to guide him, he plunged into the redemptive love of Jesus in such a vital way that they were eager for us to tell more of the Jesus-way on the following morning.

In the discussion that followed, a Buddhist priest told how he had a House of Meditation and felt that many problems could be solved better by intuition following deep meditations than by controversy and discussion. I told how it had taken me thirty years to learn how to pray the Lord's Prayer which takes only thirty seconds to recite. My method is to take a single clause, "Give us the Kingdom of Heaven on earth as it is in heaven," and then meditate on my highest conception of what the Kingdom of Heaven would be like —with the constant presence of a Loving Father, the right friends, the right ideas, and the right supply. To achieve this, I said, often requires tremendous sacrifices, but who wouldn't sacrifice much to attain such ends? I told how Gandhi, who was not a Christian, applied the Sermon on the Mount and liberated a nation. The trouble with our religionists, I said, is that too many Christian ministers do not believe in prayer and too many Buddhist priests do not believe in meditation. The Buddhist priest's wife nodded her head emphatically, and to our joy, the Buddhist priest himself gave his assent to everything we had said about Jesus.

For reasons we could scarcely explain, these testimonials had a tremendous effect upon these businessmen, men who had spent their lives in a Buddhist community. As the discussion proceeded we were helped tremendously by some members of Kagawa's Consumer Cooperatives, and also by others who had contacted the Omi Brotherhood. When we told of the eight-hour "law" of the Omi Brotherhood, they confessed what they termed "the dilemma of Japan": Their laborers are not as dependable as the Christian laborers of the Omi Brotherhood are, they said, so that eight hours of work cannot produce enough to enable Japan to undersell on the world market as they are almost forced to do in order to get a share of world trade. I ended my evening talk by saying: "A sound diagnosis is half the cure. We now see clearly Japan's labor-production problem. Let us put it into the incubator overnight and see if God will send an inspired answer in the morning."

After the night's "incubation," things began to happen. New insights came through as to how to create a more ethically minded, responsible class of working men, in achieving which, Christianity might have an important contribution or, indeed, might furnish the chief motivation. Most of the morning was spent listening to executives tell how they were putting democracy into action, with some such goal in mind. I was amazed to hear a man who claimed no religion tell how carefully his company, before accepting any employees, put them through an aptitude test, and before the work began each day, they held a quiet meditation period for everyone. Toward the end of the morning the group asked me to summarize, and I gathered the threads together, and finally turned the session over to Roland, who ended on a very Christ-centered note. The men begged us to return next year to hold a seven-day spiritual camp in Japan, several of them saying they were now planning to become Christians. Out of Retreats such as this one (not the mere "one-night stands") we hope to see produced some pearls above price.

After the evening meeting Colonel Gladstone, the officer in charge of the army post in Nara, drove us to his home, where the family is reading *I Will Lift Up Mine Eyes* for the second time, and wanted our prayers. Not only did they get our blessing but they blessed us with the most wonderful lemonade and ice cream we had had since leaving home.

The following afternoon, when the Retreat closed with the noon luncheon, Colonel Gladstone and his son brought a guide and car and drove us to the Buddhist Shrine, the largest wooden building in the world, housing the largest seated Buddha in the world, a quite remarkable sight. Hundreds of school children in their school uniforms and thousands of grown-ups were climbing the hill and assembling in the temple. Then we went to the Shinto Shrine in another great park upon a high hill, where crowds were also coming and going. The road leading to this shrine was lined with iron lanterns and scores of tame deer were seen everywhere, perfectly willing to be petted or fed.

Returning to Tokyo, we went by train to the sea-side resort of Atami where Roland and I led a Retreat of business executives of the eastern section of Japan, in the same manner we had led leaders in the western area at Nara. Twenty clean-cut men, three-fifths of them Christian, listened with intense interest, with the result that many resolved henceforth to put Christian principles to work in their business. When men open themselves as completely to the message of Jesus as the oysters are opened up in the Miki Moto factory, some "pearls above price" are sure to be produced. Pearls were produced that day.

Young Mr. Mario Yoshida, son of a co-founder of the Omi Brotherhood, was our guide and interpreter. When the Retreat was over and after the men had come to the car to bid us farewell, Yoshida took us by taxi up into the mountains where we saw the queen of all the mountains of the world, glorious Fuji. She can be seen only two days out of ten, on an average, because the clouds love her so. Previously we had passed in her vicinity three times, only to see her shrouded in clouds, but this day was perfect, and Roland got many pictures. When you have seen the Taj Mahal, made by men, and Fuji, made by God, you have seen the two most exquisite works of art in the world, at least, so we felt. Fuji, by the way, means "Nothing more remains to be seen."

And now at last we were back in Tokyo for our final week in foreign lands. We were lodged in the Marunouchi Hotel in the heart of the city. The next morning Roland addressed seventy-five missionaries at their weekly breakfast prayer-meeting hour. On Sunday, Roland and I gave three addresses each and Marcia one, and the day closed with an immense reception at Chapel Center in honor of General Harrison, who had represented the United States at the Panmunjan Peace talks with the Northern Koreans and

Chinese. Only his faith in God could have kept him serene during that long ordeal, he claimed. At the reception he shared his honors with the Browns and me by having us stand beside him in the reception line. In their courteous Japanese way our hosts announced that the reception was in honor of our coming as well as of his leaving.

For the next four days we conducted an abbreviated Camp Farthest Out at the Tokyo Union Church, with devotion in motion and prayer laboratories in the afternoon and addresses and chalk talks in the evenings. Also on two days Roland and I gave chapel talks at Ayama College, and then for three days we gave three addresses a day in the Yodabajhi Japanese Church. The meetings in the Japanese church were held at ten, two, and seven each day and each meeting lasted for two hours as they insisted on getting everything they could from us. Folks from hundreds of miles around attended these meetings, fifty of whom were ministers. The series in the Union Church and in the Japanese church were of sufficient length, let us hope, for the Lord to produce a few real spiritual "pearls."

Wonderful missionaries from all over Tokyo attended the Union services. Most of the other meetings were arranged by the army chaplains who did all the presiding and made most of the plans. I had a special noon luncheon with these chaplains at which time I shared my dreams of recruiting an army of three hundred thousand pray-ers to help usher in a world of peace. Chaplains Crist, Warren, Blair, and Anderson will long remain in our hearts. I had a closer contact with them because they all had known and esteemed my nephew, Edward Elson, former director of chaplains in Europe and now pastor of President Eisenhower's Church in Washington.

Thursday, Starr Daily arrived from his speaking tour in the southern cities of Japan and we all had breakfast together. Starr's books, *Release* and *Good News,* have been translated into Japanese and have been widely spread by a new movement which is bringing Christ into Japan through the "back door" in such floods of enthusiasm that the results are amazing. Starr Daily had run away from home when he was eight, had spent twenty-five years in the underworld, fourteen of them in chain gangs and penitentiaries. Not until a vision came to him of Jesus was he converted. His life has been one of the most dramatic stories of modern times.

"I hear that crowds attend your meetings," I said.

"Crowds is not the word for it," Starr replied. "They come in *multitudes*. Whenever I arrive in a town the railroad station is filled with the throngs waving flags and singing songs. They sit on the floor by thousands in the meetings. All my available books are sold before the meetings even start. The big majority who come are youth. They are turning away from everything in the past— the traditions of church and state, and are ripe for something new."

"I suppose that makes them susceptible to Communism," I remarked.

"Yes," he replied, "and this movement is the best bulwark against Communism. Masaharv Taniquchi, the leader, is a genius in leading people. He has drawn thousands away from Communism into this movement. He seems to have unlimited money to finance it, and as a result, no offerings are taken at the meetings. Japan must have many men of wealth and they are pouring money into this cause."

Kagawa, as we were talking with him about our conversation with Starr the next day, said, "This 'House of Growth' movement, as it is called, has the best of Buddhism and the best of New Thought, and what it needs is for someone like Starr, who is Christ-centered, to fill it with the spirit of Jesus." Some of Starr's greatest meetings in Japan were in prisons which were thrown open to him everywhere. He said that the Japanese prison system is far better and more enlightened than the American system. "Why is America so loathe to put Christianity into anything but the church?" he exclaimed. "Why let un-Christian lands surpass us in the *practice* of Christianity?"

Our last day was a glorious climax for our world-wide journey. We spent it in the home of Toyohiko Kagawa. It was the only day he was in the city and the only day we had no appointments, one of those remarkable "coincidences" that seemed to follow us throughout this journey. Kagawa embraced us as old friends, and his wife, who understands no English, served us tea and cake, and before we left, brought us coffee. He is busy evangelizing, bringing scores to Christ every week. In his own church on the previous Sunday he had had thirty-seven conversions.

He took us into his back yard where two hundred children of preschool age were playing on slides, turning-poles, and swings, laughing and singing with ecstatic glee. He took us to the kindergarten rooms lined with cases filled with sea shells and stuffed birds of all varieties. Few birds get out to Japan, as they seem to fear the overseas flight, so he has made a great collection of them to educate the children. He asked Marcia to educate him in botany when he comes to the United States. She said, "That's a date!" Science is his hobby. At sixty-six his health is fairly good and he is constantly at work for his Lord.

Helen Topping, who had taken us to Kagawa's home, has inherited two big homes from her parents; one is only five minutes walk from Kagawa's house; the other is out in the country. One of these will care for thirty-five guests and nearby homes could care for one hundred and fifty people while the auditorium of the church nearby holds three hundred people, which Miss Topping thinks would be a good location for a camp sometime. Her mother founded an orphans' home in which we saw scores of little ones finding care and love.

One question Kagawa and I considered was whether two such diametrically opposite economic systems as Capitalism and Communism can work out a method of living amiably together. To accomplish this amity, we agreed, is a necessity, as the general consensus around the world is that it must be "co-existence or co-death." I expressed my belief that the English and Russian proposal of universal disarmament and removing the arena of conflict between Communism and Capitalism from the battlefield to the market place might be the most sensible solution if properly safe-guarded and supervised by the United Nations.

Kagawa said he would go a step further. Instead of two *different* economic systems *competing* to achieve world peace, he would see them *cooperating* which he seemed to think could be done through the economic cooperative movement. "Cooperatives would not do violence to either ideologies," he said, "and would, therefore, lay the most perfect foundation for a World Government."

"But, Dr. Kagawa," I questioned, "wouldn't America be the last nation to accept this plan? And I doubt if the Kremlin would open its doors to it either."

"Then we should pray about it," he said. "For practical politics, Dr. Clark, I believe the time has arrived in world history when we must apply the Bible to our international relations. The way to do it is to practice the Golden Rule through international economic cooperatives and international government, following the example of federalism achieved by the original Thirteen States in America.

Then I asked Kagawa his opinion about re-arming Japan.

"The greatest blessing that has come to Japan," he exclaimed, "was Article Nine of Japan's Constitution which states 'The Japanese people forever renounce war as a sovereign right of the nation and the threat or use of force as a means of settling international disputes. In order to accomplish this aim, arms will never be maintained.' No matter what happens hereafter, the history of Japan in the past eight years has been a milestone on the way to world peace.

"Dr. Clark, we do ask you to use all the influence in your power to persuade the Americans to permit us to live up to our Peace Constitution. I haven't time to tell you how many benefits in reconstruction of homes, food supply, education, and other life necessities will be cut off by a program of re-armament forced on an unwilling people just struggling to their feet again after the bombing of one hundred and nineteen Japanese cities. Hence the prayer-slogan with which we live, twenty-four hours of every day now: DON'T ABANDON THE PEACE CONSTITUTION. MAKE IT THE FOUNDATION FOR THE PEACE CONSTITUTION OF THE WORLD!"

Then the little man, with eyes half-closed, and head up-raised, spoke words that I wish all the world could hear:

"A typical modern state cumbered with heavy armament, but well nigh bereft of other values, reminds one of a naked savage, lugging about his javelin and poisoned arrows. States today seem nearer to barbarism than do individuals. By the renunciation of war, we in Japan have emerged from barbarism and are accorded a chance to make ourselves progressive and civilized. If only we might have done this ten years ago, history would have taken another course. But it is not too late for us. We are going to alter the definition of a 'great' state. A truly great state is not necessarily big, nor rich, nor quarrelsome with its neighbors. The great state is wise, moral, and Godfearing. We aim to make Japan a state with which God can be pleased. Thus only may we arrive at true civilization. Our new Constitution will then become a milestone in the attainment of world peace. For the first time in human history has the warning of Christ been heeded by a national government: 'They that take the sword shall perish by the sword.'"

That afternoon a half-dozen friends saw us off at the airport. One little boy, Gary Forrester, son of a missionary in whose home we had visited, a boy whose face was very like that of Sallman's "Boy Jesus," cried when he saw me going. I had taught him how to make a coin disappear in his ear and elbow, and he had listened intently to my talk on living in the Kingdom now. A little girl, after one of our talks, said, "If everyone was like you, we would have a better world." These are all the encomiums we need!

Soon we were flying toward the last of the Seven Islands on our magic carpet. We stopped at Wake Island and I wrote the following message on cards to my six precious children, "We are leaving Wake Island at six Saturday morning May first. We are due to arrive in Honolulu at four forty-five Friday afternoon April thirtieth. Thus our magic carpet was seemingly travelling faster than sound, arriving at one destination hours before we left the last."

In Hawaii we found that some sixty people from the American mainland had flown across to welcome us—the largest single party the island has ever known, according to records of the airplane company and hotel owners. While we conducted a camp made up of mainlanders and islanders, I took time sitting by the beach to do a lot of thinking. I call this the island of Phaeacia, which for Odysseus symbolized the "Island of the Soul," where there was perfect weather the year round, trees always in bloom, fruit and grain always in harvest, every need fulfilled. If the whole world could be brought into such harmony, what a heavenly world it would be! This island, situated as it is midway between two great continents, yes, between two great hemispheres, and above all, between two great ideologies, makes a splendid vantage point from which to contemplate impartially and fairly the problems of the world, and consider ways and means of solving them.

BOOK II

THREE WAYS OF SOLVING WORLD PROBLEMS

CHAPTER I

THE WAY OF WAR

THE THREE WAYS OF SOLVING WORLD PROBLEMS ARE GRAPHICALLY portrayed for us in the well-known story of Goldilocks. When her curiosity led her into the home of the bears (a replica of our materialistic world) the first things that caught her attention were three bowls of soup representing the three needs of mankind, the physical, the mental, and the spiritual, graduating in size from that which was most visible toward that which was most invisible. First she tried the big bowl, but it was too hot. Next she tried the middle-sized bowl, but it was too cold—the cold war proving as futile as the hot war. Last of all she tried the little bowl and it was just right; but, alas, there wasn't enough of it. That was the reason we were taking this journey around the world—to build a Belt of Prayer and thus to increase the size of the spiritual bowl so there'd be enough of the right thing to fill the need.

In the concluding chapters of this book I propose to take a close-up view of these three ways of solving world problems.

The first way—the way of war—has been tried and found wanting. It was found wanting five thousand years ago. "Woe to them that go down to Egypt for help;" warned Isaiah, "and stay on horses, and trust in chariots, because they are many; and in horsemen, because they are very strong; but they look not unto the Holy One of Israel, neither seek the Lord!" Failure to accept this advice led to Isaiah's captivity by Assyria from which the ten tribes never returned.

The war way was tried and found wanting in 1914–1918. Had the United States stayed out of the First World War, according to Winston Churchill, the war would have ended in a negotiated peace, a million French, English and German boys' lives would have been saved, and Communism would not have been born. It was tried and found wanting in 1941–1945. After that war was over, which cost us over three hundred thousand lives and over three billion dollars, we found ourselves in the absurd position of depending upon the very nations we had tried to destroy, Japan and Germany, to save us from the very nations we fought to save from destruction, China and Russia, who today are threatening to destroy us.

Every intelligent being today accepts as a truism the fact that, whether or not wars ever solved any problems in the past, they certainly do not solve any problems today. The most outstanding thing the First World War accomplished was to bring Communism to birth, and the most outstanding thing the Second World War accomplished was to spread its tentacles all over the world. The most outstanding thing a third world war will accomplish will be the tightening of those tentacles until free enterprise will be banished from the face of the earth. Win or lose makes no difference in the final outcome; wars create rubble and rubble is not propitious soil for free enterprise.

Let us take a realistic look at history. The philosophy of nations has been based upon "the survival of the fittest," and due to the blindness of their leaders, people have perverted that slogan to mean the survival of the best fighters, those most adept in destroying the lives of others. Opposed to that philosophy stands the completely contrasting slogan of Jesus, "The meek shall inherit the earth." Let us put these two slogans side by side and see which has won the verdict of history.

Where are the dinosaur and the saber-toothed tiger and the cave bear today? Not only have they become extinct but the gorillas and grizzly bears are gradually slipping off the scene, the lions and tigers are fading away, and the creatures that are surviving in vast numbers are the helpless cattle and sheep, those creatures that are meek, those creatures that serve.

In the same way the nations which once waxed great through the wielding of swords and spears are being replaced by nations who cooperate and serve. What were the conquering nations in ancient times? Egypt, Assyria, and Babylon? What do they amount to now; and where are the mighty Medes and Persians? Who flee today at the approach of the "Macedonian phalanx" and who tremble before the tramp of the "Roman Legions?" Spain no longer dominates the "Spanish Main," and Britain no longer is

"Mistress of the Seas." The great armies of Napoleon under the mightiest general that ever lived succeeded in only one thing—bringing France into a period of decadence from which she has never emerged. Half a million magnificent men, tall and strong, most of them over six feet in height, marched with Napoleon to Moscow and only twenty thousand came back. The French race today is two inches shorter than it was one hundred and fifty years ago.

The reason why Russia and the United States are the strongest fighting nations today is because they are the two nations that have rarely used their fighting strength for anything but defensive wars. But unless these two nations rise above the jungle methods of imposing their ideologies upon the world, their lights, too, will go out. The survival of the fittest is still the slogan that nations live by, but it will remain a snare and a delusion, leading nations to destruction, unless the word *fittest* is properly redefined, not as the fighters but as the lovers; not those who combat but those who cooperate; not the proud but the meek. Yes, Jesus gave the best formula for survival when He said, "The meek shall inherit the earth."

Never in modern times has the futility of war been so dramatically portrayed than in the speech which General Douglas MacArthur gave at a banquet following the unveiling of a statue in his honor sponsored by the Los Angeles Council of the American Legion in celebration of his seventy-fifth birthday:

"War started in a modest enough way as a sort of gladiatorial method of settling disputes between conflicting tribes," the General began. "At the turn of the century, when I entered the Army, the target was one enemy casualty at the end of a rifle or bayonet or sword. Then came the machine gun designed to kill by the dozen. After that, the heavy artillery raining death upon the hundreds. Then the aerial bomb to strike by the thousands—followed by the atom explosion to reach the hundreds of thousands. Now, electronics and other processes of science have raised the destructive potential to encompass millions. And with restless hands we work feverishly in dark laboratories to find the means to destroy all at one blow.

"The present tensions with their threat of national annihilation are kept alive by two great illusions. The one, a complete belief on the part of the Soviet world that the capitalist countries are preparing to attack them; that sooner or later we intend to strike. And the other, a complete belief on the part of the capitalistic countries that the Soviets are preparing to attack us; that sooner or later they intend to strike. *Both are wrong.*

"Each side, so far as the masses are concerned, is equally desirous of peace. For either side war with the other would mean nothing but disaster. Both equally dread it. But the constant acceleration of preparation may well, without specific intent, ultimately produce a spontaneous combustion.

"I am sure that every pundit in the world, every cynic and hypocrite, every paid brainwasher, every egotist, every troublemaker, and many others of entirely different mould, will tell you with mockery and ridicule that this can be only a dream—that it is but the vague imaginings of a visionary.

"But, as David Lloyd George once said in Commons at the crisis of the First World War, 'We must go on or we will go under.' And the great criticism we can make of the world's leaders is their lack of a plan which will enable us 'to go on.'

"I recall so vividly this problem when it faced the Japanese in their new Constitution. They are realists; and they are the only ones that know by dread experience the fearful effect of mass annihilation. They realize in their limited geographical area, caught up as a sort of No Man's Land between two great ideologies, that to engage in another war, whether on the winning or losing side, would spell the probable doom of their race. And their wise old Prime Minister, Shidehara, came to me and urged that to save themselves they should abolish war as an international instrument. When I agreed, he turned to me and said:

"'The world will laugh and mock us as impractical visionaries, but one hundred years from now we will be called prophets.'

"Sooner or later the world, if it is to survive, must reach this decision. The only question is, when? Must we fight again before we learn? *When will some great figure in power have sufficient imagination and moral courage to translate this universal wish—which is rapidly becoming a universal necessity—into actuality?*

"We are in a new era. The old methods and solutions no longer suffice. We must have new thoughts, new ideas, new concepts, just as did our venerated forefathers when they faced a New World.

"We must break out of the straight jacket of the past. There must

always be one to lead, and we should be that one. We should now proclaim our readiness to abolish war in concert with the great powers of the world. The result might be magical."

The Way of War to solve world problems has been tried and found wanting. Let us turn next to the Way of Adjustment.

CHAPTER II

THE WAY OF ADJUSTMENT

A. *ADJUSTMENT OF ECONOMICS:*

AS ALL THE WARS OF THE PAST TWO CENTURIES, ACCORDING TO WOODrow Wilson, have been commercial wars, and as the center of contention between Communism and Capitalism has revolved around divergent techniques of economics, I could see that Kagawa was right. Before we can end war we must resolve our economic tensions.

Two possible solutions to this problem were outlined before me on this journey which I shall try to present briefly here, and let the reader meditate on their merits.

(1) The first is Kagawa's conception of Cooperatives as the ideal bridge to span the chasm that separates these two opposing Ideologies of the East and West. Could Cooperatives do for the world what they had done for Sweden? The Cooperative Movement in Sweden seems to have served as the fulcrum to hold the extremes in her economic life in balance, much as the Royal Family in Great Britain had served as a fulcrum to hold the extremes in her political life in balance?

Here is the picture of Sweden. Let us compare it with the picture of the world.

Swedish business leans to the right, deplores raids upon private enterprise, is wary of extravagance in public expenditure, and is alarmed by governmental excursions into business. Labor leans to the left, demands social security against the ravages of disease, accident, and old age and unemployment. The Swedish worker demands larger wages and shorter hours, but he knows these will be won by the slow reordering of industry and not by a legislative fiat. Swedish Labor knows how to fight but, having won an acceptable compromise, the fighting mood disappears. It will shake fists when necessary, but it knows how to shake hands. The harmonious balance between capital and labor that makes business relations run so smoothly in Sweden is largely due to the fact that the Swedish economic teeter-totter has a fulcrum, and that fulcrum is the Consumer Cooperatives.

The people who make up these Cooperatives have forged a weapon with which to rout the monopolists, regardless of which end of the scales they occupy, Capital or Labor. The Cooperative Union has become a cudgel of democracy for forcing the unruly to respect the rights of the consumer. When the Cooperative Union took over the Three Crowns Mill in Stockholm and the Three Lions Mill in Gothenburg, which were drawing dividends of 20 per cent to 35 per cent, the price of flour was lowered all over Sweden. The Cooperative Union slashed a dollar and twenty cents from the price of galoshes by the simple expedient of opening one small factory. It took only one bright new electric bulb factory on the Stockholm skyline to drop the price from thirty-seven to seventeen cents. When anyone buys oranges, coffee, tires, bread, and a host of other things he is reminded of the power of the Cooperative Union.

But the destruction of monopolies does not tempt the cooperatives to build monopolies of their own. The leaders of the cooperative movement have learned that they can determine national price levels by the control of from 5 to 25 per cent of the national supply of the commodity under scrutiny. This is the Swedish yardstick method. They fight private monopolies, but they fight with no less vigor the moves to increase government monopolies. Possessing no monopolies of their own and aspiring to none, they produce only enough goods to determine prices, no more. Private business continues and flourishes, but the consumers play the tune to which private business must march.

"One of the most hopeful things about Cooperatives as an influence for world peace," according to Kagawa, "is that they have mastered the secret of working effectively across national lines. The Swedish groups have joined their bargaining power effectively and continuously with the Cooperatives of Norway, Denmark, and Finland and are strengthening their lines of cooperation with England and all of Europe."

Since wherever Cooperatives thrive Communism is unable to take root, there is good ground for believing that if Cooperatives can spread over Europe fast enough the entire continent will be more secure against the inroads of Communism than all the efforts being made by our State Department to establish a solid armed front. If that should ever be achieved, then Cooperatives might become the bridge Kagawa hoped they might be to span the chasm that separates the two Ideologies of East and West.

(2) But since Cooperatives have not reached that strategic place of power in this country they have in Scandinavian countries and since their value would also have to be "sold" to the Communists, neither side seems ready and ripe for Cooperatives on a world scale. Would it, therefore, be feasible to accept the challenge of Malenick, head of Russia's economy, to exchange the contest in arms for a contest in economic systems?

If an agreement should be made among the nations of the world that a moratorium be declared on war for twenty-five years, and the Communistic and Capitalistic systems enter into a thirty year peace-time competition to prove to the world which way is best, we would find ourselves entering into a contest for which, in its early stages, Communism might be better prepared than Capitalism.

At the very outset, free enterprise would find itself facing a similar situation to the one that brought our undoing in 1929. Twelve million unemployed was our problem then; twenty million unemployed might be our problem when all the men in uniform and all the workers in munition plants would be released into the industrial world. When news came of the death of Stalin and the mere *possibility* of peace loomed up, Wall Street values dropped eight billion dollars. If we could adjust our American economy so that all those workers released by de-militarization could be absorbed into our economic body, I am confident free enterprise would win the race. However, to achieve this absorption of unemployed labor our nation would have to become as well organized to "wage peace" as today it is organized to wage war. It might require the emptying of the Pentagon building of its experts on war and filling it with an army of experts on peace.

Capitalism's very efficiency has often proved its liability, for it is the only system in which production can exceed consumption. The biggest problem we would face in this contest would be how to correlate our over-production with adequate distribution so as to prevent wide-spread unemployment and the consequent depression. We have already made long strides in that direction but we would have to complete the job in a hurry if we would hope to win the contest. Our continually broadening welfare programs and in addition such blessings as Social Security, old age pensions, unemployment insurance, and Federal Reserve Banks are already giving us an internal security unequalled except in the Scandinavian countries where they have practically mastered the problem through their international cooperatives. We would need to bring into effective play all the "shock absorbers" already devised to prevent another major depression and add to them a thousand more. Indeed we would need to find a genius who could do for the field of economics what Edison did for the field of electricity. To do this job we would need a man of the stature and character of Paul Hoffman who believes "the United States economy is a *mutual* Capitalism, a widely shared Capitalism sparked by all the people who could contribute to the job, as opposed to the outmoded Capitalism of Europe which crumbles before the first shock of Communism.

"With only 6 percent of the world's people," Hoffman reminds us, "the United States produces a third of the world's total goods, and almost half of its manufactured goods." He believes free enterprise can furnish an equitable distribution of these goods, not by taking something away from those who have and giving to them who have not but through devising new ways of equitable distribution of newly created wealth. To win this contest against Communism it must use to the full what Hoffman calls its "unique capacity for change." "It rolls with the punches," he says. "It continues to evolve, undertaking major changes in every decade. It remains pioneering and flexible. Marxism claims to be the wave of the future, whereas in reality it is more rigidly reactionary than any right-wing Capitalistic economy of which I have knowledge.

"There is no economy on earth," Paul Hoffman continues, "that begins to compare with free enterprise from the standpoint that decisions are made by the many rather than the few. Communism depends upon such tight little monopoly that before long only those few in that minority group are capable of making decisions." With a man like Paul Hoffman as five-star general conducting a campaign with wisdom, justice, and foresight, I believe the free enterprise system would ultimately win the world. But if an extreme right-wing or extreme left-wing general were placed in charge, the outcome might be disastrous. For this contest would not be staged on a bed of roses; it would be the most decisive contest of all time— we might reasonably say a veritable matter of life and death.

Once get this competition transferred from the battlefield to the market place, then, just as in football, rival teams would be glad to appropriate any new technique learned from their rivals. We might actually learn something from each other. Unless Communism were satisfied to lag hopelessly behind in this race, it would have to adopt some of the incentives and rewards of Capitalism and some of its adaptability for cooperation and change. On the other hand there are undoubtedly places where our profit system and freedom of enterprise might learn some valuable lessons in controlling the forces of materialism that threaten our own national life.

For instance, the most glaring evil in our present day profit system, which has undoubtedly injured our nation the most on the home front as well as in the eyes of the world, is our enslavement to the Addiction Trusts. Of the sixty-five million drinkers of alcoholic liquors in America, three million, seven hundred thousand are hopeless addicts. As leprosy was the most hopeless and the most despised affliction in the days of Jesus, alcoholism is the most hopeless affliction in America today. "I would rather have cancer than be an alcoholic," remarked a famous doctor, "for cancer is the more curable of the two."

In contrast to the three million in slave camps of Russia are three million seven hundred thousand hopeless American liquor slaves in a worse hell than Russian camps. An addict friend of mine forged my name with the definite purpose of being sent to the penitentiary. I wanted to withdraw the charge but he begged me to let the law take its course. "My only protection from this hell I am in is to get behind bars." He was in for two years. Unfortunate for him that he was not incarcerated longer. He was let out when I was away from the city and committed suicide! My beloved cousin and boyhood chum, not able to resist the temptation to drink, under the constant lure of liquor advertisements, blew his brains out. Were the Russians ever any more completely under the dictatorship of Stalin than our Congress is today under the dictatorship of John Barleycorn?

Are the three million slaves in Russian camps any more unfortunate than the three million and more slaves of our Addiction Trusts? Indeed, so obedient is our government to its master, Mr. Alcohol-Tobacco Trusts, that it furnishes six cans of beer every week to each soldier boy and all the cigarettes he can smoke. Several mothers have told me they would have been far happier if their boys had been killed instantaneously on the battlefield—an honorable quick death—than to have them come home hopeless addicts dying a slow death and bringing misery and tragedy upon their families. Boys who have never smoked or drunk previous to entering the armed services often come home confirmed addicts.

In our much touted free enterprise, democratic nation, one-third of all crime, half the divorces, and half of all accidents are caused by excessive drinking. Daily slaughter on our highways resulting from excessive drinking far exceeds the daily casualties when the war in Korea was at its height. More people were killed in automobile accidents upon our highways in the past thirty years than in *all* the wars in which America has participated in its entire history.

The pollution of our American life by the over-growth of the Addiction Trusts is only one evil, although it is probably the most glaring one, that we must bring under control if we want to win the race against Communism as the best way of life.

People in other lands have often said to me, "Russia and China have their Iron Curtain, but the United States has her Dollar Curtain."

It is time to take both Iron and Gold off the pedestal and put God there instead. Perhaps a contest between Capitalism and Communism might be a good thing. It might result in a good housecleaning for both of us.

B. *ADJUSTMENT OF IDEOLOGIES:*

The first step taken toward World Peace was the creating of the United Nations. Because the organization has disappointed some of its friends and antagonized its enemies, many have been wondering if something important in its construction has been left out. The best answer to that question will come when we compare the steps with which the United Nations was established, with the steps taken to convert a loose federation of colonies into the United States of America.

Before we adopted a Constitution for the United States we made clear our purposes in the Declaration of Independence. That Declaration became the anchor and goal of every step our nation has taken since. It was the initial step that made all subsequent steps sound and sure. Because we have neglected that initial step the history of the United Nations has been filled with confusion and conflict, with the Veto holding the center of the stage.

When the nations of the world met in San Francisco in 1945 they prepared the Constitution first, and neglected entirely the step that should have preceded it—the preparing of a *Declaration of Interdependence.* The time has come when the step that was omitted years ago should be taken now. If we could secure world-wide acceptance of such a Declaration much of the present clash in Ideologies might be resolved.

The ground work for this basic and fundamental step has already been laid. Over three hundred persons from fifty countries have studied, amended, and approved such a Declaration which I would commend to your attention at this time. The reason I believe it has the germ of reality and permanence about it is because it came not as a formal statement of diplomats, but has welled up from the hearts of individuals everywhere, of whom you who read this book can well be one. The aim is to establish continuing relationships across frontiers among men of good will living under all conditions.

It aims to engender a feeling of participation in a worldwide invisible fellowship united by common aspirations.

The Declaration stands squarely on moral and religious principles common to the great world religions. The Preamble and the Compact seek to increase faith and allay fear. The Program presents a sound structure upon which a free world may firmly stand.

The Declaration of Interdependence is not to be attached to any political party, personage, or particular nation. It aims to be an international document arrived at by wide consultation.

DECLARATION OF INTERDEPENDENCE

PREAMBLE

We men and women of different races and religions, children of a Supreme Being through whom all men are brothers, unite our needs and aspirations in this Declaration of Interdependence.

No man, no people can stand alone. Out of union of diverse elements we will form durable partnerships to withstand the pressures of conflict. The killing of millions would not diminish the mutual distrust of the survivors. Therefore, we seek to be trustworthy and to find men worthy of our trust. With the ocean's strength and the mountain's patience we will stand together in creative faith that a free and peaceful world is attainable through cooperative action.

Faith is like the bird that feels the coming light and sings when the dawn is still dark. Faith is the substance of things hoped for, the evidence of things not seen. With such faith we will use the increasing human interdependence of modern times for peaceful progress.

Realizing that man does not live by bread alone and that material progress cannot produce peace or the good life, we offer ourselves as partners in the following interlocking program:

PROGRAM

We declare our common purpose to:

Exercise reverence for life and human dignity, abolish racial barriers, and repudiate all doctrines of supposed superiority based upon national origin, color, creed, sex, or class. People are more alike than they are different.

Foster mutual understanding and respect for one another's beliefs and cultural values. Many keys are required to unlock all the gates of truth and beauty.

Uphold freedom to think, to read, to listen, to look, to speak, to assemble. Freedom of information and freedom of expression are not rights only but tools with which to create a way of life. Opinions, like the roots of a tree, require nourishment from all sides. There is no substitute for an open mind. Mutual confidence can be approached only through open minds and reliance upon free discussion. The earth is strewn with the ruins of great powers, but great ideas survive and ultimately rule the world.

Increase the opportunity of each individual to overcome ignorance and illiteracy. Famine and poverty are their result; it is hard to make an empty sack stand upright. We will press for universal elementary schooling and fundamental education.

Achieve for youth of every land the opportunity to unfold creative talents, to realize noble dreams, and enjoy fruitful, unthreatened lives.

Promote physical and mental health of all peoples as fundamental for the attainment of peace and security. Prevention is better than cure.

Work for equality of opportunity—economic, social, and political—for men and women alike.

Protect the individual against suppression or exploitation by those misusing political or economic power. Each individual is the ultimate minority. To protect minorities is to safeguard each human being. Government has evolved for the benefit of the individual, not the individual for the benefit of government.

Eliminate forced labor.

Secure freedom of association and the right of workers to form unions to bargain collectively through representatives of their own choosing, without interfering with the rights of employers.

Favor the progressive participation of subject populations in the business and government of their native lands.

Assist subject peoples toward self-government and self-determination of their changing relationships to an ever widening commonwealth.

Support land reform and relieve tillers of the soil from unjust forms of land tenure, however imposed. Injustices eat away the foundations of human relations. The impoverishment of any area is of concern to all. Peace to be durable must be endurable.

Lower trade barriers, which reduce the flow of goods essential for raising standards of living throughout the world. Whether people eat or starve depends in part upon how widely goods can be exchanged with mutual gain. Many confluent streams of trade are needed to form a world-wide flow of employment; therefore, we oppose discriminatory trade practices, which diminish access to markets and to supplies of goods and services.

Explore workable approaches to strengthen human relations through economic unions and political federations.

Encourage our respective governments to work together in cooperation for the solving of social and humanitarian problems, and the upholding of fundamental human rights and freedoms for all.

Seek a substitute for the illusion of military victory. We do not place our main reliance upon the military power of the state or alliance to which we belong. Spiritual power is superior to physical power. Wars are world disasters and after total war the distinction between victor and vanquished grows less and less.

Reject all propaganda from home or abroad which seeks to justify aggression.

Melt the cold barriers of distrust now creeping over the earth like a glacier. We enlist in a personal campaign against fear, bitterness, and prejudice, and we ask that as much thought and effort be given to the art of increasing understanding as is being given to the means of increasing fear and hatred. Through enlightenment, understanding, and cooperation we will eradicate the roots of war and plant seeds of mutual aid in the fertile soil of good will.

Advocate progressive mutual disarmament with adequate safeguards. War is not inevitable. Men are not created to destroy one another, but to work together on their never-ceasing task to build a better world.

Strengthen the United Nations and encourage its evolution as a center for harmonizing the actions of nations in the attainment of these common ends.

COMPACT *

Believing that with the assistance of divine guidance we shall succeed,

Knowing that it is better to light a candle than to curse the darkness,

Desiring to help one another to mount, step by step, toward these high summits of human aspiration, and

Voicing the longings of all people for peace, freedom, justice, and security with equal rights for all and special privileges for none,

We hereby agree as partners to champion and cherish the Declaration of Interdependence, its aims and ideals.

---

* The three hundred persons who drew up this Declaration, representing fifty nations, signed their names to this Compact.

Those desiring separate copies of this Declaration of Interdependence send to Otto Tod Mallery, President Interdependence Council, Inc., 9006 Crefeld Street, Philadelphia (18), Pennsylvania, U. S. A.

See Appendix B.

CHAPTER III

THE FINAL STEP TOWARD WORLD
PEACE: *PRAYER*

THERE WAS A TIME WHEN KNUTE ROCKNE, THE FAMOUS COACH OF Notre Dame, started every game with his reserves, holding back his first team until the game was well under way. Some other coaches adopted the same method until in one game a coach held back his first team too long with the consequence that he lost the game. Our nation can well derive a lesson from this mistake.

The story of Goldilocks reveals three ways of solving world problems: the physical, the mental, and the spiritual. Referring back to the football analogy I would rank these three ways as follows: The armed forces, the third team; the diplomats, the second team; and the spiritual forces, the first team. The goal of the "game" is to cross the white line that leads to world peace. The armed forces have borne themselves well but they have not succeeded in crossing the coveted white line. Our diplomats have done a worthy job but they have not succeeded in reaching the goal either. If there was ever a time in history when the first team was needed in the game it is now.

Our President fortunately is more aware of that fact than most of us. As Commander-in-Chief of our Armed Forces and Director of our Diplomatic Corps he has handled the second and third teams well, but he is evidently not going to make the mistake of holding out his first team too long. In all of my years of playing and coaching football I have never been so thrilled as I was when our President stood before the "first team" assembled in Evanston, Illinois, August 19, 1954 under the auspices of the World Council of Churches, and addressed them with more vigor and drive than I have ever heard a coach address men before.

"We know that there is no true and lasting cure for world tensions in guns and bombs," he began. "We know that only the

241

spirit and mind of man, dedicated to justice and right, can in the long term enable us to live in the confident tranquillity that should be every man's heritage.

"You can strengthen our faith that men of goodwill, working together, can solve the problems confronting us. Faith is the mightiest force that man has at his command. It impels human beings to greatness in thought and word and deed. Now ours is a time when great things must again be dared in faith.

"Today, the campaign for a just and lasting peace desperately needs the lifting and transforming power that comes from men and women the world over, responding to their highest allegiances and to their best motives.

"How can we help strike this spark of dedication in receptive hearts around the earth?

"THE GOAL SHOULD BE NOTHING SHORT OF INVITING EVERY SINGLE PERSON IN THE WORLD WHO BELIEVES IN THE POWER OF A SUPREME BEING TO JOIN IN A MIGHTY, SIMULTANEOUS, INTENSE ACT OF FAITH. THAT ACT OF FAITH MIGHT TAKE THE FORM OF A PERSONAL PRAYER BY THE HUNDREDS UPON HUNDREDS OF MILLIONS DELIVERED SIMULTANEOUSLY AND FERVENTLY FOR THE DEVOTION, WISDOM, AND STAMINA TO WORK UNCEASINGLY FOR A JUST AND LASTING PEACE. IF THIS MASS DEDICATION LAUNCHED AN UNENDING CAMPAIGN FOR PEACE, SUPPORTED CONTINUOUSLY BY PRAYER, I AM CERTAIN WONDROUS RESULTS WOULD ENSUE."

Note the tremendous emphasis in that last paragraph: *"Nothing short* of inviting"—whom? *"Every single person* in the world who believes in the Power of a Supreme Being." To do what? *"Join in a mighty, simultaneous act of faith."* And how many people? *"Hundreds upon hundreds of millions."* And what should they pray for? *"For the devotion, wisdom, and stamina to work unceasingly for a just and lasting peace."* Then note this cumulative climax: *"If this mass dedication launched an unending campaign for peace, supported continuously by prayer,"* what would be the outcome? *"Wondrous results would ensue."*

There is the call.

What will be the response?

A clear cut answer was given in a resolution unanimously adopted at the Annual Meeting of the Board of Managers of the General Department of United Church Men of the National Council of Churches of Christ in the United States of America, at St. Louis, Missouri, November 6, 1954. It is entitled OUR ACT OF FAITH.

"The time for decisive action is at hand.

"The manner in which people of good-will now respond to the appalling needs of mankind throughout the world may well determine whether our civilization is headed toward the horror of global annihilation or toward its most glorious hour.

"At such a time, the United Church Men, who seek to follow the Prince of Peace, have a solemn obligation. We must demonstrate by our devotion and our deeds that we are among those who are willing to dare and share in meeting the needs of the hour.

"The President of the United States has reminded us in his historic address before the World Council of Churches that 'Ours is a time when great things must again be dared in faith.'

"He further stated that such an 'Act of Faith' would comprise these things:

" 'Personal prayer for the devotion, wisdom, and stamina to work unceasingly for a just and lasting peace;

" 'Unceasing and universal study of the principal factors in the global problems that seem to impede progress toward peace;

" 'New projects for defeating the despair and suffering and hopelessness in which millions now live.'

"We would associate ourselves whole-heartedly with this inspired plan of living prayer for a just and durable peace.

"We, therefore, in meeting assembled, call upon the churchmen of America to lead in such a three-fold program of prayer, of study, and of action for peace. We ask that the men's work bodies in each of our constituent Communions set themselves to the task of implementing such a program.

"In an undertaking so vast and so urgent we invite all peoples of whatever creed, culture, or nationality to have a part.

"With confident assurance that this is yet our Father's world, we humbly and earnestly dedicate ourselves to this, our 'Act of Faith.' "

A group of church leaders, government leaders, and people of influence from all over the nation met for three days of discussion and prayer at the Koinonia Foundation outside of Baltimore to discuss some of the most effective ways by which we could "set ourselves to implement such a program."

Frank Laubach, the great apostle of literacy, who has taught two hundred nations how to read, opened the meeting with these significant words: "For ten years the Communists have been winning a strange kind of war infiltration of every country with propaganda. They arouse the unhappy, under-privileged people and organize them to overthrow their government by violence or by elections. They have won the most fantastic victories in the history of the world. In four years they captured China, one-fourth of the human race, with this war of promises, and Russia never lost a man! They are still infiltrating through Asia and Africa and Latin America and Europe, boring as termites bore where wood is dead and rotten. They promise food to the hungry people. They promise land to the landless people. They offer the dissatisfied people of Asia and Africa anything they want. Four-fifths of the people are illiterate and hungry and deep in debt, and Communist promises sound like music from heaven. These illiterates have no way of knowing that they are being lured into even worse slavery than they have known. They do not know that after the iron curtain falls over a country the Communists abandon their gentle wooing and simply liquidate everybody who opposes them. Tens of millions of ignorant, unhappy people are capitulating each year before the false promises of the Communists throughout Asia, Africa, Latin America, and Europe.

"We have not worked out an adequate, all round strategy to meet this tremendous Communist offensive of propaganda. Our soldiers and airfields and warships are powerless to stop this infiltration of propaganda. Indeed, the Communists point to these as the proof that we are oppressors. Nor will it do any good to tell the four-fifths of Asia and Africa who are hungry and unhappy that 'The Communists are lying, stay where you are,' for there is an ever increasing demand among the masses to come up out of their poverty, and they look upon any person who tells them to 'lie still' as their enemy.

"Our only answer to the Communist weapon is TO PROVE THAT WE ARE THEIR FRIENDS AND THAT WE WILL HELP THEM OUT OF POVERTY AND MISERY. And our

CAMP FARTHEST OUT, KOTOYAM, INDIA, during lecture by Glenn Clark. Interpreter standing beside him.

CAMP FARTHEST OUT, JAFFNA, CEYLON: Glenn Clark, E. Stanley Jones, Roland Brown, Selvaretnum, D. T. Niles.

TEACHERS AT UDUVIL GIRLS ENGLISH SCHOOL, who attended the Camp Farthest Out, Jaffna, Ceylon. Marcia Brown and Lucy Clark at extreme left.

STUDENTS AT HONGKONG BAPTIST THEOLOGICAL SEMINARY. Reading front row, fourth from left: Victor Frank, Roland Brown, Maurice Anderson, Glenn Clark.

CAMP FARTHEST OUT, BAGUIO, LUZON, PHILIPPINES.
Center front, Presiding Bishop Enrique C. Sobrepena.

CHILDREN OF THE TYAL TRIBE in front of Presbyterian
Church in a mountain village of Aborigines, Formosa. In back
row: Glenn Clark, Marilyn Dickson, Everlasting Life (Pastor of the
Church). The tattoo marks on face of woman at right indicate that
she is a married woman whose husband was a head hunter. Second
from her to the left is one of the most spiritual women in Formosa,
who has won scores of people to Jesus Christ.

CHURCH AT GOVERNMENT LEPERSARIUM, Taipei, Formosa, erected and supervised by Rev. and Mrs. James Dickson.

THE BLUE-ROBED CHOIR at the Leper Church, Taipei, Formosa. This is one of three choirs.

GLENN CLARK AND LILLIAN DICKSON, Taipei, Formosa.

GLENN CLARK, MERRELL VORIES, ROLAND BROWN, HACHIRO YUASA, President of International Christian University, Tokyo, Japan.

KOKICHI MIKIMOTO, world-famous "Pearl King," sitting between Glenn Clark and Marcia Brown, at his home on Pearl Island near Shima, Japan. Picture taken a few months before he died at the age of 95.

DEVOTION IN MOTION at Omi Hachiman School, Japan. Marcia Brown, back to camera, in center circle. Mrs. Merrell Vories interpreting from platform.

INDUSTRIALISTS OF EASTERN JAPAN at a two-day retreat, Atami, Japan. We lectured to two such groups, the other in Western Japan, both organized into a DIA (Democracy in Action) a year before by Melvin Evans.

TOYOHIKO KAGAWA WITH SOME OF HIS SCHOOL CHIL-
DREN, in the yard behind his residence.

TOYOHIKO KAGAWA with Glenn Clark and Roland Brown at
his residence in Tokyo.

attack against very real hunger and misery and injustice and hate must be as well integrated and as thorough as the magnificent program of the War Department in the Pentagon is against a possible atomic war.

"To do this effectively we should have a Pentagon of World Friendship as competent and as effective as the War Pentagon, which is the most efficient and effective and at present the most powerful organization in America.

"Why is the Pentagon so effective?

"Each year a competitive examination is opened to the smartest young men in America, and those who excell are sent to West Point and Annapolis where they receive the most intensive training and discipline offered anywhere in the world. When they graduate they are superbly prepared for commanding armies and navies and for winning wars.

"Some of the most brilliant officers from West Point and Annapolis are selected to work day after day in the Pentagon in Washington, pinpointing maps of the world to build a vast and powerful military strategy. The Pentagon with tireless zeal keeps up-to-the-minute plans to threaten the enemy and to destroy him if war should break out. Our country has such confidence in these men that Congress gives them almost any appropriation, however astronomical, to provide the armaments they request. Thanks to their consumate efficiency, an attack from Russia with atomic weapons seems less likely each month.

"But all these armaments are as futile against Russian propoganda as the Maginot Line was against the German invasion. This is why we need urgently and at once a highly efficient and powerful Pentagon of World Friendship and Service.

"We would have to be very careful in selecting the persons for this Pentagon of World Friendship—men and women who are as skilled in friend-making as the generals are skilled in war-making. They should be as free from prejudices and biases as the Supreme Court and the War Pentagon are supposed to be. They would have but one objective—to study and achieve World Friendship and Peace—to gain and hold friends. They would not be hurried. They would have time to think long and deeply through and around every problem. They would give careful consideration to every reasonable proposal.

"They would meet in or near the Congressional Library, where they would have available the best staff of research assistants. They would work with the best maps and the best methods of pinpointing the world's needs. They would call into their meetings day after day every possible type of organization, public and private, to help answer the question of building World Friendship."

I did not quote all of President Eisenhower's address before the World Council of Churches. His closing words made a perfect climax to Laubach's appeal for a Pentagon of World Friendship.

"There would be initiated," said President Eisenhower, "unceasing and universal study of the principal factors in the global problems that seem to impede progress toward peace. There would be generated a support for honest and devoted world leaders that would inspire them to plumb new depths of knowledge and understanding, and seek new paths toward conciliation. There would spring forth and be carried out new projects for defeating the despair and suffering and hopelessness in which millions now live. And the destruction of the conditions that shrivel the soul and starve the body would add new millions to the soldiers of the faith, the faith that the children of God can live if they so will, in the climate and the relationships that mean justice and decency and peace for all. The time has come when for mankind there is no substitute for a just and lasting peace."

This proposal of a Pentagon of World Friendship interested me so much that, accompanied by Roland Brown, I later made a careful but hasty inspection of the Pentagon Building in Washington. I found it occupied by thirty thousand full-time workers, and indeed consisting of a little city all in itself. It is the world's largest office building, twice as large as the Merchandise Mart in Chicago, with three times the floor space of the Empire State Building. The National Capitol could fit into any one of the five wedge-shaped sections. The distance around the outer edge of the building is one mile, but the total length of the corridors of the Pentagon is seventeen and a half miles.

We had the privilege of meeting and talking with leaders in all phases of war preparation, but the climax came when we reached the office of Dr. Lombard, head of the scientific research in nuclear fission. When we arrived outside his office door we saw that he was in conference with the leading researchers in America in nuclear materials and hesitated to intrude upon him. But when he was told that we were outside he rushed out and seized both our hands, exclaiming, "Just before you arrived we had come to the conclusion that this nation will never be saved by military force, but only by spiritual power."

After that experience and after talking with many of the chaplains who hold religious meetings in the building every noon for Catholics, Protestants, and Jews I realized that it wouldn't take many alterations to convert one-tenth of this great building into a Pentagon of Peace. Following the precedent of tithing wouldn't it be wonderful if one-tenth of the space, one-tenth of the personnel, and one-tenth of the appropriations were devoted to building World Friendship!

But why wait upon government to make these changes? There is a Higher Government to which we can make our appeal right now. For many years many people have been petitioning the government to add a Department of Peace to the Cabinet. Our chief argument was that the United States has never lost a war and has never won a peace for the very simple reason that we have a strong Department of War, but we have no Department of Peace.

When the government kept postponing this step we finally carried our appeal to a higher Court and our appeal was immediately granted. When we asked for an official affidavit and proof of the actual existence of such a Department our attention was diverted to this statement in a Book of Official Records that is more authoritative even than the famous Constitution of the United States:

"For unto us a child is born, unto us a son is given: and the government shall be upon his shoulder: and his name shall be called Wonderful, Counselor, The Mighty God, The Everlasting Father, The Prince of Peace. Of the increase of his government and peace there shall be no end . . . to establish it with judgment and with justice from henceforth even forever. The zeal of the Lord of hosts will perform this." Isaiah 9:6–7

Not only has there been a Department of Peace all these years, but there has been a Secretary of Peace, indeed an amazingly efficient Secretary, the Prince of Peace, Himself.

The moment a sufficient number of us turned to this Prince and united in placing "the Government upon his shoulder" things began to happen. Taking every step with prayer, and under guidance of this Prince of Peace the foundations for this Department of Peace began to appear.

The first step was to inundate the entire nation, especially the government, with prayer. Once get our land flooding with prayer and we would be sure that all the subsequent steps would follow in perfect sequence and perfect order.

Through the Camps Farthest Out, the United Prayer Tower, our mission to shut-ins, our city Camps Farthest Out groups, and our three spiritual magazines we were in touch with thousands of prayer groups and tens of thousands of praying people throughout the nation. To insure that a constant stream of prayer be sent up for our government, our nation, and the world, we set aside one day in every month for the people of every state to observe to the best of their ability for that purpose.*

Hardly had I sent out word through our magazines and other avenues of publicity to the prayer groups of the states, than Rev. Thomas Carruth, head of the Department of Evangelism of the Methodist Church visited my office and laid before me the wonderful around-the-clock system he had set up for the Methodist Church. He had hoped three hundred and sixty-five churches would pledge themselves to share these twenty-four hour vigils, but to his joy over a thousand volunteered. So that would mean that three churches would be in prayer at the same time sending up a stream of prayer that would continue without abatement all year long.

The next step was to organize the Prayer Groups in Washington, D. C. to have some one in prayer in the galleries of Congress every day Congress convened. This was accomplished on my next trip to Washington. Twenty-eight persons will take over this responsibility in relay style. Once a month these carefully selected, dedicated people will come together under some great spiritual leader for rededication and new inspiration.

Another step, and perhaps a climactic one, is praying for the President and his cabinet. As the twenty-eight who take turns in the House of Congress serve as a sort of funnel to channel our prayers for Congress, the National Presbyterian Church in Washington, which the President faithfully attends, has served a similar purpose for some of us in channelling our prayers for him. As Dr.

---

* See Appendix C.

Edward Elson, the President's pastor, happens to be the husband of a remarkably spiritual niece of mine, "Uncle Glenn" has had the honor and privilege of giving the first Sunday night address every year in the National Presbyterian Church. From many inner sources, even more convincing than the remarkable evidence given in the preceding pages of this book, I knew that President Eisenhower trusts in prayer more than any president, unless we should except Lincoln, and will rejoice in knowing that millions are praying for his continued "devotion, wisdom, and stamina" as he works "unceasingly for a just and lasting peace." *

But while centering our prayers on the national leaders we must pray for the men in factory and farm. We want to reach men right down where they live. Norman Vincent Peale, through his books, speeches, and Guideposts is doing that splendidly. Melvin Evans through his Democracy In Action movement is doing well. Bishop Sheen over the radio is reaching many, Protestants and Catholics alike. The Moral Rearmament Group is very effective in changing men who are going the wrong way and turning them in the right direction. Billy Graham is converting thousands.

One of the most effective instruments for reaching men right down on the street level where they live is the International Christian Leadership movement that has established hundreds of men's breakfast groups all over the world, most outstanding being the Senate Breakfast Group and the House of Congress Breakfast Group.

But while these men in the front lines are bringing God more and more into our national and world statesmanship, we must not lag for one moment in keeping the unseen centers of prayer working day and night. Perhaps the most unseen of all the groups are the shut-ins. This is an untapped reservoir of prayer power consisting largely of the old folks and war veterans who think their lives are useless. We have often referred to them as the Fanner Bees, a term used to describe the bees, too old and weak to go on excursions for honey, who therefore spend their time fanning in the fresh air and driving out the bad, keeping the beehive sweet and fresh. If we had enough "fanners," and if they were as keen on their

---

* Since writing these words, President Eisenhower has added to the Cabinet Harold Stassen as Secretary of Disarmament, a perfect beginning for a Department of Peace.

jobs as those bees, it would go far toward keeping the great hive of the world sweet and fresh! One of our undertakings of the Peace Department is to find a Queen Bee in every city who will organize some worker bees to help build up this army of praying Fanner Bees.

In *A Man's Reach* (1949) I made a promise: "Should there be another war, there will be no defense against total destruction that can be worth the name, excepting defenses of Love and Prayer. Therefore, if in my time another war looms as a seeming certainty, I shall call for an army of three hundred thousand people for three months." . . . and then I went on to tell what an army of prayer could do.

I now know of a far more effective way than the method outlined in the book referred to, for since writing *A Man's Reach* I have written *God's Reach* and instead of asking the Leader of the United States for permission to recruit an army of three hundred thousand and for the facilities and the financial backing necessary to train them, I am asking the Leader of the Universe for His permission to recruit such an army, and the financial backing and the leadership necessary for training them effectively in the most dynamic weapon ever devised for delivering a world out of danger— PRAYER.

The method of recruiting and training an army for war furnishes a perfect model in parable form for recruiting and training an army for peace.

The first step in preparing a wartime army is not first to train the entire army but to establish officer training camps. If we want to train an army of three hundred thousand, we would spend three months training three thousand or more who can go out and train the rest. The Camps Farthest Out can do just that, and the Ashrams of Stanley Jones can do it, also the Disciplined Order of Albert Day, and the many church camps will reach far more than three thousand. But as these are to be an *officers'* training camp we should redouble our efforts especially to draw leaders and prospective leaders. The best material for that purpose are ministers and seminary students. If a thousand ministers were really set on fire each year with that living something "strangely warm" stirring within them so they would go back to their churches and set their congregations on fire with power to pray effectively, within three years we would have an army of three hundred thousand prayer recruits from the best place in the world to find them, right out there in the churches.

Let us pray that all ministers might become John Wesleys, George Foxes or Martin Luthers to give the Revival, which is already here, impetus.

There should be one or more "teams" making a circuit of the globe every year developing these training centers around the world much as we have been doing in the journey described in this book. Taking a leaf from the Communists' Strategy book *we should keep up this process of indoctrinating people all over the globe* in the solid doctrines of the ways of peace under Christ.

The need for a year-round training place is being met by the Koinonia Foundation Training Center just outside of Baltimore. After a few months conditioning here, the trainees are prepared to build bridges of friendship in foreign lands. For instance, last Christmas Holidays the Foundation Farthest Out financed the bringing together of a remarkable group at Koinonia of forty Korean students who are attending universities all over America. These are all returning to their native land as trained leaders in their various fields and the spirit they caught at Koinonia may help to change Korea.*

To find this Pentagon of World Friendship, and this Department of World Peace we do not need to make pilgrimages to the mountains of Samaria or to the temples at Jerusalem, but we can find it in the hearts of men. I am such an irrepressible optimist whenever perfect harmony abides among the leaders, and unlimited faith in God abides in leaders and followers alike, that I know a spiritual movement is afoot that cannot be stopped—a program that will bring us a long way toward the realization of the vision of Isaiah 2:2–5:

"And it shall come to pass in the last days, that the mountain of the Lord's house shall be established in the top of the mountains, and shall be exalted above the hills; and all nations shall flow unto it. And many people shall go and say, Come ye, and let us go up to the mountain of the Lord, to the house of the God of Jacob; and he will teach us of his ways, and we will walk in his paths: for out

---

* See Appendix D.

of Zion shall go forth the law, and word of the Lord from Jerusalem. And he shall judge among the nations, and shall rebuke many people: and they shall beat their swords into plowshares, and their spears into pruning hooks; nation shall not lift up sword against nation, neither shall they learn war any more. O house of Jacob, come ye, and let us walk in the light of the Lord."

END OF BOOK

APPENDIXES

APPENDIX A

THE CAMPS FARTHEST OUT: THIRTY YEARS AGO WHEN I WAS visiting Monhegan Island, the "Island Farthest Out" off the Coast of Maine, it dawned on me what a wonderful blessing it would be for a hundred people to come together at an isolated spot like this, away from the morning newspaper, the telephone, and the neighbor's gossip, and spend a week or longer learning how to fall into balance, physically, mentally, and spiritually so completely that they could stay in balance all year.

Thus the first Camp was born at Lake Koronis, Minnesota, as an adventure in finding the wholeness of the spiritual life, a period where spirit, mind, and body are developed in wholesome orchestration.

Materialists tell us that there is no world except what we can see and feel—that is as far as we can go. Psychologists tell us that the materialists are wrong, that there is a realm farther out from the material realm, called the subconscious world. Spiritual leaders tell us that the materialists and psychologists both stop too soon, that there is a Realm Farthest Out, called the superconscious world. The only message bringers at these Camps are people who have gone farthest out in surrendering their lives to Christ. They don't talk of and about the Kingdom of Heaven, they immerse their listeners in it. Only two or three lectures are given a day, the rest of the time all those present share in singing, painting, writing, praying, and spiritual exercises.

The Camps Farthest Out is not a place where the material and intellectual forms of religion are studied—the temples and shrines, the cults and the creeds and theologies. It is a place where people learn how to pray and practice the presence of God, and go home prepared to apply it in every avenue of life; business, home, politics, recreation, hospitals, and above all our churches.

For fuller description and location and information of the forty and more camps, write to the Camp Coordinator, 1571 Grand Avenue, St. Paul 5, Minnesota.

APPENDIX B

THE DECLARATION OF INTERDEPENDENCE: IS THE RESULT of twelve previous drafts which were studied, amended, and approved by people in the following fifty lands: Algeria, Argentina, Australia, Austria, Belgian Congo, Bolivia, Brazil, Canada, Chile, Colombia, Costa Rica, Denmark, Ecuador, Egypt, England, Finland, France, French Cameroons, French Equatorial Africa, Germany, Gold Coast, Guatemala, Holland, Honduras, India, Indonesia, Israel, Italy, Japan, Jordan, Liberia, Mexico, Morocco, Nigeria, Norway, Pakistan, Panama, Paraguay, Peru, Philippines, Salvador, Saudi Arabia, Sierra Leone, Sweden, Switzerland, Turkey, Union of South Africa, United States of America, Uruguay, Venezuela.

Texts in Spanish, French, German, Portuguese, Italian, and Japanese are obtainable from Regional Vice Chairmen. English editions are printed in England and the United States of America.

Those desiring copies of this Declaration of Interdependence, send to Otto Tod Mallery, President Interdependence Council, Inc., 9006 Crefeld Street, Philadelphia 18, Pa.

APPENDIX C

IN THE OCTOBER–NOVEMBER, 1954, ISSUE OF THE *Fellowship Messenger* a call was sent out to the prayer groups everywhere to share in a constant stream of prayer for "devotion, wisdom, and stamina" of the rulers and lawmakers of the world in general and of our nation in particular to "work unceasingly for a just and lasting peace." A specific day of the month was appointed for the prayer groups of each state to join together in a concerted prayer for peace. These dates have been kept with wonderful results.

DAY OF MONTH	STATES	DAY OF MONTH	STATES
1	Maine and Idaho	5	Maryland and Montana
2	Mass. and N. Dakota	6	Virginia and Utah
3	Conn. and S. Dakota	7	N. Carolina and Rhode Island
4	New Jersey and Nevada		

Any prayer group or individual wishing to be enrolled in this movement for world peace is requested to write to Mrs. Ethel Dow, the coordinator of prayer groups, 3124 West Calhoun Blvd., Minneapolis, Minnesota.

APPENDIX D

KOINONIA IS A LOVELY ESTATE JUST OUTSIDE OF BALTIMORE FOR the training of prospective candidates for foreign service, whether it be under government auspices, for example, Point Four work, or under church mission boards. There they all get a sound orientation in the dynamics of faith and love, build a broad Christian attitude, and an integrated attitude based upon imagination, sympathy, and understanding between peoples. The trainees come to Koinonia with their specific knowledge and technical skills, and while there achieve a personal integration, spiritual orientation, and cultural understanding that sends them forth as dynamic influences for world peace. Over fifty trainees have gone forth from Koinonia and the reports coming back are thrilling. In several instances they are changing the attitude of the entire embassy in ways that effect the entire nation. One foreign government reports, "We could use sixty more." Secretaries are especially in great demand. Many who go forth with technical skills in various fields have risen to executive positions.

Letters of inquiry regarding Koinonia should be addressed to the Executive Director, Box 336, Pikesville Station, Baltimore 8, Md.

APPENDIX E

ANYONE IN NEED OF PRAYER FOR PHYSICAL OR SPIRITUAL WHOLENESS is invited to write his needs to the United Prayer Tower, 1571 Grand Avenue, St. Paul, Minnesota. This service is rendered free as the Prayer Tower is supported by the love offerings of its friends.

All checks made out to the United Prayer Tower, the Koinonia Foundation, or to the Foundation Farthest Out are exempt from income tax.